THE LAWYER'S GUIDE TO

Microsoft® Word 2010

BY BEN M. SCHORR

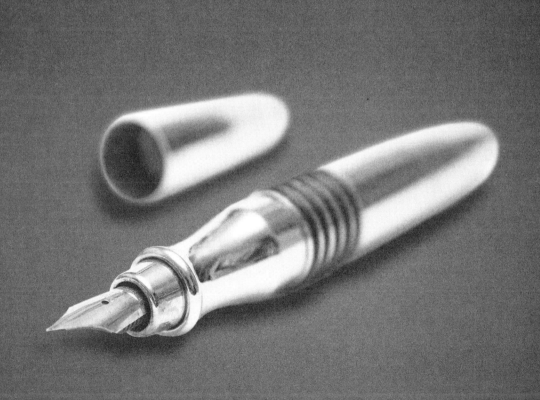

ABA **LawPracticeManagementSection**
MARKETING • MANAGEMENT • TECHNOLOGY • FINANCE

Commitment to Quality: The Law Practice Management Section is committed to quality in our publications. Our authors are experienced practitioners in their fields. Prior to publication, the contents of all our books are rigorously reviewed by experts to ensure the highest quality product and presentation. Because we are committed to serving our readers' needs, we welcome your feedback on how we can improve future editions of this book.

Microsoft is a registered trademark of the Microsoft Corporation.

Cover design by RIPE Creative, Inc.

Nothing contained in this book is to be considered as the rendering of legal advice for specific cases, and readers are responsible for obtaining such advice from their own legal counsel. This book and any forms and agreements herein are intended for educational and informational purposes only.

The products and services mentioned in this publication are under trademark or service-mark protection. Product and service names and terms are used throughout only in an editorial fashion, to the benefit of the product manufacturer or service provider, with no intention of infringement. Use of a product or service name or term in this publication should not be regarded as affecting the validity of any trademark or service mark.

The Law Practice Management Section of the American Bar Association offers an educational program for lawyers in practice. Books and other materials are published in furtherance of that program. Authors and editors of publications may express their own legal interpretations and opinions, which are not necessarily those of either the American Bar Association or the Law Practice Management Section unless adopted pursuant to the bylaws of the Association. The opinions expressed do not reflect in any way a position of the Section or the American Bar Association, nor do the positions of the Section or the American Bar Association necessarily reflect the opinions of the author.

Printed in the United States of America.
15 14 13 12 11 5 4 3 2 1

Library of Congress Cataloging-in-Publication Data
Schorr, Ben M.
   The lawyer's guide to Microsoft Word 2010 / Ben M. Schorr.
      p. cm.
   Includes bibliographical references and index.
   ISBN 978-1-61632-949-5
1. Microsoft Word. 2. Word processing—United States. 3. Legal composition—Automation. 4. Legal correspondence—Automation. 5. Law offices—United States—Automation. I. American Bar Association. Section of Law Practice Management. II. Title.
   KF322.5.M53S363 2011
   005.52—dc23

                                          2011029733

Discounts are available for books ordered in bulk. Special consideration is given to state bars, CLE programs, and other bar-related organizations. Inquire at Book Publishing, American Bar Association, 321 North Clark Street, Chicago, Illinois 60654-7598.

www.ababooks.org

Dedication

To my amazing wife Carrie. You make everything in my world a thousand times better.

Contents

Chapter 1
Introduction 1

Chapter 2
A Quick Tour 7

Chapter 3
Creating a Basic Document   63

Chapter 4
Formatting   77

Chapter 7
Working with Other Programs
145

Chapter 10
Troubleshooting   201

Chapter 11
Mistakes Lawyers Make with Microsoft Word   215

Chapter 12
Tricks to Impress Your Law School Classmates With   229

Chapter 13
Keyboard Shortcuts   245

Acknowledgments

I'd like to give some special recognition to the following people:

At Microsoft, Jensen Harris, Jamie Sloan, Ed Hickey, and the Microsoft Word team in Redmond for being terrific and accessible and giving so much of their time to help me understand how the product works.

Beth Melton, Stephanie Krieger, and Shauna Kelly: great ladies who've forgotten more about Microsoft Word than most people will ever know. Adriana Linares and Barron Henley for reminding me of things I forgot to include in the first draft.

My business partner, Matti Raihala, and the rest of the Roland Schorr & Tower team for keeping things running smoothly so I could spend all this time banging out yet another book.

Sharon Nelson and John Simek for their support and friendship. Sharon's unending faith and enthusiasm and John's steady whip-cracking are what got me to finish this book and only be six months late.

And last, but most definitely not least, to my beautiful Carrie Rae who came along at exactly the right time and brought with her hope and happiness. Thank you for giving me a new reason to achieve.

About the Author

Ben M. Schorr is a technologist and Chief Executive Officer for Roland Schorr & Tower, a professional consulting firm headquartered in Honolulu, Hawaii. In that capacity he consults with a wide variety of organizations including many law firms. He is frequently sought as a writer, teacher, and speaker for groups as diverse as the Hawaii Visitor and Convention Bureau and the American Bar Association. More than eleven years ago Microsoft named Mr. Schorr as an MVP in their Outlook product group, and he has been supporting Outlook, Exchange, and most recently OneNote ever since. Prior to co-founding Roland Schorr, he was the Director of Information Services for Damon Key Leong Kupchak Hastert, a large Honolulu law firm, for almost eight years.

Mr. Schorr was a contributing author for *Using Microsoft Office 2000* by Que and has been a technical editor or contributor on a number of other books over the years. For several years he was half of the "Ask the Exchange Pros" team for Windows Server System magazine. He is the author of the forthcoming *The Lawyer's Guide to Microsoft Outlook 2010*, which is being published by the American Bar Association.

In October of 2005 Mr. Schorr was named by the Pacific Technology Foundation as one of the Top 50 Technology Leaders in Hawaii. He is a member of the Institute of Electrical and Electronics Engineers' (IEEE) Computer Society, the American Bar Association, and the United States Naval Institute. In his free time Mr. Schorr enjoys coaching football, running marathons, reading, playing softball, and kayaking in the ocean, and he has completed the Tinman triathlon three times. His dog is not impressed. You can reach him at bens@rolandschorr.com.

Introduction

1

Microsoft Word is one of the most venerable elements of the Microsoft Office suite—there are few applications more fundamental than putting words on paper—and one of the most important applications in the practice of law. No matter what area of law you practice, you probably have to put words on paper almost daily.

> "One of the hardest things in life is having words in your heart that you can't utter."
> —*James Earl Jones*

Just as with the last book, I began this project by asking myself the key question:

How can I make this book even better than the last one?

Not surprisingly the answer was essentially the same as last time: Most lawyers use Word, but few of them get everything they can from it. With this book I want to help you get the most out of Microsoft Word to make you more effective, more efficient, and more successful. I'm hoping you'll find this book to be useful, powerful, and maybe even a little enjoyable. I'm also hoping this book finds its way into the hands of legal assistants and paralegals—each of whom also spends a great deal of time in Microsoft Word and will, I hope, get some benefit from reading this.

To accomplish my goals I'm going to tell you about Word through my eyes. Through the eyes of a fifteen-year veteran of Microsoft Word who is also a twenty-two-year veteran of law office technology. I'm hoping that you'll keep turning the pages because every new page will bring a series of moments. "Gee whiz" moments, "Holy cow!" moments, and "Light bulb" moments. Hopefully, you'll put this book down repeatedly as you rush to your computer to try that new trick. If this book ends up on your desk with a colorful array of sticky notes protruding from the pages, I'll know I've succeeded.

What's So Special about Word Processing?

We all use Word and it seems like typing, saving, and printing are relatively simple tasks. So why do you need a book to explain how to do it? Because the documents we create are complex and important—your law practice depends, to some degree, upon the quality of the documents you produce and the efficiency with which you produce them. In this book I'm going to try to help you do it more productively, more efficiently, and more enjoyably. And since this is a book aimed at lawyers and law firms, I'm going to skim over the features I don't think are very useful to lawyers and try to focus on those tools that you'll actually use. For example, I don't think most lawyers care much about SmartArt, so I'll not waste a lot of time on it in here. I could easily do 700 pages on Microsoft Word 2010 if I tried to cover every feature and option in depth. I'll save your time (and mine) and try to keep my emphasis on those features and capabilities that will matter to law firms. If you really want a large, comprehensive work on Microsoft Word 2010, there are some excellent general books on the market—anything with Beth Melton's or Stephanie Krieger's name on it is undoubtedly worth reading if that's what you're after.

Those Who Love Software or the Law Should Not Watch Either Being Made

I thought an exploration of how the Office 2010 suite was made would be enlightening here. The story really begins with Office 2003. When you installed Office 2003 or 2007, a funny little icon was added to the system tray (down on the task bar, next to the clock) where it sat, mysteriously, staring at you. When you eventually clicked on it, a dialog box was presented that offered to let you opt in to something called the "Customer Experience Improvement Program." The Customer Experience Improvement Program (CEIP) sends a lot of non-identifiable data back to Microsoft about how you actually use its software. Don't worry, it doesn't send any actual documents or e-mail addresses or anything like that. Instead it's primarily concerned with *how* you use the software—what buttons you click, how many documents you have open, how many sub-folders you create, how long you spend in each program (that's how we know that

Outlook stays open longer than any other Office application). The reason for gathering this historical usage data (known internally at Microsoft as "SQM" or "Service Quality Monitoring" data) is to make the next version of Microsoft Office better.

> "Designing Microsoft Office is like ordering pizza for 400 million people."
> —*Steven Sinofsky, Microsoft*

Prior to the CEIP, boxes of dry erase markers were used in brainstorming sessions. Huge quantities of Chinese food were consumed behind one-way mirrors in the usability labs, and survey after survey after survey was analyzed all in the name of trying to figure out how users actually used the products. The results of all of that work became Office XP, the immediate predecessor to Office 2003. Clearly a better way was needed, and the CEIP is it. Microsoft receives a mind-boggling volume of data from the CEIP; in fact, as of April 2006, the company had received more than 1.3 *billion* sessions of Office 2003 usage. That data taught a lot of interesting, useful, and surprising lessons and was of tremendous help in designing Microsoft Office 2010. As a result, Office 2010 has been built with volumes of direct feedback from real end-users in real-life situations.

The most commonly clicked toolbar button in Microsoft Word 2003, and it's not even close, is "Paste"—followed, in order, by "Save," "Copy," "Undo," and "Bold."

Those results can be seen in several areas, most notably in the user interface (UI). Outlook 2007 replaced the old "File, Edit, View" menu structure with what is called the "Ribbon." (See Figure 1.1) Developed using CEIP data, the Ribbon is intended to be a more discoverable interface where every feature in the product is easy to find and use. The CEIP data also was used to find out what desirable features—features that users asked for—were rarely used, indicating that they were too hard to find.

FIGURE 1.1

One key indicator that Office needed a new UI was that four of the top ten feature requests received from Word 2003 users were for features that were already in the product. People just didn't know how to find them! According to Jensen Harris, group program manager for the Microsoft Office User Experience Team (which means he's the lead dog on the team that designed the new UI), features like adding a watermark to Word documents were so hard to find that a lot of users asked how to do it or didn't realize you could. With Office 2010, the feature is prominently located on the "Page Layout" tab, and Jensen has had a lot of users comment on what a "great new feature" it is.

More Bits for Power Users

Office 2010 is the first version of Microsoft Office to be offered in both 32-bit and 64-bit versions. It's not too important that you understand the technical details of that distinction. All you really need to know is that as computers have evolved, the number of bits they can handle at a time has grown. When I first started in law office technology we were beginning to see the migration from 4-bit to 8-bit computers. For most of the 15 years or so, 32-bit computers have dominated the landscape. In the last few years 64-bit computers have become more commonplace.

> "640K ought to be enough for anybody."
> —*Bill Gates*

Microsoft introduced its first 64-bit operating system for workstations with Windows XP 64-bit. Never heard of it? Almost nobody used it. Windows Vista came in a 64-bit flavor too, and it got a little more adoption than Windows XP 64-bit did, but not much. Now, with Windows 7, the 64-bit market is truly mature. It's almost impossible to buy a new computer that isn't 64-bit today, and it's almost always a better choice to buy Windows 7 in the 64-bit flavor. Why? I'll give you two reasons.

1. For all practical purposes, 32-bit operating systems are limited to 4GB of RAM. That sounds like a lot, but if history has shown us anything it's that RAM usage has tended to increase as programs have become larger and more powerful and the price of RAM (the memory that the computer uses for active processes) has fallen dramatically. As a general rule, the more RAM you have, the faster and more stable your computer will be. It's hard to find a new computer these days with less than 2GB of RAM, and we usually recommend clients start at 4GB and consider 6GB or 8GB if the budget allows. The 64-bit operating systems make that possible.

2. Windows 7 may be the last version of Windows Microsoft makes that is even available in 32 bit. It's fairly universally accepted that the 32-bit platform is on the luge ride to obsolescence. Investing in a new 32-bit system at this stage makes no sense unless you have key legacy hardware or software that demands it. And if you

> do have such legacy hardware or software, you should be thinking hard about your ongoing commitment to that gear.

Most 32-bit hardware and software will work just fine with a 64-bit operating system.

When it comes to Microsoft Office, however, I'm going to temper that advice slightly. As of this writing, the 32-bit version of Office is still the wiser choice for most firms. The reason: few people really need a 64-bit version of Microsoft Office, and a number of add-ins and other pieces of software just don't work properly with the 64-bit version of Office (even though they run fine on the 64-bit version of Windows). Confused? I hope that by the time you're reading this book those problems have faded into the past, but as I sit here writing it, there are still some issues.

So Why WOULD I Want 64-bit Office?

The 64-bit version of Office is good for power users who are using *extremely* large files. The advantage, primarily more speed and stability, shows itself mostly on very large Excel workbooks and very large Microsoft Outlook mailboxes. Other than that, you probably won't see a lot of difference between the 32-bit and 64-bit versions of Office. Except, of course, that your add-ins will probably work better in the 32-bit version.

Making the Choice

Luckily, making the choice between 32-bit and 64-bit versions of Office is pretty easy—in fact *both* versions are in the box when you buy Office. You just have to decide, when you install, which version you want. If you're installing on an older computer (you can install Office 2010 on systems as old as Windows XP Service Pack 3), you're probably going to be forced into the 32-bit version anyhow. If you're installing on a 64-bit operating system, then you'll have the option to install the 64-bit version.

If you install the 32-bit version but find, down the road, that the 64-bit version becomes desirable and viable for you, you can always reinstall Office and choose the 64-bit version at that time.

So, to Be Clear . . .

We recommend that most of our clients getting new machines opt for Windows 7 Professional, 64-bit, and Microsoft Office 2010, 32-bit.

And Now, by Popular Demand . . .

Since you've probably already bought Word 2010 (seeing as how you're reading a book on it), I'm not going to try to sell you on why you should go get it. Let me just briefly highlight some of the key new features of Word 2010 that lawyers are going to love. I'll explain them in more detail later in the book, but here's the teaser:

1. Improved Ribbon—it's a little cleaner in Office 2010 and a bit customizable, too.
2. New numbering formats.
3. Checkboxes available for forms or lists.
4. New Compare Documents option.
5. Metadata checking and cleanup, to protect your client and yourself.
6. Navigation pane helps you navigate long documents quickly and easily.
7. Save to PDF natively lets you create basic PDF files without additional software.
8. Building blocks help you assemble standard documents more quickly and easily.
9. Collaborative editing (If you have SharePoint).
10. Improved picture handling—use images to illustrate your point.
11. Backstage View—easier access to things you want to do with your document, like print or share.
12. Available 32- and 64-bit versions for real power users.

A lot of the other new features will really excite your consultant or IT person but might be a tad esoteric for you. I'll mention them throughout the book, but mostly I'll focus on the features and tools that you're going to use and care about in your daily practice.

So, let's get right into it. Turn the page for Chapter 2—A Quick Tour.

A Quick Tour

2

Word 2010 is quite a bit different from previous versions of Word in that it features the new Fluent interface, which is most prominently evident in the "Ribbon" at the top of the screen. (See Figure 2.1.) This may be a bit of a shock to users who are used to the old "File | Edit | View" menu structure. So while this chapter is titled "A Quick Tour," the tour may not be all that quick after all.

FIGURE 2.1

You may want to settle in with a refreshing beverage as we dig into the new interface. We're not going to spend a lot of time explaining the features here—the idea is that you come out of this chapter feeling comfortable with the interface and like you know where to find everything you need. In subsequent chapters we'll go into how you use what you need.

> Note . . . If you're already familiar with Word 2007 you might just want to skim this chapter. You'll want to read the section on Backstage, but otherwise the rest of the interface has changed in only very slight ways.

Backstage

In Office 2007 Microsoft replaced the File menu with the "Office" button, a round icon at the top left corner of the screen. Unfortunately many people didn't realize that actually *was* a button, believing it to be mere decoration, and so they never thought to click on it. Equally unfortunate was the fact that many key features of the product, such as Print, Open, and Save, were located behind that button, and thus people were rather confused about how to print or save when there weren't any obvious buttons for that.

Lesson learned. In Office 2010 the File menu is back . . . sort of. Office 2010 introduces a nifty new way to handle your documents called "Backstage." It's cleverly located behind the File tab of the Ribbon. Click that tab and you'll see Backstage, as you do in Figure 2.2.

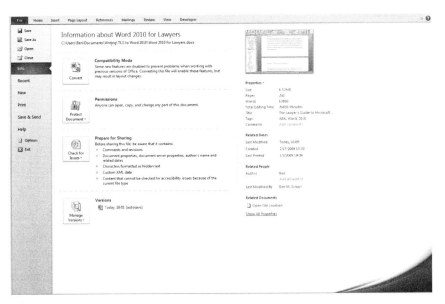

FIGURE 2.2

▼▼▼▼▼

Every Frustrated Actor's Lament . . . How Do I Get Out of Backstage?
Since Backstage doesn't really look like a tab the way the rest of the Ribbon tabs do, it's not entirely obvious how to get back to your document once you're in Backstage. I've seen a lot of users actually close Word just trying to get back to their document. All you have to do, though, is click any of the tabs on the Ribbon (Home, usually) to return to your document.

The first four commands listed under Backstage are familiar to Microsoft Office users: Save, Save As, Open, and Close. (See Figure 2.3.)

FIGURE 2.3

Save does exactly what you'd expect it to do—it saves the current document in its current format and in its current location. In other words, if you're editing \My Documents\resume.doc, it will save it as resume.doc in the My Documents folder. If you're editing \marketing\great letter.docx, then it will save it as "great letter.docx" in the marketing folder. It's as easy as that. If you're editing a document that hasn't been saved before, Save will behave exactly as Save As does. And that means . . .

Save As is a little more flexible. Save As lets you save a brand new copy of this document, leaving the original document (if there is one) unaffected. When you click Save As, Word will prompt you to name the document and give you the option to change the format (from Word 2002 .DOC format to Word 2010 .DOCX format, for example) and the location (to any folder or other accessible storage location) if you wish. (See Figure 2.4.)

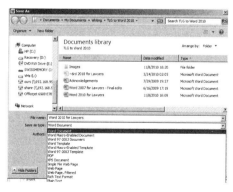

FIGURE 2.4

Open gives you a way to open a document or file from a storage location (hard drive, flash drive, network drive, etc.). Figure 2.5 shows you how that looks. Click Open and you'll be presented with a dialog box that lets you select the file (or files, see Chapter 12) that you want to open. You'll notice that on the right side of the window is a preview pane that gives you a glimpse of the document you're about to open. If you want to turn off the previewer, and you may want to for performance reasons if you notice lags in accessing documents across a network, just click the button next to the "Help" button above the preview pane.

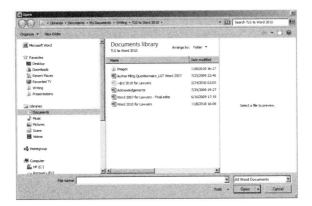

FIGURE 2.5

One handy feature of the Open dialog box in Office 2010 is the Search box in the top right corner. If you have a folder with a lot of documents in it, rather than the four I have in my sample folder, you can very quickly navigate to any of those documents by typing the name in the search box. If you have Windows Desktop Search installed (and Windows Vista/7 users do), that search box will search the text *inside* the documents too. So you aren't just relying on the names of the documents—you can search for a text string that appears inside the document, too. Just click in the search box and type.

Close . . . well, close puts the document away. If you haven't saved it first, Close will ask you if you want to save before closing.

Info

When you first open Backstage, the Info group will be displayed. (See Figure 2.6.) The Info group gives you access to tools that let you do things with the current document. Specifically which tools are displayed depends on the document you've opened and whether you've saved it yet. We'll talk about some of these tools in more depth later; I'll just introduce them here.

- Compatibility Mode—disables certain features of Word so that the document will transfer more smoothly to people using older versions of Word or using word processors from other suites like Corel WordPerfect or OpenOffice.
- Permissions—lets you encrypt the document with a password, securing it (sort of) from prying eyes; mark the document as final; digitally sign it; or set up the Information Rights Management (IRM). We'll talk more about IRM in Chapter 6.
- Prepare for Sharing—the description of the Prepare for Sharing tool doesn't include the one word that might clue you in to what it really does . . . it cleans metadata. You'll learn more about that in Chapter 11.

■ Versions—one handy feature of Word is the ability to manage multiple versions. That feature is improved in Word 2010, and our discussion of it is improved in Chapter 6.

FIGURE 2.6

Metadata

Speaking of metadata, much of the metadata about this particular document is displayed on the right side of the Info tab. Here you'll find total editing time, how many pages the document is, and last modified and created (even last printed!) dates. (See Figure 2.7.) You can see the author's name, the name of the last user to modify the document, and more.

Word's password protection feature is like a grocery-store padlock: good enough to deter amateurs or casual browsers, but will barely slow down a determined or experienced intruder.

FIGURE 2.7

Recent

The next tab on the Backstage navigation pane is Recent. Clicking on that will show you something like what's in Figure 2.8. On the left side is a list of files you've edited recently. The most recently used files will be at the top of this list, and as you work with more and more files they will gradually get pushed toward the bottom. By default you'll see your 20 most recently used files here, but you can change that by going to File |

Options | Advanced and scrolling down to the Display section. Eventually the oldest files will scroll off the bottom of the list, unless you pin them (we'll get to that in a moment).

On the right side you'll see a list of folders you've accessed recently. That's especially handy because you probably often work with documents from the same folders, if not always the same document. This way, even if the document doesn't appear on your Recent list, the folder it's in might, and that lets you get to the document faster. Like the documents, the most recently used places will be at the top and will gradually scroll down the list.

FIGURE 2.8

Two other points I want to make about this group:

1. If there is a document or folder you want to keep on the list permanently, you can pin it to the list by clicking the Pushpin icon on the right side of the list. Naturally, the more items you pin, the fewer the slots available for recently used documents, so you may want to be modest in your use of this feature. Typically I'll pin half a dozen or so of the documents I want easy access to. Keep in mind that if you use a document every day, you don't need to pin it . . . it'll almost certainly always be on your Recently Used list anyhow.

FIGURE 2.9

2. If you want to save yourself a step, use the checkbox sitting quietly at the bottom of this screen that lets you add a certain number of recently used documents (up to the maximum number of recent documents you're letting Word display on the Recent tab) to the Backstage navigation pane. Click it and you'll see something like Figure 2.9. This saves you from having to click the "Recent" group on the navigation pane to get to those items.

New

The New group Backstage gives you a bunch of options for creating a new document. As you can see in Figure 2.10, it really encourages you to use a template to start your new document. Here you can select from any number of templates that you've created or that you download from other sources. We'll introduce templates in Chapter 4 and get a little friendlier with them in Chapter 8.

Just select the template you want to start with (including the Blank document) and click the "Create" button on the right side to get started.

FIGURE 2.10

Print

Printing is something lawyers do a lot, and Word 2010's print dialog has improved over the old version. The first thing you'll notice when you go to the print tab in 2010 (see Figure 2.11) is that there is now a print preview right there on the screen. Don't overlook the value of print preview—too often I've had clients find out after they printed a document that something didn't line up or paginate properly. Print preview lets you see that *before* you waste the paper. Take a moment to look at the print preview before you click "Print."

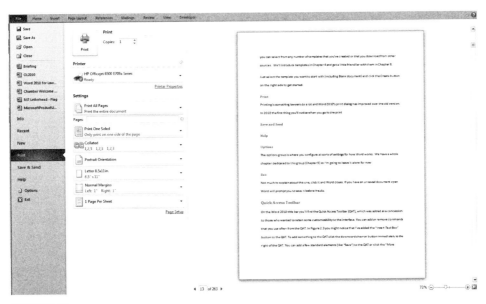

FIGURE 2.11

The rest of the settings in the Print tab should be pretty familiar, and they will vary slightly depending upon what kind of printer you're connecting to. Among the settings you'll use most often:

■ Copies: Right at the top, this lets you print multiple copies of the document in a single pass.

■ Printer: If you have more than one printer, you can select which printer you want to use here. Office 2010 adds a couple of virtual printers when you install it, including "Send to OneNote 2010" and "Microsoft XPS Document Writer."

■ Print all: Hiding under this option are settings to let you print only the current page or a specific selection, as well as the ability to print metadata reports about the document—such as a printout of all of the markup in the document (Figure 2.12).

FIGURE 2.12

We'll talk more about printing in Chapter 3, so I'm not going to get too deep on it here.

Save & Send

Microsoft Office 2010 emphasizes collaboration, sharing, and taking word processing beyond the printed page. The Save & Send group Backstage is a good example of this.

Within this group there are several sections:

Send Using E-mail

In the Send Using E-mail section (Figure 2.13) you have up to 5 different ways to share this document via e-mail.

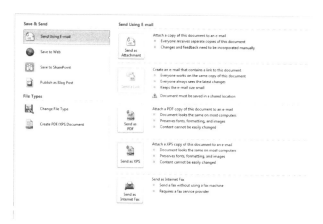

FIGURE 2.13

- Send as Attachment—the conventional way Word documents are shared. Click this button and Word will start a new e-mail message for you in your default e-mail program (probably Outlook) and attach the document as a .DOCX file. Unless the other party needs to be able to edit it, I would avoid sending Word documents in Word format, if for no other reason than to minimize the metadata issues (see Chapter 11).

- Send a Link—there's a good chance that this option is going to be grayed out for you. Why? Because in order to send somebody a link, there has to be a shared location for it to link *to*. Documents on shared network drives can be shared with a link. Documents in the My Documents folder on your laptop? Not so much.

- Send as PDF—I wish this were the first option because it's usually the best. It creates a new e-mail message just like Send as Attachment, but instead of attaching a .DOCX file it creates an Adobe PDF file and attaches that.

- Send as XPS—XPS is Microsoft's version of PDF. Do you ever use it? Know anybody who does? Me neither, so let's move on.

- Send as Internet Fax—faxing is a dying technology as scanning and e-mailing become the predominant way to fill that need. If you still use fax though, and have an account with a fax service provider like eFax, you can use this option to send your fax directly from Word.

Save to Web

Save to Web offers just one option—but it's an option that has gotten a lot more powerful recently—and that's Save to SkyDrive. SkyDrive is Microsoft's free Internet-based storage site. If you have a free Live.com or Hotmail.com account, then you have a free SkyDrive account with 25GB of free storage.

I'll talk more about SkyDrive in Chapter 6.

Save to SharePoint

SharePoint is becoming the preferred document collaboration site for a lot of law firms. If you have a Windows server of even slightly recent vintage, then you already have SharePoint, even though you may not be using it. Not surprisingly Word (and the rest of the Office suite) ties in with SharePoint fairly tightly. Saving to SharePoint is easy to do and almost immediately gains the advantages SharePoint can provide, such as version tracking and full-text indexing.

We'll look at SharePoint in more detail in Chapter 6.

Publish as Blog Post

Back when it was creating Word 2007, Microsoft decided that some folks might like to use Word to author their blog posts. If your blog is hosted on

WordPress, Blogger, Windows Live Spaces (which has now been largely migrated to WordPress), TypePad, or a few other popular services, then you can use Word 2010 as your blog editing tool. To be honest, I don't know many people who actually *do* use it for that, but you can. I'll talk more about how to do that in Chapter 12.

Change File Type

If you have a document that has been saved as one file type, such as the Word XML format that is standard in Word 2007 and 2010, but you'd like to change it to a different format, this is the place to do that. You might use this feature if you need to share a document with somebody who still uses Word 2003 (and refuses to install the converters) or if you have a document you'd like to convert to a template to use as the basis for future documents. (See Figure 2.14.)

FIGURE 2.14

Create PDF/XPS Document

If you'd like to create a PDF version of your document but don't have Adobe Acrobat, you can do that natively right here. Just click the "Create PDF/XPS Document" button (it's the only button on that screen) and the Save As dialog will appear with PDF already selected as the default type. (You weren't really going to save it as an XPS file, were you?) This is an excellent solution for creating basic PDF files.

Help

At first glance the Help group (Figure 2.15) seems redundant. We have the little blue Help icon out on the Ribbon (Figure 2.16), and clicking it takes you right into Help. So why do you need the Help group Backstage? Well, as you can see from Figure 2.15, there's a lot more back there than just a place to get answers to questions.

On the left side of the screen is a link to the help system, and below that a very useful link to the Getting Started with Word 2010 site. This site

FIGURE 2.15   **FIGURE 2.16**

offers free resources (including training videos and online courses) to help you get up to speed on Word 2010. It's almost as good as this book.

The Options setting on the left side is actually the same as clicking "File | Options" off the main Backstage menu—nothing special there. The Check for Updates button connects you to Microsoft Update to see if there are any new updates, hotfixes, or patches for Office. If you have Automatic Updates installed on your machine (and most of you should), then this isn't really necessary, but it doesn't hurt to check it.

▼▼▼▼▼

Automatic Updates

All software needs updating and patching from time to time. New features, bug fixes, security vulnerabilities . . . all software goes through those issues, and all major vendors (Microsoft, Apple, Adobe, and others) have a mechanism for distributing those patches and updates to their users. Microsoft releases new patches for its software on the second Tuesday of each month, unless it's an urgent patch, which is released as soon as it's ready. You can get these patches at http://update.microsoft.com. However all modern versions of Microsoft Windows include the Windows Automatic Update service, which automatically checks for and installs new updates on a regular basis. You can find it in the Control Panel for your particular operating system, if you want to see if it's turned on and how it's configured. I encourage you to enable it, unless you're one of those few users who have some legacy third-party software that gets broken if you install updates. If that's the case, I'd rethink that legacy software—many of Microsoft's patches are critical security patches that you really should have.

On the right side of the Help screen you'll see some useful information about your application—most notably whether it's currently activated. When you first install Microsoft Office, you'll be able to use it 25 times without activating it; after that, if you still haven't activated, then Office will automatically start in "reduced functionality" mode. This basically means that certain important features won't work . . . until you activate.

If Word isn't activated, you should be prompted to activate it every time you start the product. Just go through the wizard and in moments it will activate. If you don't see that wizard, or you skipped it and went into the product but want to activate now, you can do it through the Help menu in Backstage. Where it says "Not Activated" you'll find a link to the Activation Wizard, which will let you activate Word.

Also on the right-side of the screen you will find your version number, such as "14.0.5128.5000 (64-bit)," and a link to the End User License Agreement. I know how lawyers love to read license agreements!

> **Version 14?**
>
> Microsoft uses incremental version numbers internally. The "Office 2010" is just what the marketing department labels the product. Version 14 is Office 2010. Office 2007 was Version 12. Notice how Microsoft skipped the 13? I was in a meeting with the Microsoft VP who owned Office when 2010 was being developed, and he was asked if the company was skipping Version 13 because Microsoft is superstitious. He smiled and said, "No, but some of our customers are."

Options

The Options group is where you configure all sorts of settings for how Word works. Chapter 9 is dedicated to this group, so I'm going to leave it alone for now.

Exit

Not much to explain about this one; click it and Word closes. If you have an unsaved document open, Word will prompt you to save it before it exits.

Quick Access Toolbar

On the Word 2010 title bar you'll find the Quick Access Toolbar (QAT), which was added as a concession to those who wanted to retain some customizability to the interface. You can add or remove commands that you use often from the QAT. In Figure 2.17 you might notice that I've added the "Insert Horizontal Line," "Quick Print," and "Insert Address" buttons to the QAT. To add something to the QAT, click the downward chevron button immediately to the right of the QAT or right-click almost anywhere on the

FIGURE 2.17

Ribbon. You can add a few standard elements (like Save) to the QAT or click the "More Commands" option to select from a list of every command or macro in the program. With some time and patience you can build out the QAT to be a powerful personalized toolbar of commands.

There is another command on the Customize Quick Access Toolbar menu that you will want to get to know:

- Show Below the Ribbon. This will, not surprisingly, move the Quick Access Toolbar to a line of its own at the bottom of the Ribbon. This gives you much more space to work with, if you're adding a lot of commands to the QAT, and reduces the distance you have to move your mouse to get to the QAT by an inch or two. Word 2010, you'll find, has made a few efforts to reduce the amount of mileage you put on your mouse to reach your commonly used commands.

The Ribbon

The most noticeable difference in Word 2010 is the Ribbon. The Ribbon is the name for the new interface at the top of the screen where all of the program commands are found.

The key elements of the Ribbon are the Office Quick Access Toolbar and a series of Ribbon tabs that contain various commands. The Ribbon

▼▼▼▼▼
Minimize the Ribbon

One of the first things people say when they first see the Ribbon is "Wow, that takes up a lot of screen." If you're one of those users who would like to reclaim some of your screen real estate, then you can minimize the ribbon to a single line (much like the old menus) which tucks it nicely out of the way. You can also minimize (or restore) the Ribbon by right-clicking any empty area on it or the QAT and selecting "Minimize the Ribbon" on the resultant context menu. You can also minimize the Ribbon by double-clicking on any of the group labels (like "Home" or "Insert"). They say Eskimos have a lot of words for "Snow" because it's important to them. Well, there are a lot of ways to minimize the Ribbon.

is far less customizable or variable than the old menu structure was. It will change a bit if certain document elements are selected on screen, but otherwise it will, by design, remain basically the same. An example of when it will change is when you add a table to your document. In that case, a couple of extra tabs, related to tables, will be added to the Ribbon. (We'll talk more about Tables in Chapter 4). The tabs on the ribbon are made up of groups, which collect the commands.

"I don't know the key to success, but the key to failure is trying to please everybody."
—*Bill Cosby*

Some of the groups have a tiny "button" to the right of the group name, called a dialog launcher. I've circled them in Figure 2.18. Clicking that dialog launcher opens a larger dialog box containing more commands for working with that family of commands. We'll spend time with the dialog launchers as we go through the book.

FIGURE 2.18

One thing to keep in mind with the Ribbon is that it will adapt to the size of your window and your screen resolution. If you don't have Word running full-screen and you drag and drop the Word window wider and narrower, you'll notice that the Ribbon changes as you go so that the various groups compress and expand to fit the available space.

To be fair, not all users like the Ribbon. Some have such a long history with the old menu structure that the change to the Ribbon is uncomfortable. Some have long ingrained habits that they'll have to break, and some simply don't like it. It *is* a significant change from the old way. On balance, however, most users do seem to like it, at least eventually. I've heard from a number of users who didn't care for it initially but grew to appreciate the Ribbon after spending some time with it.

So let's introduce you to the Ribbon and see if you don't hit it off. . . .

Home

The Home tab (see Figure 2.19) on the Ribbon is the default tab and contains the most commonly used editing commands.

FIGURE 2.19

Clipboard

At the far left you can see the clipboard commands such as Paste, which we've learned was the most commonly clicked-on toolbar button in Word 2003.

▼▼▼▼▼

Tricks of the Pros

To display the contents of the Office Clipboard, click the dialog launcher at the right end of the "Clipboard" group label. The Office Clipboard can hold up to 24 items at a time, and by exposing it you can select which of the items you want to paste. Unlike pressing CTRL+V, with this method you don't have to paste the last thing you cut or copied to the clipboard. Figure 2.20 shows you what it looks like.

This is especially handy if you want to paste the same word or phrases in various places of your document without having to re-copy them (or worse, re-type them). To close the clipboard again, just click the "X" at the top right corner of that pane.

FIGURE 2.20

Font

Next to the Clipboard group you'll find the set of Font commands, which include the typeface (such as "Times New Roman"), font size, font color, highlighting, and change case.

The fonts listed in your document (Times New Roman, Arial, etc.) depend entirely upon the fonts supported by your currently selected printer. Change the default printer for the document or system and the list of fonts may change slightly, although most modern printers support a fairly common set of fonts.

One feature I find very useful is the Change Case feature. Occasionally I'll type something, especially a section heading, that I want to have in "Capitalize the First Letter of Each Word" format. In the past you might have had to retype the sentence or at least the first letter of each word.

Now just select the sentence, click the "Change Case" button, and select that option. Word takes care of the rest. This is one of those great "new features" that has been in Word forever but that many users are just now discovering thanks to the Ribbon.

Paragraph

Next to the Font group you'll find the Paragraph group, which contains buttons for bulleted or numbered lists, justification, fill color, line spacing, borders, sorting, and other features. We'll talk more about most of these options in Chapter 4.

Notice that the Paragraph group has a dialog launcher at the bottom right corner. Clicking it will fire up the Paragraph dialog box you see in Figure 2.21. In that dialog box you can do some tricky things with indentation, line and page breaks (notice the tabs at the top of the dialog?), line spacing, and more.

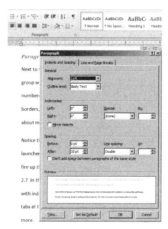

FIGURE 2.21

The last thing I want to call your attention to is the Tabs button at the bottom left, which launches the dialog box you see in Figure 2.22. This lets you customize your tab stops quite easily. You can create or customize tab stops on the ruler, but I've found that some people have trouble

FIGURE 2.22

getting the tabs just the way they want them using only the ruler, so this dialog box may be a little more intuitive for you.

We'll explore this in more detail in Chapter 4.

Styles

The next group contains the Styles Galleries, which let you apply a style to selected text. It's also easy to modify or create new styles from this part of the Ribbon. Like most of the options on the Home tab, we'll be spending some time with Styles in Chapter 4. This is a nice example, however, of the Galleries feature in Word 2010 that gives you WYSIWYWGIYCT (What You See Is What You Will Get If You Click This) capabilities. Despite my doubts that the acronym will catch on, the feature certainly will. If you select some text in your document and then hover your mouse over one of the elements in the gallery, such as "Heading 3," the selected text changes temporarily to show you what it will look like if you click. That eliminates the need for trial and error like the old days; now you can quickly "try" a bunch of formats just by moving your mouse through the Gallery.

To see more styles, click the down arrow at the right end of the Styles gallery. Or click the bottom arrow there to see the entire list at once (Figure 2.23), along with a couple of other options . . . that we'll discuss in more depth in Chapter 4.

FIGURE 2.23

Editing

Finally, the curiously named Editing group contains three buttons: "Find," "Replace," and "Select." These options have changed a bit in Word 2010. In Word 2007 the "Find" and "Replace" buttons both did essentially the same thing: pop up the Find & Replace dialog box. In Word 2010, however, "Find" will take you to the navigation pane (or open it for you if it's not already open) on the left side of the screen, where you can type the text you're searching for in the Search Document box. You can do some neat and tricky things with Find, and I'll get into those in Chapter 3.

Notice the Find tab in Figure 2.24? That's another way to get to the Advanced Find feature you can access through the navigation pane. More on that in Chapter 3. Be patient, it's worth it.

Clicking "Replace" will open the dialog box you see in Figure 2.24 and take you to the Replace tab.

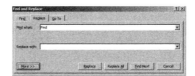

FIGURE 2.24

Find and Replace are pretty handy tools when you're working with large documents. Find lets you search your document for instances of specific text—a witness's name, for example. Replace lets you replace something with something else—if you just realized you've misspelled that witness's name throughout the entire document, it's fast and easy to change the 37 instances of "Smith" to "Smyth."

The Select tool is one of the most underused tools in Word and, honestly, for good reason. Of the three capabilities it has, two of them are much easier to do otherwise. Select All is most easily done by just pressing CTRL+A on the keyboard. Select Object is awkward to do with the Select tool; it's easier to just click on the object with your mouse.

The one option in the Select tool that I find marginally useful is the ability to select all text with a similar formatting. Of course, if you're using Styles (as you should be), then you don't really need to do that with the Select tool either. Moving on. . . .

▼▼▼▼▼
But Wait, There's More

The sharp-eyed among you may have noticed in Figure 2.19 that there is an additional group on my Ribbon in Word—something you may not have seen before. It's called "Ribbon Hero," and it's a game that Microsoft created to help people get more comfortable with the Ribbon. There's plenty of precedent for this; the original Solitaire game was added to Microsoft Windows way back in the day to help people get better with that new-fangled mouse thing. Ribbon Hero, which you can download from Microsoft for free, gives you a set of tasks to perform in the application. Things like converting text to a table, or vice versa. As you successfully complete each task, you're awarded points. What makes it extra clever is that you can compete against your friends if you want to—Ribbon Hero actually has some integration through Windows Live and even Facebook, so you can post your scores and compare scores with other people. It's not Farmville, but it's surprisingly addictive and I can almost guarantee you'll learn some things. I've been using Microsoft Office for the better part of sixteen years, and I learned a thing or two playing the game. It's available for Word, Excel, PowerPoint, and OneNote, and you can find it easily by just Googling or Binging for "Microsoft Ribbon Hero."

Insert

Next up is the Insert tab (see Figure 2.25). The Insert tab, as you might suspect, is filled with things you might want to insert into your document: clip art, page breaks, QuickParts, that sort of thing. Let's take a quick look at each group on this tab.

FIGURE 2.25

Pages

The first group you'll find on the Insert tab is the Pages group, which includes the Cover Page gallery that lets you select from a number of pre-created cover page templates or allows you to create your own cover page to save to the gallery.

The second and third buttons in the Pages group are the Blank Page and Page Break buttons. The page break button inserts a page break at the current cursor location—that forces all of the text after the current cursor location to move down to the next page. Those of you who've used older versions of Word are probably thinking "Wait, doesn't CTRL+ENTER do the same thing?" Yes, it does. The Blank Page button inserts a blank page into your document at the current cursor location. "Wait, couldn't I just press CTRL+ENTER twice?" Yes, you could.

Tables

The next group over on the Insert tab is the little group that could. It has only one button, but it's one button you will want to remember the location of, and that's "Table." To use it, click the button to open the Insert Table tool and then just drag your mouse from top left to bottom right to create a table that matches your needs. Everything from 1x1 (which you may also know as a "Text Box") to 10x8—it's a quick and easy way to create a table that's just the size you need. If you need to make more, we'll talk about ways to do that in Chapter 4. For now Figure 2.26 gives you a teaser.

FIGURE 2.26

Illustrations

The Illustrations group gives you a handful of tools to insert all sorts of pretty pictures, from actual pictures (photos, scans, or other graphics files) to clip art, shapes, SmartArt, or charts.

The Picture tool is pretty self-explanatory. You click it and a dialog box opens that lets you browse your storage devices (hard drives, flash drives, inserted SD cards, CDs, or DVDs) for one or more pictures that you might want to insert into your document. This can be handy if you want to include photos of certain exhibits, properties, or pieces of evidence in your document.

Clip Art is basically eye candy—small graphics that just add some color and visual elements to a document. They're great in presentations and probably have a role in marketing materials, but you're not going to use them in your legal documents so we won't spend a lot of time on them in this book.

When you click the Clip Art button you'll get the search tool you see in Figure 2.27. You can search for clip art, photographs, and other media based on keywords. When you find one you like, either double-click it or drag and drop it to insert it in your document. If you use a lot of clip art, you can manage "collections" of clip art, download more clip art from the

FIGURE 2.27

Web (including Office Online), and even create your own. Again, handy for the brochures and occasional PowerPoint presentation, but not something lawyers use in Word that often. So we'll leave it there.

Unlike the fluffy Clip Art, SmartArt and Charts are both tools that might be useful to you in client communications or to illustrate concrete ideas and principles.

SmartArt lets you create custom graphics like cycle and process diagrams. Not only does it work in Word 2010 but also Excel and PowerPoint as well. I'll give an example of using SmartArt in Chapter 5.

The Chart tool lets you embed a wide variety of charts and graphs into your documents to illustrate comparative data—for instance, revenue over time or to graphically show relative ownership in a disputed piece of real estate. If the interface for the tool looks like Excel, that's because it is Excel. And you can embed or link to Excel workbooks and/or charts in your Word documents, too. We'll talk about that in Chapter 7.

There is one new button in this group for Office 2010, and it's a handy one . . . "Screenshot." Screenshot lets you capture the image of any window that you currently have open. There are a few instances where that can be handy, for example if you're handling a case in which a Web site is part of the dispute—you can open the site in your browser, grab a screenshot of it, and paste that screenshot directly into your document.

Links

The next group on the Insert tab is the Links group. This is a deceptively useful set of tools—the first is the Hyperlink tool that lets you insert a hyperlink into your document. Most people think of this as inserting Web links (e.g., http://www.officeforlawyers.com), but you could also use this to insert a hyperlink to an internal source like a file on your intranet or a link to something else, like a note in OneNote. This feature does make your documents highly interactive, but of course you have to keep the ultimate form of the document in mind. If this is a document that is intended to be printed, then it doesn't do you any good to insert lots of links—they won't translate to paper in any meaningful way.

Figure 2.28 gives you a look at the Insert Hyperlink dialog box.

FIGURE 2.28

The next tool in the Links group is one I use a lot. As you can imagine, I write lots of long documents (like 250-page books), and I don't usually write them in a single sitting (no matter how many Frappacinos I drink), so I frequently have to save my place and come back to it later. I also don't tend to write these books sequentially. Right now I'm writing Chapter 2, but I've already written most of Chapter 12. (It's a good one, but wait for it.) I can't just press [END] and go to the bottom of the document to pick up where I left off. To make matters even slightly more difficult, I also tend to write multiple chapters at once. Obviously here I am in Chapter 2, but I've also written some of several other chapters. So how do I quickly get back to where I left off in a particular chapter? Bookmarks.

▼

Also remember who your audience is . . . if this document is going to stay electronic but be transmitted outside your organization, then it does you no good to create hyperlinks to documents inside your internal systems—the recipients probably won't be able to access those links from their location. This is a mistake I see made *a lot*, by the way. I often receive documents from clients that contain dead hyperlinks . . . because the link points at a location on a private network that I can't access.

The Insert Bookmark tool (see Figure 2.29) lets you create a new bookmark at your current location, delete an existing bookmark, or go to a bookmark you've already defined in the document. As you can see in Figure 2.29, I currently have at least twelve bookmarks defined. You can have as many as you'd like and sort them either by name or by location. A location sort will place them in the order they appear in the document from page 1 forward. The way it works is pretty simple; you click in a spot or select a block of text and then go to the Insert tab of the Ribbon and choose Bookmark. (Or you can press CTRL+SHIFT+F5 if you're mouse-averse). The Bookmark dialog box will appear, and you can type a name for your new bookmark. You can't use spaces or many of the punctuation characters (like hyphens) in your bookmark name, but you can use underscores ("_") to separate words.

FIGURE 2.29

Notice the checkbox for Hidden bookmarks? Those are a special case, generally. Word uses them for a variety of purposes—usually without your realizing it. One example is the Table of Contents. When you add a Table of Contents to your document and flag an item for inclusion, Word puts a hidden bookmark at that spot so that the hyperlink from the Table of Contents can take you back there when you click it.

The third item in the Links group is the Cross-Reference tool. This lets you build links between text and figures, pages, tables, and so forth. The key to it is that if the table or figure is moved, the cross-reference can be "automatically" updated. I am a little disappointed to have to put "automatically" in quotes, but the reality is that it doesn't quite get automatically updated—you have to initiate the update by pressing F9. To update all cross-references, you just use CTRL+A to select the entire document, then press F9.

If you've got a lot of cross-references in a document, and you've been doing some editing, you should make a habit of reconfirming your cross-references by doing a CTRL+A, F9 before you save and finalize the document. Even small edits could have caused things to move around and repaginate in the document, so it's always a good practice to recalculate tables of contents, indexes, cross-references, and any other similar elements you may have in your document.

Header & Footer

Next to Links you'll find the Header & Footer group. One of the more straightforward groups, this is where you can add a header or a . . . wait for it . . . footer. A header is the section at the top of a page that frequently might include the name of the firm, the name of the case, or other title information. The footer is the section at the bottom of each page that might include the date, page number, or other information.

The Header & Footer group contains good examples of one of the better features of Word 2010, and those are the galleries. Figure 2.30 shows what happens when you click the drop arrow under Header. You're presented with a fairly long gallery of predefined headers you can choose from—and if you don't like any of the predefined ones, you can just choose "Blank" and then edit it to create your own header. You can also remove your header from here if you've accidentally added one or just decided you don't want a header on this document after all. Footer works

TRICKS OF THE PROS

Tired of stacks of outdated letterhead sitting in your supply closet? Got more scratch paper than you can use? A lot of firms have taken to creating templates of their letterhead in Word, using the Header & Footer features for much of the static information, and then printing their letters (including the letterhead template) on blank paper as needed. No more ordering overpriced letterhead, some of which will end up stacked in a back closet when you move to a new office or have turnover among the associates.

in much the same way. Clicking the drop arrow opens a large gallery of pre-defined footers. We'll talk more about headers and footers in Chapter 4.

FIGURE 2.30

The third feature in the Header & Footer group is Page Number, which, when clicked, gives you a number of galleries to view in four categories:

- Top of Page creates a header for you that contains the page number in a variety of formats.
- Bottom of Page creates a footer that contains the page number in a variety of formats.
- Page Margin creates a page number on the left or right side of the page—depending upon the option you choose.
- Current Position will let you insert the page number right where you are on the page.

We'll cover page numbering more in Chapter 4.

Text

The next group you'll find is the Text group. This contains a number of items you can add to your document, such as Text Boxes (graphical boxes that contain text), Quick Parts, and others. WordArt lets you create text with artistic graphics, while drop caps are a stylish way to open a paragraph and are especially useful in newsletters and other marketing materials. Figure 2.31 shows the WordArt gallery.

FIGURE 2.31

QuickParts are where you'll find AutoText and the Building Blocks Organizer, a very useful tool that we'll talk about more extensively in Chapter 8. Pay attention to this one; you'll probably use it a lot, once you learn how.

The other things you'll find in QuickParts are Document Property and Field, which let you automatically populate a document with information like the author name or a large selection of formulas.

There are three more options in the Text group, the first two of which are very useful to attorneys:

> **Signature Line** lets you save and insert a standard signature line for use on letters, contracts, and other documents. It can also insert a digital signature for use in electronic documents.

> **Date and Time** is a feature you'll likely use often; it inserts the current date and/or time in a variety of formats (as you can see in Figure 2.32).

FIGURE 2.32

One option you have with Date & Time is the "Update Automatically" option. If you check this box Word will automatically update the date and time. This is handy if you're creating a template and want the date to always be the current date. But be careful . . . if you're creating a letter where you want the original date to be persistent, you should leave this unchecked.

The Object feature in the Text group has two options in it, both of which can be very useful for attorneys. The first option is to insert an object, and that's how you embed items from other applications, as you can see in Figure 2.33. What you're going to see in this window will vary a bit depending upon what applications you have installed. We'll look at some uses of this feature in Chapter 7, and it might make an appearance in Chapter 12 as well. You can either create a new item from that application or insert an item from an existing file.

The other option you'll find if you click the arrow next to the "Object" button is "Text from File." This is a deceptively helpful feature that will insert all of the text from an existing file. Let's say you have a document on your hard drive and you want to incorporate all of that text into your document, but you don't want to have to retype it or open that document separately and do a Copy/Paste. Use Object | Text from File, and Word will just insert all of the text from the file you select at the current insertion point. It's a great way to reuse content from other documents. You may know this feature as "Insert File" from previous versions of Word.

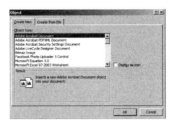

FIGURE 2.33

Symbols

The last group on the Insert tab is the Symbols group, which contains two commands. The equation button launches a gallery that lets you select from a wide variety of items like Pythagorean Theorem and Quadratic Equation. Probably not something lawyers are going to use very often, to be honest, but if you have kids over the age of 13, they may find it useful in doing their homework. The second command in the group, Symbol, is more useful to attorneys, however. Δ, §, and © are among the law-useful symbols you'll find under this command. Note also that if you use a command from the "More Commands" list, it will be added to the initial gallery of symbols so that next time you go to use the same one you don't have to click into More Symbols to find it. (See Figure 2.34.)

FIGURE 2.34

Page Layout

The Page Layout tab (Figure 2.35) contains the features and commands that let you control how your page will appear on the printed sheet. Most notably it covers things like page margins, paper type, and themes.

FIGURE 2.35

Themes

The Themes group includes four commands related to the look and feel of your document. The first one is a Themes gallery that lets you select one of many built-in themes, manage the currently applied theme, download additional themes, or even create your own theme.

What does that mean?

For the most part I think it's pretty rare that attorneys will ever need to tweak those things. The vast majority of your documents are going to be black text on white paper and with a relatively small number of fonts or "effects." The reality is that many of your documents are mandated to a certain look and feel by the court, and I don't care how liberal your judge is, he or she probably doesn't want pink or green type on yellow paper. Accordingly, we're not going to spend much time on Themes in this book.

The next three options are all nicely related to the theme—in fact, they are the elements that the theme controls: Colors, Fonts, and Effects. Each of those buttons launches a gallery that lets you set the text colors, available fonts, and graphical effects that will be used in your document.

Page Setup

The Page Setup group contains commands that let you control the basic layout of the page, most notably things like margins, paper size, and columns.

Margins (Figure 2.36) are a feature that is pretty familiar to folks who work with documents—they control the white space around the edges of your document. Clicking the "Margins" button opens a gallery of common margins that you can use for your document. If none of those are exactly what you need, you can always click "Custom Margins" at the bottom of the list to create your own. Keep in mind that if this document is going to be printed, your printer almost certainly has an unprintable area. Very few printers can print all the way to the edge of the paper—the vast majority will have some small area, on the sides especially but also at the top and bottom, that they just can't put ink or toner on. So no matter what you set your margins to in Word, your printer will generally enforce some minimal unprintable area.

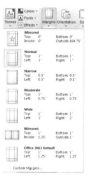

FIGURE 2.36

▼▼▼▼▼
Caution: Geek Content!
Why can't you print all the way to the edge? Pretty simple, actually: your printer needs to have some way to handle the paper. Almost every printer uses rollers to move the paper through the printer, and it can't print on an area of the paper that is under the rollers. Modern printers have gotten pretty good at using very small, or carefully positioned, rollers to minimize that problem, but there is still almost always a bit of the page that the printer can't reach. Some very high-end printers, used almost exclusively by professional printing companies, are able to work around this. Few law firms will have (or need) that kind of equipment.

The old dot-matrix printers used tractor-feed strips attached to the sides of the paper to allow them to handle the paper and still print all the way to the edge. Tearing those perforated tractor strips off the sides was an unwelcome chore, however.

Orientation is fairly simple—there are only two choices there: Portrait or Landscape. Portrait is the typical vertical alignment, like this book. Landscape is with the page rotated 90 degrees, more like how the typical computer monitor is or an HDTV.

Size lets you set the size of the paper you're going to print on. We're all used to "Letter" (8.5x11) or "Legal" (8.5x14), but you can also choose from a variety of other sizes like A4 or Envelope, or you can specify a custom paper size.

Columns are a little trickier to work with, and we'll talk about those in more depth in Chapter 4. Clicking the Columns button here, however, drops down the Columns gallery like you see in Figure 2.37. You can choose from five default column settings, or you can click "More Columns" to set something custom. Generally speaking, if you need something other than one of the five default column selections, then you might consider using a Table instead of columns, but there may be occasions when you'll want some sort of fancy custom column arrangement.

FIGURE 2.37

The Breaks command gives you a number of choices for breaks you can insert. As you can see in Figure 2.38, the gallery is actually pleasantly notated. Not only does it give you a graphical hint of what the command will do, but there is some explanatory text as well. That's a big improvement over the old File, Edit, View menus that never really told you what a command was about.

Page breaks are probably the most common breaks you'll use, aside from Column breaks. If you're using sections in your documents, perhaps to separate exhibits, then you have some choices there as well.

The important thing to remember about Section breaks (so important that I'll probably repeat this in Chapter 4) is the difference between a Next Page and a Continuous break. A Next Page break is actually going to create a new page for you and start your section there. A Continuous break is going to start your new section right at the point of the page that you place the break. Usually lawyers will want a Next Page section break.

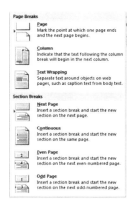

FIGURE 2.38

Page Background

The Page Background group has three commands that affect what goes around and behind the text in your document. For lawyers the first one, Watermark, is generally the most useful.

▼▼▼▼▼

Jensen Harris, the lead dog on the User Interface team at Microsoft, has been heard to say that he got a lot of compliments on the "new" watermark feature in Word 2007. What users didn't realize is that watermark has been in Word for years . . . they just never knew where to find that feature before. The Ribbon exposes it readily, so now they realize it's there.

Watermark, which we talk about in more depth in Chapter 12, lets you create a faded bit of text or image that sits behind your text. It is most often used in law firms to apply words like "DRAFT" or "CONFIDENTIAL" to a printed or digital copy so that the reader is aware of the status of the document. You can see an example of that (which I darkened to make it easier to read for this screen shot) in Figure 2.39.

FIGURE 2.39

Page Color lets you change the background color of the document. This is mostly useful for digital versions of the document, if you want to make a document that is white text on a blue background, for example. For printed versions it's usually a lot easier and cheaper to just use the font color you want and print the document on colored paper. Plus, the sort of documents a lawyer would normally print with colored backgrounds are most likely to be brochures or flyers, and if you're printing that kind of quantity of those sorts of documents, you'll probably send your text to a commercial printing company rather than rely on Word's Page Color settings and your own color printer.

Page Borders lets you create graphical "boxes" around the text in your documents. As the name implies, the borders you create with this feature will encircle the entire page. Note that you can apply the page borders to the entire document (that's the default) or just to a particular section.

Paragraph

The Paragraph group contains two related sets of commands for controlling your indent and spacing. As you might suspect, these settings apply on a paragraph by paragraph basis. I'm not going to really get into these here, but we'll discuss them in some depth in Chapter 4. Suffice it to say that these commands on the Ribbon are an example of direct formatting, and you'll generally be better served by the indirect formatting provided by Styles. If this is a subject you're passionate about, you'll have to flip to Chapter 4 to enjoy more of it.

Arrange

The arrange group controls how text and items on a page interrelate. This is especially useful when you have a graphic image, chart, text box, or other item on the page and you want to be able to control exactly where it appears and how the surrounding text will behave.

Many of the commands in this group will be active only if you have an object (like an inserted image) selected.

The "Position" button opens a gallery (Figure 2.40) that helps you align the object with your text. You can position it so that the text wraps around your object or so that the object stands by itself on the page. Like all galleries in Word 2010, this demonstrates a powerful feature—if you move your mouse over the various gallery options, Word 2010 will temporarily alter the display of your document to reflect how the change will look if you actually make it. This saves a lot of time in trial and error for aligning text and objects.

FIGURE 2.40

The next two commands (Bring to Front and Send to Back) demonstrate a surprising capability of Microsoft Word—the ability to have multi-layered documents. There are more options than just having text next to images. You can actually have text in front of (or behind) images or multiple images stacked on top of each other. You can use the Front/Back commands to arrange the images the way you like them. This really isn't a feature lawyers use often, so I'm not going to spend additional space on it in this book.

The Selection Pane solves a common problem with multi-layered documents. It can be very hard to manipulate images that are layered simply because it's hard to select them. Click the Selection Pane icon to turn on the Selection Pane, and you'll find it easier to handle them. As long as you're in there, rename your images to make them easier to identify on the page.

Figure 2.41 shows the Align group, which lets you tune how you want to align a selected image (or images) on the page. You can even turn on gridlines for precision text and image layout. Not really a feature lawyers will use very much, so we're not going to spend a lot more time on it here.

If you have multiple images that you want to be able to link together, then the Group command is for you. With images grouped you can move

TRICKS OF THE PROS

One of the rare times I do see lawyers use this feature (or want to) is if they are annotating exhibits. Perhaps you've pasted in a satellite photo of a piece of real estate in dispute and you want to type (or draw) annotations on top of it. Then "Bring to Front" and "Send to Back" are features you might want to get cozy with.

and format them together. Clicking the "Group" button offers two options: Group or Ungroup. For reasons that may be obvious, only one of them will be active at a time.

FIGURE 2.41

Finally if you insert an image that is not aligned on the page the way you would like it to be the Rotate button gives you the option to rotate or flip the image either left or right.

References

The References tab on the Ribbon, shown in Figure 2.42, can be very powerful for attorneys creating complex documents, as it helps to automate some of the more challenging and time-consuming tasks.

In Chapter 5 we'll see examples of using many of these features.

FIGURE 2.42

Table of Contents

The Table of Contents group contains tools that help you create and maintain a table of contents. In Word this is primarily accomplished by using the Header styles, but you can also use the Add Text command to add a current bit of text, such as a custom heading, to your table of contents.

Update Table does just what you think it does, making another pass through your document and updating the table of contents with any new headings that you've added since the last update. Also, it will correct for any headers that have moved to a different page number—making sure your table of contents is always correct. It's important to do this before you finalize a document that has a generated table of contents in it.

Footnotes

Lawyers love footnotes. With the Footnotes group you have some powerful tools for creating and maintaining footnotes and endnotes.

Insert Footnote lets you create a footnote at the bottom of the current page. Insert Endnote creates a note at the end of the document.

The Show Notes feature takes you to the actual notes area. If you're working in a document that has both footnotes and endnotes, then Word will politely ask you which one you want to see.

Citations and Bibliography

The Citations and Bibliography tool has a lot more than meets the eye. At first glance you may not realize that it helps you maintain a database of sources and insert them, consistently, where and when you need them. The feature is powerful enough and useful enough that we'll devote a little space to it in Chapter 5. For now . . . this is where you find these tools.

Captions

The Captions tool is for images or graphics inserted into a document. It should be really useful, and in some cases it probably is, but to be honest every time I've tried to use the feature I found it was more in my way than helping me. The problem with it is you don't have much control over how the caption is created. Unless you really love the way the tool chooses to create the captions, you'll spend a lot more time trying to fix them than if you'd just created the captions manually.

If you do decide to use the Captions tool, I'd advise not applying them until you're nearly done with the document. If you caption images and then reorder the them (or insert one), the caption numbering can stay in the original order . . . meaning that your "Figure 3-6" may end up after "Figure 3-7," which is confusing to everybody. Applying the captions last will give you a better chance to get them right.

Index

The Index group does for indexes (typically found at the end of your document) what the Table of Contents group does for tables of contents (typically found at the beginning). This is a really useful set of tools that lets you create and maintain an index. You can mark any term or phrase as an entry for the index, and Word will automatically add it. Best of all, if, that text should move to a different page, through subsequent editing, simply clicking "Update Index" will correct the page numbers associated with the terms in the index. As with the table of contents it's important to update your index before finalizing any document that contains one.

Table of Authorities

Lastly, Table of Authorities employs commands essentially similar to the Table of Contents and Index groups to create and maintain a table of authorities. Using this tool is actually pretty easy. When you create a citation in your document that you want to add to the table of authorities, you just highlight that text and then click the "Mark Citation" button on the Ribbon. Once you've gone through and marked your citation, just go to the place in the document where you want to place your table of authorities and click the "Insert Table of Authorities" button. The table will be nicely created for you.

If you later want to add more citations to the table of authorities, just mark them as the others, then click the "Update Table" button. Yes, we'll spend more time on this in Chapter 5, too.

Mailings

The Mailings tab on the Ribbon (Figure 2.43) is primarily concerned with helping you create mail merges; very handy for doing large "personalized" mailings, but it also contains the commands for creating envelopes or mailing labels.

FIGURE 2.43

Create

A feature I've always used in Word is the ability to create and print envelopes. We'll talk about it more in-depth in Chapter 12.

Creating mailing labels is a fairly similar process—clicking the command on the Ribbon launches the "Envelopes and Labels" dialog box to the Labels tab. You'll notice right away that it offers you a large field to type the address you want to appear on the label. Less obvious is the tiny "Address Book" icon just above the address field (it looks vaguely like an open book), and you can see it next to the "Use return address" checkbox in Figure 2.44. Clicking the address book icon will let you access your Outlook address books, especially your Contacts folder, so that you can select one or more addresses from those lists to print on the labels. Yes, that's really handy.

FIGURE 2.44

Tricks of the Pros

One of my client firms uses this tool to print a whole page of mailing labels when they open a new file for a client. My clients know there will be a number of mailings and deliveries to this client, so after adding the client to Outlook, they come into this tool and print a full page of labels, which they then put in the paper file. Anytime they need to send something to the client, they can just peel the next label off the sheet and they're ready to go. If they run out of labels it's trivial to just print up a new sheet.

Start Mail Merge

"Start Mail Merge" is the button you'll click to initiate the mail merge. It has a whole collection of options that let you specify what kind of document you're going to merge to. Select Recipients and Edit Recipient List are tools used to manage the source data for your mail merge. I won't spend much time on these here because we're going to go into mail merge in detail in Chapter 7.

Write & Insert Fields

The Write & Insert Fields group contains the tools you'll use to build your merge documents. This is another group we'll spend a lot more time with in Chapter 7. One of the features I do want to point out here, though, is the "Rules" command. This lets you take your mail merges to a whole new level, by letting you add some logic to your mail merge that you never really had before. For example: if you know the address of the property in question, you may be able to use a rule to automatically insert the address of the relevant courthouse.

Preview Results

Preview Results is an underappreciated set of tools—they let you see what your merge results are going to be without having to waste paper to do it. Click "Preview Results" to get a test merge on-screen, and then you can use the forward and back arrows to scroll through your merge set and make sure everything looks right before you commit to printing or sending it.

Finish

The Finish group seems a little silly because it contains only a single command: Finish & Merge. This is the command you'll use when you're confident that your merge is ready to go. Clicking this button will perform the final mail merge of your data and template and create the finished documents for printing, e-mailing, or whatnot.

> **Tip**
>
> If you have Adobe Acrobat installed, you may have a "Merge to Adobe PDF" (Figure 2.45) group and button on the right end of the Ribbon. It's a handy way to create a set of merge files as PDFs instead.

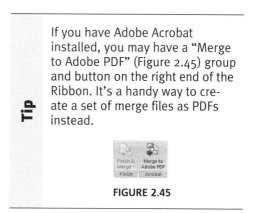

FIGURE 2.45

Review

The Review tab contains a number of tools you'll use to collaborate with other parties on documents as well as to review and finalize a work in progress. You can see the tab in Figure 2.46.

FIGURE 2.46

We'll dig into many of these features in Chapter 6, but let's introduce them to you here.

Proofing

The proofing group contains some tools that you can use to check and finalize a document before sending it out. The spelling and grammar tools are largely active as you type—we've all seen the red squiggly lines that appear beneath text that Word believes is misspelled.

The Research tool is very handy for making sure that you're using exactly the words you want to use—it helps you check the definitions of words or phrases as well as find alternatives that might be better. See Chapter 12 for a lot more coverage of the Research function.

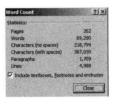

The Thesaurus can help you to find exactly the word you want—showing you synonyms (and antonyms) of the word you select so that you might decide to use something else. To use it, just select the word you're interested in, then click Thesaurus (AKA Lexicon, Vocabulary, Glossary, Phrasebook, Wordlist . . .).

"Never use a big word when a diminutive one will do."

The last option in the Proofing group is the "Word Count" button. This gives you quick access to a bit of statistical information (more than just the word count) about your document, as you can see in Figure 2.47.

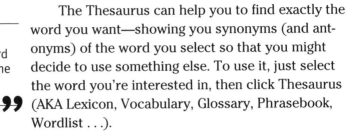

FIGURE 2.47

Language

Translate is one of those features that you won't use often, but when you do need it you'll be happy to have it. Word 2010 has the ability to help you translate text from more than a dozen languages into more than a dozen languages. Is that pretty cool in our very international world? *Creo que sí.*

> ▼▼▼▼▼
>
> ## CAUTION! (*CUIDADO! AVERTIR!*)
>
> The Word translator is not perfect and should not be used as a substitute for a capable human translator. If you use it to translate anything important, you should have that text proofread by a person who is fluent in the language you're translating to or from.

The translation screen tip, which is turned off by default, allows you to highlight a piece of text in your document and Word will pop up a screen tip that shows you information about the word and its translation in one of four languages.

The Set Language command lets you specify that a piece of text was written in a particular language and that the spell checker should treat it accordingly. Word does a pretty good job of automatically detecting what language text is in, but there may be times when you'll need to give it a hand and tell it what language you've used.

The Word Count tool shows you how many words, sentences, paragraphs, etc. you have in your document, but this isn't the best way to get

▼

Anybody notice that one of the language choices is Hawaiian?

to this tool. Keep reading; later in this chapter we're going to talk about the Status Bar, which you'll find is a really powerful tool.

Comments

If you're going to review a document, you'll almost certainly want to include comments. You won't believe the number of comments my editors will be inserting in this manuscript before they send it back to me! Comments can be colorful, and those colors are automatically assigned to each reviewer through a magical algorithm involving page count, margin size, and the phase of Jupiter . . . OK, I'll be honest, I can't find anybody who knows exactly what the algorithm is, and it really doesn't matter. The bottom line is that you can't readily control what color you're assigned without manually assigning everybody's colors.

The comments (you can see one in Figure 2.48) are identified not just by color but by the intials of the reviewer ("BMS" in my case), followed by a number indicating which comment (sequentially) that is. My next comment, predictably enough, would be "BMS3." You can't easily control the colors, but you can easily control the initials. Click File, then Options, and on the General group you'll find a place to specify the user's initials. You'll want to change the initials if you inherited the machine from another user or if another user you collaborate with frequently has the same initials as you.

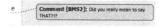

FIGURE 2.48

▼▼▼▼▼
TRICKS OF THE PROS

There is a little hidden shortcut for getting to the General group to change your initials from here. The next group over is "Tracking" (we'll be talking about it in a moment), and under the Track Changes button there are three options—the third of which is "Change User Name," which will just open that same dialog box that you get to via File | Options.

Tip

Be very careful with comments. This is one of those document elements that can get you into trouble if you get careless. Before you finalize any document and prepare it to be sent out of the firm, even to the client, be sure that there are no comments in the document that you wouldn't want to see on the front page of the New York Times.

Other than being able to add or delete comments, there are also buttons here that will help you navigate to the previous or next comments in the document.

Word 2010 includes the ability, if your machine is suitably equipped, to do Ink comments. Click the Ink Comment link and you can draw your comment on the page with a stylus (or mouse, if you're talented enough). That's handy for people who like to annotate that way, but I find that the quality of the inked comments are often such that it's hard for anybody else to read. I prefer to stick to the typed comments myself.

If you don't see the Ink Comment button, don't be concerned. That just means the feature isn't currently enabled on your machine.

Tracking

The tracking group is one of the most important groups on the Ribbon, especially for attorneys. This is one place where you can control track changes and adjust how (or even if) Word displays those changes.

The "Track Changes" button lets you turn tracked changes on or off, and the options you'll find under the drop-arrow on that button let you have more control over how Track Changes behaves. Clicking the "Change Tracking Options" command will get you the Track Changes Options dialog box you see in Figure 2.49. We'll get into this more deeply in Chapter 6.

FIGURE 2.49

The next two options in the Tracking group are very important, so you may want to read this section twice. In fact, I recommend buying a second copy of this book and opening both copies side by side just to get the full effect. The first is the "Display for Review" drop list, which you can see in Figure 2.50. I'll explain it in more depth in Chapter 6, and I'll mention it again in Chapter 13. More than a mere shameless attempt to reuse content to inflate my page count, this really is an important discussion about a feature of Word that attorneys need to be aware of. Yes, really. It's no less than the way you display, or hide, markup and metadata in the document.

FIGURE 2.50

The next option, Show Markup, is equally important because it controls what kinds of markup the "Final/Original Showing Markup" views will reveal. Figure 2.51 shows what you'll see there. Of particular interest to us are comments, insertions, and deletions.

The "Balloons" button gives you options for how (or if) you want Word to use balloons to show the revisions. You can see an example of a balloon in Figure 2.48; even though that's a comment balloon, it looks basically the same. For the next version of Word I'm suggesting that Microsoft let us make balloon animals! The primary function of the "Balloons" button is to let you control if you want your tracked changes to appear inline or off to the side (AKA "in balloons"). Generally speaking I tend to prefer inline unless there are so many changes that it makes the document difficult to read. Since this is just a display setting, there's no harm in leaving it set to "Inline" and then switching to balloons later if the inline starts to annoy you. Or vice versa.

FIGURE 2.51

Changes

The Changes group (Figure 2.52) contains tools that you'll use to specify what you want to do with tracked changes made to the document. Accept and Reject will accept or reject (of course) the currently selected change and then move on to the next change. Note that the Accept and Reject drop-down menus include the ability to accept or reject *all* of the changes in the document in one shot. That can be really handy—especially if you're finalizing and you know that you want to accept all the changes. Accepting the changes, then turning off track changes, then running the metadata checker is a good way to finish your document before you send it off.

FIGURE 2.52

Generally when I'm reviewing a document I will reject the changes I know I don't want and leave the other changes alone until I'm done with the review. Once I've completed my review, and I may take multiple passes at it, I assume that all of the remaining, un-rejected, changes are changes I want to accept, so I'll simply Accept All to the remaining changes and go from there.

If you don't want to accept or reject the currently selected change, just click Previous or Next and it will take you to the previous (or next) change and leave the current change unresolved. I don't think I need to explain those beyond that, do I?

Compare

Compare is another feature that lawyers use *a lot*. We'll demo this a bit in Chapter 6, but these tools have been significantly improved in Word 2010. The compare feature lets you put two documents side by side, and it will show you the differences, what used to be called "Redline" but now seems just as often to be called "Blackline." Whatever color you like to call it, that's what this tool does—shows you the two documents side by side and gives you a copy of the documents that merges the changes and shows you what they are.

▼

Most of you will find the Block Authors button grayed out with no obvious way to enable that functionality. That's because it's only available on documents that are saved to a SharePoint 2010 site that supports Workspaces. The seven of you reading this who have that kind of environment just smiled.

Protect

The Protect group has been expanded in Word 2010. It now contains two commands: Block Authors and Restrict Editing.

Block Authors protects a specific section of a document from being edited.

Restrict Editing is an extremely handy way to protect some or all of a document. We'll talk more about it in Chapter 6, but just remember that this is how you configure restricted editing and document protection.

Ink

If your machine supports digital ink, you may have a group called "Ink" and a single button called "Start Inking." That's used to turn on the ink annotation features—we'll mention it a bit more in Chapter 6.

OneNote

Office 2010 is the first Microsoft Office suite that includes Microsoft One-Note right in the box. That means almost all of you will have the OneNote group and its single "Linked Notes" button. We'll explore this a bit more in Chapter 7—put briefly, if you want to take notes about your document in Microsoft OneNote (as opposed to in the document itself), you could use this feature to link those notes to the document. It remains to be seen how many attorneys actually avail themselves of that capability.

View

The View tab gives you the controls to handle how Word is going to display your document (see Figure 2.53). There are a number of useful commands here, so let's dig in.

FIGURE 2.53

Document Views

The Document Views group lets you switch between the five basic views that Word offers.

- Print Layout—this is the default view that most people use, most of the time. It lays out the document on the page more or less how it's going to look if you print it. It's a familiar, comfortable, and capable view, and that's why most people use it. Note . . . which printer you currently have selected under File | Print may affect how pages display and paginate in the Print Layout view. If you're going to use this view, and I'll bet you are, try to have the printer you're actually going to print on already selected in the print settings to reduce the chances of a nasty surprise later.

- Full Screen Reading—this was a new view in Word 2007 and one that users tend to either love or hate. When you open a Word document from an e-mail message, for example, Word 2010 defaults to showing it to you in Full Screen Reading view. This is a read-only view, no editing allowed by default (see sidebar), so you probably won't choose to use it that often. If you don't like it for viewing received documents, by the way, I'll show you how to turn it off in Chapter 9.

- Web Layout—this view shows how your document will look as a Web page. Very few lawyers will use this view; there aren't any page margins and the pagination and layout are going to be different from how the document will look when you print it or send it.

- Outline—the Outline view is a view optimized for outlining. There's no formatting, and switching to Outline view turns on the Outlining tab on the Ribbon (see Figure 2-54). It's occasionally useful for highly structured documents (or if you just like to use Word to create outlines), but you should be sure to switch back to the Print Layout view to finalize your document formatting and layout.

- Draft—the Draft view is a clean look at your document without all the bells and whistles that some find distracting. It can be somewhat faster than the Print Layout view because it doesn't do foreground repagination, which is a fancy way of saying that it won't stall you while it tries to do administrative stuff with your long document. Do note, however, if you have images, charts, or clip art pasted into your document they won't show up in Draft view. You'll need to switch to one of the other views (Print Layout, most likely) to see them. I don't like to use Draft view because it uses a very utilitarian font that I find uncomfortable to work in.

If you'd like to enable editing in the Full Screen Reading view, click the "View Options" at the top right corner of the view and choose "Allow Typing."

FIGURE 2.54

Show

The next group is the Show group, which is just a small collection of checkboxes that turn on and off some common features of Word.

- Ruler—turning off the ruler saves you a tiny bit of space at the top of the document and does give you a slightly cleaner look. I, personally, like to turn it off, especially since it's so easy to turn it back on for those rare instances when I want or need it. You can also turn the ruler on or off with the very discreet button at the top of the vertical scroll bar on the right edge of the window.

■ Gridlines—if you need to do some really precise alignment of elements of your documents, or if you just have an odd fetish for typing on graph paper, you can turn on the gridlines. Primarily this is used when you're doing some more advanced graphic design, such as laying out a graphically complex newsletter. I can honestly say that in twenty years of working with lawyers and technology, I've never seen an attorney who turned the gridlines on. And I've never had one ask me if there was a way to turn the gridlines on, either.

■ Navigation Pane—in Word 2007 this was called "Document Map," and it's been greatly improved in the new version. The navigation pane (Figure 2.55) is a text-based outline that shows you your document based upon the headings and helps you to navigate readily up and down in a long document. I use it quite often, especially when writing a document like this book. We'll talk about it more in Chapter 12.

FIGURE 2.55

Zoom

The Zoom group gives you some quick controls that help you display your document in the most productive way for you. It's important to note that all of these buttons and settings are basically just presets of various zoom levels. Clicking "Two Pages," for example, sets the zoom level to a percentage that will show two pages on the screen, side by side, at the same time.

▼

Want to get to the Zoom dialog box without having to go to the View tab on the Ribbon? Just click the percentage indicator on the zoom slider on the status bar at the bottom right of the document window.

Clicking the "Zoom" button will open the Zoom dialog box you see in Figure 2.56. From there you can more precisely control how your document is zoomed, including some of the pre-created zoom options like "Text Width" or "Page Width." What's the difference? Text width excludes the right and left margins; page width doesn't. Whole Page is going to zoom the document so that you see the entire page, top to bottom and left to right, on the screen at once (the same as clicking "One Page" on the Ribbon).

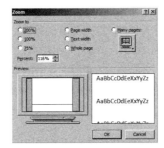

FIGURE 2.56

The other buttons in the Zoom group give you quick access to popular zoom options. Selecting 100% takes you quickly to the 100% zoom level; One Page and Two Pages set the zoom to display either one or two pages.

Window

Word has always allowed you to work with multiple documents at once in multiple windows. With Word 2010, the tools are just right out on the Ribbon instead of hidden under a Window menu.

If you already have a document open, clicking "New Window" might surprise you just slightly. Rather than opening a new, blank, Word window, it actually opens a second copy of your open document in the new window. That can be really handy if you're copying/pasting text from one part of your document to another, or if you're using cut/paste to move text from one part to the other and you want to be able to see both bits of the document at the same time.

Once you have opened one or more "New Windows," you can use the "Arrange All" command to lay those windows out side by side (actually one on top of the other, stacked vertically) on the screen. This will arrange all Word 2010 windows for you, by the way, not just windows you open using the New Window command. Most of the time, if you have multiple instances of Word 2010 running, it's because you opened multiple documents from your document management system, from Windows Explorer, or by just starting another instance of Word from the operating system—as opposed to using the "New Window" command.

If you'd like to quickly arrange those multiple windows on the screen, the Arrange All command is your answer. Naturally, if you have only one instance of Word open, you can click "Arrange All" as often as you like and it won't do anything other than make your one window of Word full screen.

▼▼▼▼▼
CAUTION

If you use multiple monitors, be aware that "Arrange All" isn't going to respect your current settings. If you have some or all of your documents on a second monitor, Arrange All is going to move them to the first monitor. That can be a minor annoyance as you have to start dragging them back to your preferred screen.

Another tool that lets you see multiple parts of your document at the same time is the Split Window tool. When you click it you'll get a horizontal line you can place anywhere on the screen. When you place it Word will split the screen at that point. You'll get two sections of the window, each with the same document, as you can see in Figure 2.57.

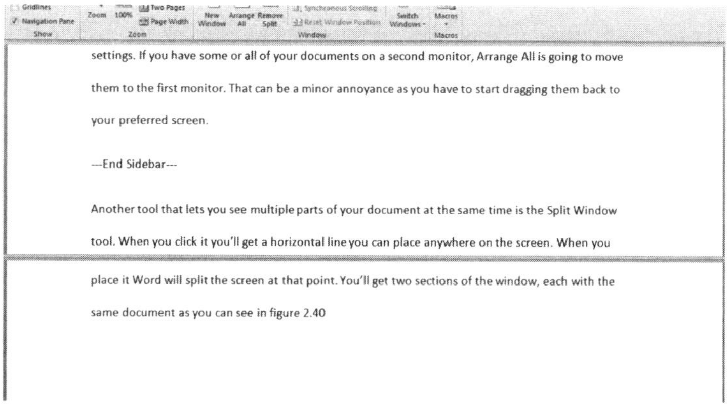

FIGURE 2.57

You can scroll up or down in either window to compare, copy, or paste text. When you're done with the split, just click "Remove Split" to turn it off. Really, this is just another way to view two bits of the same document side by side (actually, one above the other). You could also do it with "New Window"; using "Split" just does it within a single window.

Word 2010 provides you with a lot of tools to compare documents, and one of them is the "View Side by Side" option. In this regard Microsoft really heard the feedback from the users because this feature has been asked for a lot. And it's even got a couple of nice bells and whistles. This button is enabled only if you have two or more documents open.

Clicking the Synchronous Scrolling command (which works only if you have View Side by Side enabled) sets the two Word windows to scroll in lockstep. So if you scroll up or down in one, the other will follow. This is a great feature when you're trying to compare two documents as it makes it easy to be sure you're always in sync.

If you happen to move or resize your documents when they're in Side by Side mode—so that one document is larger or off to another place on the screen—and want to restore them to be equally sized and side by side, you can click the "Reset Window Position" button and it'll put your Word windows back the way they were when you first viewed side by side.

The Switch Windows command (Figure 2.58) is reasonably self-explanatory—clicking that will let you choose among all of the Word 2010 windows you have open. You can do the same thing on the Windows task bar, and I invariably do.

FIGURE 2.58

Macros

The final group on the View tab is the Macros group, and it contains just one command. Clicking the "Macros" button will give you the options to record or manage Word macros. I suspect Microsoft put this command here because . . . well . . . it didn't really belong anywhere else. (See the next section.) We're going to talk more about Macros in Chapter 8.

Developer

I know what you're thinking . . . "Developer tab? *What* Developer tab?" Well . . . the Developer tab is sort of an odd hybrid tab. There are some tabs that are standard: Home, Insert, Page Layout, etc. There are some tabs that are contextual: the Table or Drawing Tools tabs appear only when you have a table or when you have a drawing selected. There are tabs that will appear only if you have certain software installed—for instance, Adobe Acrobat adds a tab if you have Acrobat installed. But the Developer tab is a slightly different animal—it's a tab that you can turn on and off in the Word Options (see Figure 2.59). By default it's turned off, so if you're one of the few folks who want it on you'll have to hit File, then Options, and on the Customize Ribbon group you can check the box to enable the Developer tab.

FIGURE 2.59

Once you've turned it on (Figure 2.60), however, you get a number of features that are interesting to people who want to extend Word 2010 with some custom code. We'll touch on this a bit in Chapter 8, but since most attorneys don't have a lot of interest in programming Word, we're not going to spend much time on it. If Visual Basic for Applications fascinates you and you really want to develop your own elaborate Word extensions, I'll list a few books and resources for you in Chapter 8. For now, let's just take a cursory run around the tab so you know what's on it and why.

FIGURE 2.60

Code

The Code group contains the starting points for developing custom Word solutions. The Visual Basic button is going to launch the Microsoft Visual Basic editor, which you can see in Figure 2.61. From here a talented programmer can make all sorts of magic happen. And even a total amateur can probably stumble around and at least create a program that inserts "Hello, World" into a document over and over again with just a little time and effort.

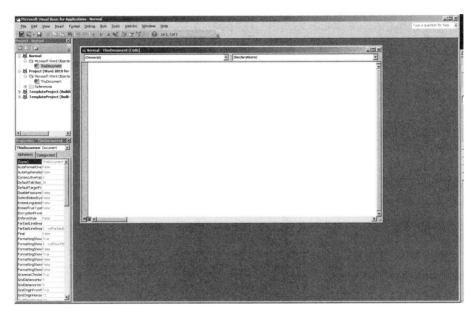

FIGURE 2.61

The Macros button launches the Macros dialog box you see in Figure 2.62. From here you can also launch the aforementioned Visual Basic Editor to create or edit macro code, or you can manage (read: Delete) your macros.

FIGURE 2.62

For most of you, the more useful option here is going to be the "Record Macro" command, which lets you create a custom macro simply by starting the recording, performing a set of tasks, and then stopping the recording and saving that result as a macro. Anytime you want to do that set of tasks again, simply "play" the macro. Cool, huh? If that concept has your juices flowing, then I suggest you hurry up and get to Chapter 8 because we'll go over it in more detail there. If that idea doesn't interest you at all, then maybe you'll skip straight to Chapter 9. It's fun, too.

The final option of the Code group actually doesn't have a lot to do with creating code and has a lot more to do with securing Word against other people's code. Clicking the Macro Security command will open the Trust Center dialog of Word Options and let you control how Word handles a document it encounters that has macros in it. The default setting is to "Disable with Notification," which I recommend you leave as is. That will *not* allow macros in a document you receive to run, but it will tell you there are macros in the document, just in case you didn't know, and give you the option to enable them. Continue with Chapter 9 if you want to learn more about these settings.

Add-Ins

The Add-Ins group offers two controls that help you determine what templates and COM Add-Ins are currently installed in Word. We'll talk about these a little more in Chapter 9, but as a general rule you should leave these settings alone. Some of the crashes and instability we see in Word 2010 can be directly traced to misbehaving or misconfigured add-ins.

Controls

The Controls group gives you a tribe of little controls you can use to insert things like date pickers and drop-down lists into your document. Mostly these are used when creating custom document templates that include some level of automation. Chapter 8 will mention these further and give a little demonstration on their use.

XML

If you're an XML guru and really want to get in and wrap your hands around the new Open XML Document structure, then this group is your playground. Here you can play with the schema, view or add XML Expansion Packs, and even work with linked CSS style sheets. Sound like something you'd love to do? I didn't think so. Which is why I'm not going to waste much time talking about it in this book.

A "schema" in this context is a structure that describes an XML document. The XML schema defines the data elements (like city, state, and ZIP) that can be tagged and identified in a document.

Protect

The Protect group may look familiar—that's because it's identical to the one you found on the Review tab. Same buttons, same purpose, same function. I guess anything worth doing is worth doing twice.

Templates

The Templates group rounds out our tour of the Ribbon and does so in style. It's one of those groups that are actually pretty useful if you're doing Word development (and if you're not, why are you on the Developer tab?). From here you can manage your templates and document information panels.

We'll talk more about templates throughout the book—most notably in Chapters 5, 8, 11, and 13. But keep your eyes open; you never know where the little fellas might turn up.

Document Information Panels are a different animal, however. They give you access to some of the basic metadata about the document in a handy panel.

From this panel you can see and edit information such as the document's title, keywords, and author and even add comments about the document. You can manually display the panel by clicking File and going to Prepare and then Properties. And you can see a sample panel in Figure 2.63.

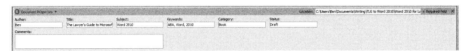

FIGURE 2.63

Clicking the "Document Panel" button in the Templates group, however, will present you with the Document Information Panel Options dialog box that you see in Figure 2.64.

Here you can specify a custom Document Information Panel if you want to, or simply select different settings to have displayed by default. Most significantly, though, you can choose to have the panel automatically displayed when a document is opened or saved for the first time (Figure 2.65). This is a great way to remind you what the document is about and to prompt you to add information (like the aforementioned Comments, Title, Subject, Keywords, etc.) to a document when you save it.

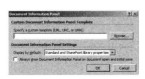

FIGURE 2.64   **FIGURE 2.65**

Those of you who are using document management systems like Docs Open or iManage, which prompt you for a document profile, are familiar with the concept already. If you are using a document management system like that then you probably don't need to use the Word document panel much.

Customizing the Ribbon

One of the things people complained about the most in Word 2007 was the inability to customize the Ribbon. That's been somewhat addressed in Word 2010. Right-click anywhere on the Ribbon and you'll get the option to customize it (see Figure 2.66). In this dialog box you can turn on or off any tab (but not Backstage) or any group or icon of the Ribbon, or even add your own custom tabs and groups. You can also add features from the left-hand column (change "Choose Commands From" to see more features) to an existing Ribbon tab or to your custom tab(s).

FIGURE 2.66

If you've made a hash of your Ribbon, the "Reset" button is here to rescue you—it'll put the Ribbon back to the way it looks out of the box.

The Status Bar

At the bottom of the Word window is the new and improved status bar. This is one of the underappreciated features of Word, and it's an area that lawyers can really get a lot of value from. From left to right across the status bar you'll (usually) find the page count ("Page 9 of 30"), which tells you which page you're on and how many total pages you've got. The tricky thing about this display is that it's also a button—if you click it you'll get the Find and Replace dialog box we discussed previously that lets you go immediately to any page, lets you search for text (and replace it if you want to), and even lets you jump straight to bookmarks.

The reason I said "usually" is that this status bar is very configurable. Right-click the bar and you can choose a number of things to add to it. Among the choices you'll have:

- Formatted Page Number: This shows you the page number you're currently on. I usually don't bother with this one because I like the "Page Number" option (below) better and I find them redundant.

- Section: If you're using section breaks this will tell you which section you're currently in. In my experience most firms don't use sections as often as they should, so it will probably usually read "1" for you.

- Page Number: This is on by default and it tells you which page you're on and how many total pages you have—"Page 53 of 125," for example.

- Line Number: Many documents prepared for courts have very specific line number requirements, so it can be handy to know which line number you're on.

- Column: This field is a little deceptive. When you first see it you might think, as I did, that it refers to columns like newspaper columns. Legal documents frequently have multiple "columns," especially in the headers. So you might expect that "Column" was going to tell you if you were in column 1, 2, or 3. But that's not what it is at all. In fact "Column" in this context refers to the horizontal cursor position. In other words, when your cursor is all the way on the left end of the line that will read "1." As you move across the line from left to right, that number will increase. Usually it's not that handy, but sometimes if you need to vertically align two words or characters it can be useful to know that both of them are at "Column 17" or wherever.

- Word count: Right next to the page number you'll find Word Count, which tells you how many total words you have in the document at the moment. And yes, it updates live. Oooh, there's 18,043 for me. 18,046. 18,047. If you happen to select one or more words, this item will tell you how many words you've selected. Selecting that previous sentence told me I had "19/18,066," for example.

- Track Changes: A very handy tool that I recommend *all* lawyers turn on—this will tell you at a glance if Track Changes is currently on or off for this document. (It's on.)

- Overtype: This item tells you if you're in "Insert" mode or "Overtype" mode.

▼▼▼▼▼

Insert mode lets you place your cursor somewhere on the screen—between two characters, for example—and whatever you type will be inserted, moving any content to the right of your insertion point. Overtype mode will replace the content to the right of your insertion point with whatever you happen to type. If you typed "Farrah Majors" and wanted to add the "Fawcett," you'd make sure you were in Insert mode, click in front of "Majors" and type "Fawcett" to get "Farrah Fawcett Majors." If you typed "John Cougar" and wanted to change it to "John Mellencamp" (without having to release another album), you'd place your insertion point to the left of the "C" in Cougar, make sure you were in Overtype mode, and type "Mellencamp" to replace the "Cougar."

Typically changing modes involves simply pressing the INSERT key on your keyboard—it's a toggle that switches back and forth. In Word 2010 you can also just left-click on the "Insert" (or "Overtype") on the status bar to switch back and forth between them. There are no features in Word 2010 that let you disable obscure '80s Pop Culture references, however.

Just to the right of the status bar you'll find some controls that affect how Word displays your documents.

First up are buttons that let you select one of the five document views that we discussed previously:

- Print Layout
- Full Screen Reading
- Web Layout
- Outline
- Draft

Next up is the zoom level indicator previously discussed. To the right of that is a zoom slider that lets you zoom in and out on your document—great if you're like me and your eyes aren't quite what they used to be, or if you have an especially large monitor and want to pull back to see more of the page at once.

All of the settings on the status bar, even the zoom settings on the right end, can be turned on or off quite quickly and easily in the Customize Status Bar dialog we talked about previously.

Mini Toolbar

Word 2010 has another little time-saver in store for you. When you select some text in Word, a small floating toolbar will appear that contains some of the most common functions that people do with selected text—for instance: bold, font size, font color, or even Format Painter. If you want to use one of these functions, just click the button on the floating toolbar and you're done. This saves you from having to mouse all the way to the top of the screen and possibly having to change to a different tab on the Ribbon to find the command you want.

▼

The Mini Toolbar, like many Office functions, has gone through several names internally at Microsoft. At one point it was called the "Minibar." At another point it was called the "Floatie." Mercifully the company ultimately settled on "Mini Toolbar."

The Mini Toolbar will appear automatically any time you use the mouse to select some text in Word 2010, and it will go away automatically if you ignore it—it only persists if you actually move the mouse to it and use it. It can take a little practice to get good at the Mini Toolbar; it appears and fades away like a mischievous puppy hiding behind the couch. Once you've mastered the art of mousing with the Mini Toolbar, however, I think you'll find it quite handy. If not, you can easily turn it off; just click File, go to Options, and the very first option on the very first tab is to turn on or off the display of the Mini Toolbar.

Summary

Word 2010 is a very nice update to the groundbreaking Word 2007. The Fluent interface has been refined and updated to address some of the concerns raised in Word 2007. The Ribbon is the most distinctive change and brings all features of the product out in front where you can find them. Other features of the new interface include the more sophisticated, useful, and configurable status bar and the handy Mini Toolbar that appears when needed to save you time in performing common formatting tasks.

Creating a Basic Document

3

At some level, creating a basic document is just that: basic. If you know how to navigate the program, it becomes a matter of using the basic tools. In this chapter I'll try to familiarize you with those tools and give you some tips for using them more effectively.

Start from Scratch

We'll talk about using templates in Chapter 4, but for now let's look at how you can use Word to start from a blank sheet of paper. To get a clean sheet of "paper" go Backstage by clicking File, then New.

The New Document window will appear (Figure 3.1), and Blank Document should be selected by default. You can double-click it or just click the "Create" button on the right-hand side to get a blank sheet of paper in Word that's ready to type in.

Another option for creating a new document is to right-click on the folder where you want to locate the new document and choose New | Microsoft Office Word Document. This will create a blank document in the folder, which you can then double-click to open it in Word. When you create a document this way, you'll notice that Windows will have the name highlighted so you can change it. Presuming you don't want to call it "New Microsoft Office Word Document.docx," you should change it. But don't change the .docx extension or Windows won't know what to do with the document anymore.

FIGURE 3.1

Adding and Editing Text

Adding text in Word is quite easy. Just point and click the mouse to place the insertion point where you want to put the text, and then start typing. The ability to click anywhere on the page and begin typing—introduced in Word 2003—eliminates the need to insert a lot of carriage returns (enters) and tabs to get your cursor to a particular place on the page.

> If, for some reason, you don't like Click and Type, you can turn it off under File | Options | Advanced. I've never seen anybody intentionally turn it off yet.

Selecting Text

Frequently when working in Word, you'll want to select a word, sentence, or paragraph so that you can delete it, move it, or apply formatting. (In Chapter 4 I will caution you about using direct formatting too much.) Word provides some handy tricks for quickly selecting text.

- Click once to place the cursor on the page.

- Click twice to select the word you're pointing at.
- Click three times to select the paragraph you're pointing at.
- Hold down CTRL and click once to select the sentence you're pointing at.
- Hold down CTRL and double-click to select an additional word—for example, if you want to select two words that are not contiguous. If I wanted to select "additional" and "example" in the preceding sentence, I would do that by double-clicking on "additional" and then holding down CTRL and double-clicking on "example."
- To select a part of your document, click at the starting point of your selection, then hold down SHIFT and click at the end point of your selection.
- To cancel any selection, just single-click anywhere on the page.

Find and Replace

Have you ever typed an entire document and then discovered that you repeatedly misspelled the defendant's name? Or maybe you're reusing a document from a previous client and making only relevant changes. Well, if you've ever had to search a long document for every instance of a word or phrase to change or correct it, then Find and Replace (Figure 3.2) is a feature you're going to adore. It does exactly what the name suggests: you tell it what text to find and what word or phrase to replace it with, either with or without prompting you at each instance. Want to change every instance of "Smith" to "Brown?" Simply go to the Editing group on the Home tab of the Ribbon, click "Replace," and type "Smith" into the Find What field and "Brown" into the Replace With field. Click "Replace" if you want Word to prompt you on each instance, or "Replace All" if you're confident that you need to change it everywhere. This is also handy if you need to change every instance of "Smith" to "Smyth."

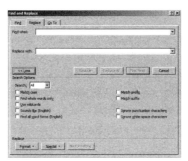

FIGURE 3.2

▼

Be careful with "Replace All." There is a famous story of a newspaper that let its computers correct text in one of its news stories, and the next day its readers were surprised to discover that the budget for the State of Massachusetts was "back in the Afro-American." It's usually worth letting a human approve the changes, or at least proofread the results.

If you look closely at the advanced options on the Find and Replace dialog (click "More" if you don't see them), you'll notice that you can match case so that only exact matches, case-sensitive, will be affected. That's helpful when John Matter sues Case Tractor Corporation and you want to replace the names but not the lowercase words.

There are three other useful options on this tool I want to point out:

- Use Wildcards—this option lets you use wildcards in your search terms to find a broader set of matches. A "?" replaces a single character. "The?" will find "Them" and "They" but not "Their" or "Thessaly." An "*" replaces a string of characters. "Tw*" will find "Two" and "Twain" and "Twitter." An "*" by itself will find every word in the document, handy if you're just messing around with Find/Replace and want to see what a document consisting of 53,213 instances of "Pancake" looks like.

- Sounds Like—this should be an amazing feature, but as it stands it's only pretty good. You can type a term and have Word find (and replace, if you'd like) words that sound like the word you specify. That can be a fantastic way to find not only your specified term but also perhaps misspellings of the word. It's also handy if you're not entirely sure how to spell the word. The downside to it is that it's not that accurate. It often finds words that are similar to your word but don't sound that much like it. Still . . . this feature works relatively well and can be useful.

- Find All Word Forms—this is a great tool because it will find variations on a word. For example, searching for "run" will also find "running" and "ran," but not "jog."

Find and Replace has a lot of other nifty uses as well. At the bottom of the Find and Replace dialog are two more buttons of interest.

Format

The format option lets you search for (and replace, if you want) different formatting options. In fact, nearly every formatting option in Word can be accessed through this option. Need to change all of your bold formatted text to small caps? Find and Replace can do it. You can also remove all highlighting throughout your document. Before you look at this as the best tool for controlling text formatting in Word, though, you should read Chapter 4, where we talk about Styles. But if you need to change direct formatting (we'll get to that in Chapter 4), this can be a good tool.

Special

The "Special" button in Find and Replace lets you find (and replace) special characters. Click the button and you'll get a list of the characters you can work with, like the one shown in Figure 3.3. One character that law-yers are likely to want to find is the section character (§).

Tips of the Pros
You can also use this tool to remove manual page breaks. Just do a Replace, select Manual Page Break from the Special menu as the thing to find, and leave the Replace field blank.

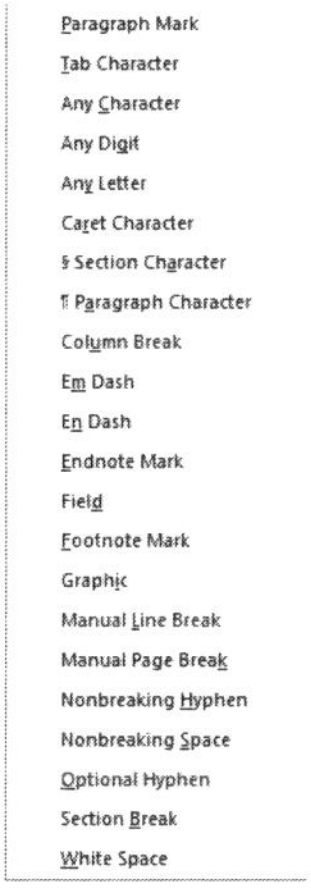

Paragraph Mark
Tab Character
Any Character
Any Digit
Any Letter
Caret Character
§ Section Character
¶ Paragraph Character
Column Break
Em Dash
En Dash
Endnote Mark
Field
Footnote Mark
Graphic
Manual Line Break
Manual Page Break
Nonbreaking Hyphen
Nonbreaking Space
Optional Hyphen
Section Break
White Space

FIGURE 3.3

Spell Check

Microsoft Word 2010 includes a powerful spell-checker that is designed to help you with document creation. I have to confess that I make con-siderable use of it myself. You don't have to do anything to invoke it; it's running all the time by default (unless you turn it off). If Word thinks you've misspelled a word, it will underline it with a red squiggly line that indicates a possible problem. Right-click the word and Microsoft Word will offer you suggested corrections.

If you're confident you have spelled the word correctly but Microsoft Word thinks otherwise (as it often will for proper names, for example), you can add it to Word's dictionary by right-clicking the word. (See Figure 3.4.) Then Word will recognize it when it sees it again in the future.

FIGURE 3.4

AutoCorrect

AutoCorrect is a Word feature that enables you to type quickly and fixes little mistakes for you as you go. For instance, it will auto-capitalize the first word in a sentence, in case you forget or don't want to be bothered with it, and fix common typing mistakes such as "teh" instead of "the."

If you really want to type "teh," just click Undo or CTRL+Z the first time Word changes it to "the," and it will change back. You may have to click "Undo" twice.

The AutoCorrect options can be set Backstage if you click File | Options, then go to the Proofing group and click the "AutoCorrect Options" button to get the AutoCorrect dialog box you see in Figure 3.5.

FIGURE 3.5

Grammar Check

A feature that was added to Microsoft Word a few versions back and has slowly improved is the grammar checker. This works in conjunction with the spell checker and will underline any perceived errors of grammar with green squiggly lines. I find it mostly useless myself—it generally points out sentences it thinks are fragments and not a lot else. As you may have noticed, I have a specific writing style, and some of what I write is probably not grammatically impeccable . . . but I probably wrote it that way for a reason. Somewhere Mrs. Selsor from Walter Reed Jr. High is weeping, but it's just how I write. It's very rare that Word suggests a grammatical correction that I accept, so I usually turn the grammar checker off, just to save that tiny bit of performance. Besides, if my grammar were perfect, how would my editor earn his keep?

Saving

If you're creating documents you care about, and presumably you are, you will at some point want to save them. Saving a document in Word is pretty simple: you can click the "Save" icon, which is one of the few default icons on the Quick Access Toolbar or you can click the File | Save. The mouse-averse among you can press CTRL+S to save. If it's the first time you've saved the document, Word will prompt you to name the document and choose a location (if you want to save it somewhere other than the default location). If you've saved the document before, Word will just quickly and quietly save it, overwriting the previous version.

▼▼▼▼▼
CAUTION!
One of the biggest mistakes lawyers make with Word (see Chapter 11, where I will beat you over the head with this one again) is reusing an existing document from another client or matter, making changes and then accidentally saving the new edits over the old version. Be careful!

Your other basic saving option is to click "File" and "Save As." What that does is prompt you for a new filename and/or location to save the file. This is great if you want to leave the original file as is (See the sidebar. I know, read it again.) and save this as a new file. The other reason you might want to use Save As is if you want to save this file in a different format—like Office 97-2003 or Rich Text Format—or update it from an older format to an Office 2010 OpenXML file. You can also get to the Save As option by pressing F12 on your keyboard.

New File Format

Either way you choose to save your documents, Word 2010 uses the same default new file format, Office Open XML, as Word 2007. You can readily identify documents saved in that format by their file extension. .DOCX is the default Word extension (replacing .DOC); the "X" tells you it's an XML document. .DOTX is the default extension for Word 2010 templates. You might occasionally see .DOCM or .DOTM—those are macro-enabled documents and templates, respectively. They don't necessarily contain macros, but they can (and in practical usage usually do).

The Office Open XML documents have a few notable advantages. First and foremost, they are quite a bit smaller than the old .DOC files. .DOCX files are actually ZIP files—compressed—containing several discreet files. A .DOCX file can be as much as 50 percent smaller than the same document in .DOC format. If you have a large document library, that can pay off in terms of significantly reduced storage space requirements, significantly faster backups, and faster transfer speeds when e-mailing documents or working with them remotely.

▼▼▼▼▼
CAUTION: Geek Content Ahead

If you really want to see what's under the hood of a .DOCX file, just rename the file and change the extension to .ZIP. Then open it like you would any other ZIP file (compressed folder). You'll be able to see the individual files that make up a .DOCX file. Can you add outside files to this ZIP file, rename it as a .DOCX, and use that to sneak files to somebody? Yes, although if anybody tries to open the file, Word 2010 will warn that the file contains unreadable content and will offer to recover it. That might tip off an observer that something's up with the file and prompt him or her to take a closer look.

Another advantage of the new file format is interoperability. XML is a popular open file format and is much easier for vendors to work with than the old, proprietary, binary, .DOC files were. Exchanging documents with other applications or working with .DOCX files in other applications (like document management or indexing tools) is also much easier in the new format.

.DOCX files are both more resilient and more recoverable than the old format documents were. They're less likely to corrupt or fail, and if they *do* corrupt you're a lot more likely to get your data back. That's because rather than being one big file, as I mentioned above, the .DOCX is actually a compressed file that contains a number of smaller files. For example, the text is stored in one file and the formatting in another within the .DOCX file. If a bit of your formatting gets corrupted, Word can probably recover your text by simply deleting the file containing the formatting. You may have to reapply your formatting throughout the document, but that's a lot better than losing all of your text, too. And, frankly, it's pretty unusual that you'd even have to do that with the new formats.

Naming Files

Folks who've used computers for a long time are familiar with the "8 point 3" naming convention. Back in the old days, before flash drives and Wikipedia, we used to have to name our documents things like "jonesbrf.doc" because of the limitations of the File Allocation Table (FAT) file system. But since FAT gave way to FAT32 (the 32-bit version of FAT) and NTFS (NT File System; the preferred file system of Windows XP, Vista, and Windows 7) long filenames became possible and preferable. That means you can use up to 255 characters in a filename, including some symbols. You can now name your documents things like "Jones v Smith Memo.docx" or "Letter to Judge Steffey regarding jury selection in Brown matter.docx."

Especially if you're not using a document management system like DocsOpen or Worldox, you should implement a sensible naming system for your documents to facilitate finding them later. Once you settle on a system, stick with it.

Don't be tempted to get crazy with the filenames. Just because you *can* use up to 255 characters doesn't mean you should. If you start naming documents "Letter to Amstutz, Huddleston, and Malcolm requesting electronic production of all documents including but not limited to those documents relating to sales of Widgets in the Northeastern and surrounding sales territories during fiscal 2006.docx" then . . . well . . . just don't. It's excessive, annoying, and ultimately not useful.

▼

Discuss your naming system with others in your firm so that you're all on the same page. Don't restrict the discussion to partners or lawyers; encourage paralegals and legal secretaries to participate, too. An experienced legal secretary can have valuable input to help you come up with the best solution. Plus, if you involve others from the beginning, you'll make it that much easier to implement whatever policy you come up with.

Folders

If you're going to use the basic Windows file system to organize your files, I would encourage you to adopt a system of folders. Don't just throw everything into one folder and then hope you can find it. The system you use is up to you, but I would recommend something along the lines of:

- Clients
    - Client A
        - Matter 1
        - Matter 2

- Client B
- Client C
  - Matter 1
  - Matter 2
- Administrative
  - Accounts Payable
  - Advertising

You can add on from there. With an intelligent hierarchy of folders it's easier to find what you need. In this example, Client B has only one matter (and isn't expected to have a second), so subfolders aren't needed. Some attorneys will create subfolders of the Matter subfolders for different kinds of documents, but I think that adds a needless layer of complexity. Use the long file names to specify what kind of document it is and keep all of those documents in the single "Matter x" subfolder. Unless you have hundreds of documents, further division of the subfolder isn't necessary. In Chapter 12 I'll explain full-text search—that's another tool you can use to help find files you've stored in subfolders.

Tags

When you save your document, Word will give you the option to apply a tag to the document (Figure 3.6). Tags can be useful for categorizing your documents and making them easier to find later. You might tag items with the client or matter number of the case, or perhaps with an explanation of the kind of document it is (memo, brief, etc.). It's tempting to use the Tags feature to include keywords from the document, but you usually shouldn't bother because Instant Search already locates documents that way. Tags are better used for keywords *about* the document that don't actually appear *in* the document. To add a tag just click the Tags field and type in whatever you'd like to add. Separate multiple tags with a comma.

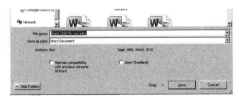

FIGURE 3.6

Printing

Before we go too far, it seems appropriate to tell you how to Quick Print. The fastest way to print is by using the Quick Print tool on the Quick Access Toolbar. Don't see it? That's because it's not there by default. Click the little drop-arrow next to the QAT and select "Quick Print" to add it. Now you can print with one mouse click.

Keyboarders, take note: Adding Quick Print to the QAT helps you, too. Tap the ALT key, and you'll see a number appear over the Quick Print icon. On my machine it's "5," but the number you see will depend on where your icon appears. You can now Quick Print by simply pressing ALT+[number] (the number that appears over the icon).

Most users print Word documents by clicking File and then Print, but Word 2010 has a lot of powerful printing tools that can be extremely useful. You can also press CTRL+P to launch the Print dialog box (Figure 3.7), just like you have for years.

FIGURE 3.7

The Office team had a lot of SQM data (remember that from Chapter 1?) to go by, and so it tried to design these dialogs to highlight the tools people use most often. Naturally, what people want to do most often when they come to the Print dialog is . . . print. So the "Print" button is the first option at the top left. Next to that is the setting that lets you choose how many copies you'd like. You don't need to print a copy and then run to the copier to make nine more. Just change "Number of Copies" to "10" and print. Of course, it helps if you have a really fast printer.

The next option in the dialog box lets you choose which printer you want to print to. If you have multiple printers in your firm, you can pick the one you want to print to here. Keep in mind that different printers have different features, and so the printer you choose will slightly affect the options you have—in fact pretty much everything else within the "Printer" box is affected by which printer you have selected. Printing to a color printer will

▼

Most of today's walk-up copiers also can be used as printers. If you're not already doing that, ask your copier support folks if your copier supports that option. Chances are, if your copier was made in the last five years, it already has a network card in it. You'll just need to run a cable to it and do a minute or so of configuration to add it to your network. Then you can print to it (and probably scan from it) like any other printer . . . any other really fast printer with cheap consumables. If you're going to print ten copies, or a large document, it will probably be faster and cheaper to print it to the copier. Plus, most of those copiers can collate, staple, duplex, and do all those great things as you print — saving you time and effort.

give you color printing options, while printing to a network-attached copier may give you options for duplexing and stapling, for example.

One classic option you may not see is a "Print to File" checkbox, which sends the print job to a file on disk instead of to the printer. In previous versions of Word it was right out here in the open. In Word 2010 you have to click the Printer selection tool to drop down the list of printers. You'll find Print to File at the bottom. When you select that and click Print, it will prompt you for a file name and location (such as your Documents folder or a flash drive). When you save it, Word will create a .PRN file that contains all of the printer instructions like fonts and colors that will be needed to print the file later. Typically, you would use this option if you were creating a document, such as a flyer or brochure, that you were going to send to a commercial printing company. You'd get it just the way you want it, print it to a file, and send that file to the commercial printer. Don't use this option to share a document with another lawyer—that's what Adobe PDF files are for.

Clicking the "Properties" button in the Printer box will give you access to that printer's properties (just like accessing it through the Control Panel | Printers tool) so you can change to low-level printer settings for your current print job. This tool can be different from printer to printer, so I won't even attempt to explain it here. Your printer documentation will probably cover that adequately.

Pages

You may not always want to print the full document, and that's when the Page Range section comes in handy. For instance, you may need to reprint just pages 11–14 of a contract because somebody—and I'm not saying who, Kim—accidentally spilled coffee on them. Just type the page range you want in the Pages box. Separate the range with a hyphen (like "11-14") or print non-contiguous pages by separating the page numbers with a comma (like "3,6,11,20").

If you have a more complex print range in mind, click the "Print All Pages" button to drop down a list of other choices. (See Figure 3.8.)

FIGURE 3.8

Here you can print only the current page, document properties (like a list of styles in the document or only the markup from a document you've been collaborating on), or a specific selection of text.

If you'd like to print one paragraph or some specific bits of a document, but not an entire page or a range of pages, you can use the mouse to highlight the text you'd like to print, then press CTRL+P (or click File | Print) and choose "Selection" under Print All Pages.

Zoom

Another option I find helpful when I print is Zoom. If I'm printing a long document and it's just for internal use—for example, so I can proofread a draft on paper—I'll often choose to save paper by having Word print two or four pages on a sheet. The end result comes out looking something like Figure 3.9. The text is small but still readable and, especially if I also use duplexing, I can save an awful lot of paper this way.

FIGURE 3.9

To do this, just click where it says "1 Page per sheet" at the bottom of the Print dialog, and you'll get a drop menu like Figure 3.10. I generally don't go any smaller than four pages per sheet . . . sixteen per sheet would be impossible to read unless you're printing on enormous paper.

FIGURE 3.10

Note: Don't be concerned that your print preview doesn't reflect the change—for some reason changing the Zoom doesn't show up in Print Preview.

The Zoom section also is useful if you need to resize a document's printing. Let's say you have a document that was initially created for 11x17 paper and you decide to print it on 8.5x11. Just changing the paper type in Word isn't going to solve the problem—you need to also go into Zoom and under Scale to Paper Size be sure to select the proper sized paper ("Letter" in this example).

Summary

Creating a document in Microsoft Word is a fairly straightforward process. Once you've mastered the basics, learned to use the tools that Word provides (such as spell check and AutoCorrect), and gotten a handle on the many print options available, you can do some powerful things.

Formatting

4

Word has two basic kinds of formatting: direct and indirect. Direct formatting is formatting that you apply directly to text—for example, when you select a word, sentence, or paragraph and then click the "Boldface" button on the Mini Toolbar. Or you select a paragraph and change the font from the Ribbon.

Indirect formatting is formatting that is applied via a style. Many of the formatting problems you'll encounter with Word come about because of a conflict between an underlying style and some direct formatting applied on top of that style.

Generally speaking you should use indirect formatting (styles) whenever possible. It'll make your life a *lot* easier. (Well, at least that part of your life that creates and edits documents in Word.)

Styles

A style is a predefined collection of formatting properties—fonts, typefaces, spacing, text colors, and so forth—that you can apply to a word or paragraph. There are a lot of good reasons to rely upon styles for most of your formatting needs. Not the least of them is consistency and the ability to modify the formatting of vast amounts of text very easily. You can set a style to have 11-point text, for example, and apply it broadly across your document. If you later decide you want to change it to 12-point text, you need only adjust the style and, just like magic, all of the text assigned that style will be updated.

Word 2010 gives you quick and easy access to some commonly used styles right on the Styles Quick Gallery on the Home tab of the Ribbon (Figure 4.1).

FIGURE 4.1

To apply a style, just click on the paragraph you want to apply the style to and click the style you want to apply . . . simple as that.

Depending upon the style you're applying, that style may or may not persist as you continue to type succeeding paragraphs. How do you know? Right-click the style you want to apply and choose Modify. You'll get the dialog box you see in Figure 4.2. Notice the "Style for following paragraph"? That tells you that when you hit "Enter" to create a new paragraph, the next paragraph will be in the designated style—in this example you can see that the Heading 1 style will be followed by the "Normal" style.

FIGURE 4.2

Can you modify that setting? You bet you can. That can be really handy if you want to save yourself a little time, and you know that every time you use Heading 2 you want to follow it with a custom "subtitle" style before you move on to "Normal" body text. Lots of possibilities here.

If you were to look at the "Style for following paragraph" setting for the Normal style, you'd find that the following paragraph is set to automatically be . . . Normal. Makes sense; generally you'd be using Normal to bang out paragraph after paragraph of body text.

So what other settings can you modify in a style?

Fonts

A font is the combination of the typeface and other elements like size, pitch, and spacing that determine the shape of the letters in your document. You can take a basic typeface like Times New Roman and apply other characteristics to it like Boldface, 13 point, and underlined. One thing that can be a little confusing in Microsoft Word is that the font is sometimes used to refer only to the typeface (like "Courier" or "Times New Roman") and sometimes used to refer to the typeface *and* the various characteristics applied to it (like "Calibri 12 point Italic"). I wish I had an easy answer for you on that one; you'll just have to try to understand from the context what is meant. For the purposes of this book I'll try to use "typeface" when I mean just the typeface ("Courier," "Arial," etc.) and "font" when I mean the whole thing.

Paragraph Options

In Word the Paragraph is an important concept. Most of the styles you'll use will be paragraph styles, and most of the formatting applied will be applied on a paragraph level. There are a number of options that apply to a paragraph in Microsoft Word.

Line Spacing

Line spacing refers to the amount of space between lines of text—single, double, etc. You can control your line spacing on a paragraph-by-paragraph basis using direct formatting with the "Line Spacing" button on the Ribbon (see Figure 4.3), or (better still) you can modify the line spacing for the style that your text is based on so that the line spacing is consistent across all of your paragraphs assigned to that style. Generally speaking, in legal documents your line spacing is going to be specified by the court anyhow, so you probably won't have a lot of discretion in what it should be. But for correspondence, marketing materials, and other personal documents you can probably make your line spacing whatever you'd like it to be.

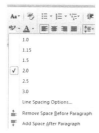

FIGURE 4.3

Justification

Justification relates to how the text aligns on the page horizontally, or from left to right. Typically our text is left justified, which means that it aligns to the left side of the page. As you type, your text moves across the page from left to right, but it's always in a straight line down the left side of the page. The right end of the line can be somewhat ragged, as mine is here, depending upon the words in the line and how long it actually is.

Right justification aligns the text to the right side of the page. For illustration, I'm right-justifying this paragraph and you can see that my text lines up perfectly along the right side . . . but now the left side is a bit ragged, depending upon the length of the line.

The next option is center justified, like this paragraph is. Now the lines won't necessarily line up on *either* side but they'll all be perfectly balanced along the horizontal center point of the page.

Finally, you have full justification. A line that is full justified will line up both left *and* right, but Word will play around with the word spacing in the line to make the line fit fully across the page if it can.

Creating Your Own Style

My favorite way to create a new style is to start with a style that is pretty close to what you want, use direct formatting to make whatever adjustments you need (bigger font, different color, italics, line spacing, etc.), then select your carefully crafted paragraph and click "Save Selection as a New Quick Style . . ." at the bottom on the Styles gallery (see Figure 4.4). Word will ask you to name your new style, and then it will appear on the Styles gallery right along with the rest.

FIGURE 4.4

Sharing Styles

It may come to pass that you've created a style that you want to share with others in your firm. Or maybe just copy to another machine that you own or use (like a laptop). Luckily, it's not too hard to do that.

The first thing I do, before copying the first styles, is create a new, blank document called "Transfer." I locate it in my Templates directory to make it easy to find. Note—you only have to do that once, unless you want multiple transfer documents. I reuse the same transfer file over and over.

Next, click the dialog launcher on the Styles group (circled on Figure 4.5) to get the Styles Task pane. Then click the Manage Styles button at the bottom (circled) to get the Manage Styles dialog box (Figure 4.6). In the Manage Styles dialog, click the "Import/Export" button to get the Organizer dialog you see in Figure 4.7. Click "Close File" on the right side, then "Open File" to select your Transfer document.

FIGURE 4.5   **FIGURE 4.6**

FIGURE 4.7

Once you have Transfer selected on the right side, select the styles you want to copy from the left side and click the "Copy" button to copy them to the Transfer file. When you're done, click "Close."

Copy that Transfer file to the computer you want to copy the styles to—then repeat the process. Open Transfer, go to the Styles Task Pane (see Figure 4.5), Manage Styles, Import/Export . . . and now you should see Transfer on the left and Normal on the right. Unless you want these styles to be available only in certain documents or templates, go ahead and copy those styles to the Normal template. Done.

Themes

One of the options that Word 2010 offers for formatting is Themes. Themes are sort of like the superset of styles—they control the colors and fonts and basic look and feel of the document. I don't think most lawyers are going to take any notice of Themes so, other than observing that they exist in Word 2010 and giving you the heads-up about what they do (control the color and font scheme), I'm not going to spend too much time talking about Themes. The vast majority of what lawyers and law firms do in formatting can be addressed with direct and indirect formatting, and especially styles in the default theme. I seriously doubt many of you will ever care to change the theme.

Page Options

Just as you have options that apply on a paragraph-by-paragraph basis, there are also options that are relevant on the page level.

Margins

Margins are a concept that's pretty familiar to anybody who has worked with documents in the past—they are the white space on the left, right, top, and bottom of your document. Generally speaking, in your legal documents your margins are probably going to be specified by the court. For your non-official documents, like letters or internal memos, you'll have a lot more leeway, but you'll want to consider this when it comes to margins:

1. You almost certainly have to have *some* margins, especially if the document is going to be printed. Very few printers are capable of printing all the way to the edge of the paper, so your printer will probably enforce some minimal margins.
2. If it's a document that is intended to be studied and/or commented on, you may deliberately want to leave ample margins for note-taking.

You control the margins on your page on the Page Layout tab of the Ribbon. Look for the "Margins" button.

Columns

Columns help to break up the text in your document. You are probably most familiar with columns in the context of a newspaper or magazine. Some legal documents can make use of columns in the headings; for example, pleading headers in many jurisdictions have traditionally been formatted with three columns (the middle column just being a container for a graphical border). They can be quite useful in other cases as well, to help break up large blocks of text for style and readability.

To set up columns in your document, go to the Page Layout tab of the Ribbon and click the "Columns" button to get what you see in Figure 4.8.

FIGURE 4.8

▼▼▼▼▼
Tricks of the Pros

Preprinted letterhead is just so 1997. These days all the cool kids are printing their letterhead on demand as part of their documents. Just create a template with the margins you want, put your firm header at the top, create a column on the left (or right) to list your addresses, partners, associates . . . all the stuff you've got on your preprinted letterhead now. A good graphic designer or Microsoft Word expert (heck, even a savvy legal assistant!) can set up a Word Template for you that looks almost identical to your preprinted letterhead. Now that you've got that template, create all of your letters and such using that template and just print on plain blank paper (or bond if you like). It'll look like you printed on preprinted letterhead, but it'll save you a lot of costs both up front and in the future. Tell the truth . . . how many boxes of letterhead do you have in a closet preprinted with the names of attorneys who are no longer with your firm, or featuring the address of your old office? If you're printing your letterhead on demand, from a template, you make a simple change to the template when somebody joins or leaves the firm or when an address or phone number changes and voilà . . . your new letterhead is ready. And, with Word 2010's new file formats you can even retroactively change the template applied to previously created documents—so if you ever reprint those documents in the future they can be printed with the current letterhead template instead of the template that was in use months or years back when the document was originally created.

Here you can choose from the gallery to have one, two, three, or more columns. You can also do some unbalanced columns like left or right—which are excellent for setting up letterhead, by the way.

Most of the time lawyers are happy with one of those default column choices presented in the gallery. For the rare instance when you need custom columns rather than what you see there, just click the More Columns command at the bottom of the gallery to get the Columns dialog box you see in Figure 4.9. Here you can set up some extremely specific columns, with custom spacing and everything.

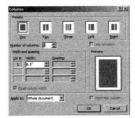

FIGURE 4.9

There are two really useful settings in this dialog box that I sometimes use even when I've only created a basic two-column page:

- Line Between: This will create a nice vertical line between your columns. It's handy in pleading headers and other places where you want a vertical line to separate your columns. No need to create a bogus center column just for a graphical divider in your headings anymore.
- Apply To: The default is "whole document" but the other option in that box is "This point forward." I'll use that to turn off columns— by setting the columns to "One"—if I want to have only two columns for part of a page or if I want subsequent pages to have a different column layout.

Page Borders

Page borders sound like margins but they're actually quite different. Borders refer to a line that you draw around the page. Again, probably not something you'll have the option to use on a legal document, but in some cases, like brochures or certificates, you may want to use them as a stylized element of your document. Click the Page Borders control on the Ribbon to get the Borders and Shading dialog box you see in Figure 4.10. This dialog box is actually somewhat more powerful than simple page borders, though we'll start there. Here you can set a border around the page, or even have the entire page shaded. The border can be a solid line or a broken line or a dashed line or a . . . you get the idea. And, of course, you can specify the thickness of the line. You can have the border apply to the entire document or just to certain sections of it.

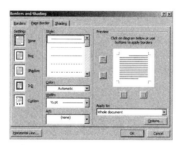

FIGURE 4.10

If you click the Borders tab of the Borders and Shading dialog box you can create paragraph borders. For lawyers these are actually somewhat more useful, though not something you'd use in a pleading, most likely. They let you enclose a particular paragraph (or more) within a border, setting it off graphically for emphasis.

The other useful tool that's here is one that you may have used before and that you've spent *a lot* of time looking for, and that's Horizontal Line. When I create training or instructional materials, I sometimes like to divide sections of the page or document with a horizontal line. When I first started using Word 2007, I probably wasted far more time than I needed to trying to find out where this command had gone, and it took me two or three uses before I remembered that it was now semi-hidden under the Page Layout | Page Borders command. (I kept looking for it under Insert | Shapes).

Tricks of the Pros

If you like to insert horizontal lines, you may want to add this command to the Quick Access Toolbar. To do that right-click the QAT and choose "Customize Quick Access Toolbar. . . ." Change "Popular Commands" to "All Commands" and scroll down until you find "Horizontal Line" to add it.

Headers and Footers

Headers and footers are text elements that appear at the top and bottom of each page. In some cases these may be empty or blank—simply margins. In other cases they can contain highly formatted or dynamic data such as a letterhead masthead at the top; page numbering, dates, and document titles in the footer; and so forth.

To create a header, just go to the Insert tab of the Ribbon and click the Header command on the Header & Footer group. You'll get the gallery you see in Figure 4.11 with a number of standard headers you can add. You can start with one of those and then modify it, or even start with a blank header and create your own content.

FIGURE 4.11

To delete a header from your document just click the "Remove Header" option.

Creating a footer is essentially the same process but with a slightly different gallery (see Figure 4.12).

FIGURE 4.12

In either case, if you build a custom header or footer and think you'll want to use it again, you can simply select your custom header or footer, pop the appropriate gallery (header or footer) as described above, and then click the "Save Selection to [Header/Footer] Gallery . . ." button. The gallery is stored with the template, so any future documents you create with the same template (Normal.dotm, usually) will have your custom header or footer in the gallery for your easy access.

When you have a header or footer in your document and you double-click the header or footer area to edit it, another contextual tab is added to the Ribbon. That's the "Header & Footer Tools: Design" tab, as shown in Figure 4.13.

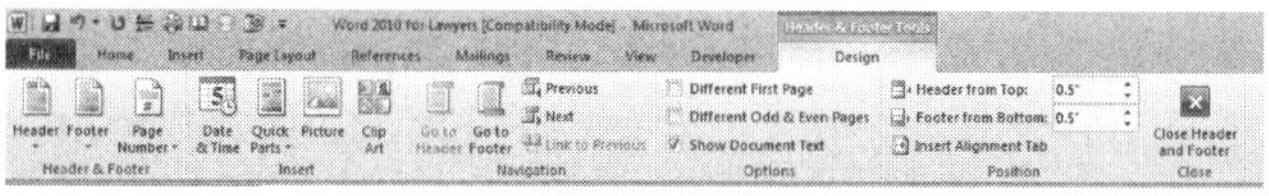

FIGURE 4.13

The Header & Footer group contains the same tools that the Header & Footer group on the Insert menu does, and those tools, naturally, work the same way here. The Insert group contains four commands that you'll also find on the Insert tab of the Ribbon—these are things you might commonly insert into a header or footer. Honestly, I doubt that many attorneys will be inserting too many pictures or bits of clip art into a header or footer (although you could use that to insert a firm logo, I suppose). Date & Time, though, would be a pretty common thing to insert, and the Quick Parts include document properties like author and fields like the document's path, which is quite popular with lawyers. You can also create and save custom Quick Parts like boilerplate text (a disclaimer, perhaps?) that you want to reuse again and again.

The Navigation group has tools that make it a little easier for you to move around between headers and footers, though I rarely see these commands used by attorneys in practice.

The Options group, however, has some *very* useful commands in it; in particular, "Different First Page" and "Different Odd & Even Pages," which lets you create documents that don't have to have the same header and/or footer on every page. That's especially handy if you're creating a document with a cover page (which you might not want the same header/footer on) or if you're creating a book-style document where the even and odd pages will face each other, and you want to put unique information on those facing pages. We get a lot of questions about how to omit the footer from a first page of a document, and "Different First Page" is the answer.

The Position group includes two very useful but confusingly named commands: Header from Top and Footer from Bottom. These commands actually let you specify the height of the header and footer, respectively. If you have a lot of information you want to fit into your header or footer, you can make it larger, or if you want an especially svelte header or footer, you can make it smaller. These are also handy if you're trying to match up the header or footer to a preprinted form or piece of letterhead. The third command in the position group lets you create an alignment tab in the header or footer. Alignment tabs were a new feature in Word 2007 and, unlike other tabs that have an absolute position on the page ("at 2.5 inches," for example), alignment tabs are relative to the margins of your page. So if you create an alignment tab that is 2.5 inches from the left margin and you later change the margins, then the alignment tab will move as well. In theory, it's a handy way to align text within your header or footer without having to worry about realigning it if you later change your page margins. In reality, legal documents have fairly well-defined and inflexible margin settings anyhow, so the chances you'd be changing the margins in a way that affects your header or footer text are pretty slim.

Finally, the "Close Header and Footer" button gets you out of the header and footer and back to editing your page. You can accomplish the same thing by merely double-clicking anywhere on your page (other than in the header or footer). If you want to get back into the header or footer . . . just double-click it.

Page Numbering

Another area we get a lot of questions on with Word is how to do page numbering. To start with, click the Insert tab of the Ribbon and go to the "Page Number" button. It's not a coincidence that this is located in the Header & Footer group. Click the button and you'll get the menu you see in Figure 4.14. Clicking any of the first four options will open a gallery of appropriate choices.

FIGURE 4.14

Top of Page puts the page number in the header, and Bottom of Page puts it in the footer. That seems pretty obvious. Current position puts the page number . . . well, where your cursor is right now. That's an intriguing idea, but I've never seen it used. The final option is Page Margins, which, interestingly, will create your page number in either the left or right margin, as an accent bar or other effect. It's actually quite stylish, and I've been meaning to use that in a document or article sometime.

Format Page Number lets you make some blanket changes to the page number format, including letting you force the page number to start at a particular value. That's handy if you're creating a document that will be part of a larger document and you want the page numbering to account for the 17 pages that came from the other document . . . so you can start your numbering at 18, for instance.

Sections

There may be times when you want certain parts of your document to have significantly different formatting from the rest. Different margins, page orientation (landscape or portrait), headers and footers, page numbering, etc. You could try to do that manually, but it would probably be a nightmare—especially if the document changed in any substantial way and you had to add or remove pages.

The better way to do it is to create a separate section. To create a section you have to insert a section break—which you'll find on the Page Layout tab, cleverly hiding under the "Breaks" button.

Click "Breaks" and you'll get the menu that you see in Figure 4.15. Below the page breaks you'll find the Section Breaks.

FIGURE 4.15

- Next Page: This starts your new section on the next page. It's similar to inserting a page break.

- Continuous: This starts your new section right there where the cursor is. You can actually have more than one section on a page by using continuous breaks. This is another good way to create a page that's partly in columns and partly not, for example.
- Even Page/Odd Page: This starts your new section on the next Even/Odd page. It's handy if you have chapters broken out as sections and you always want your next chapter to begin on an even (or odd) page.

You can't actually *see* section breaks on your page normally. If you need to delete one (or just be reminded where it is), you'll want to turn on formatting marks by clicking the pilcrow (¶) on the Ribbon or pressing CTRL+SHIFT+8. The section break looks like what you see in Figure 4.16. Click on it and press DELETE if you want to delete it.

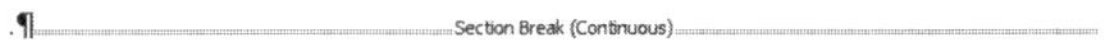

.¶··Section Break (Continuous)··

FIGURE 4.16

Tabs and Indents

Tabs and Indents are related, but different, concepts. Both are used to align content horizontally on the page but with a subtle difference. Tabs set anchor points for you to align text on the current line. Indents move the entire current line or paragraph. You can have text on either side of a tab, but the indent acts like a temporary margin that moves the text inward from the side of the page the specified distance. You can have multiple tabs across the line, but a given paragraph will have just a single indent setting. (Well, one on the left and one on the right, if you like.)

Controlling how tabs and indents are set up in your document can be done one of two main ways:

1. Using settings on the horizontal ruler at the top of the page.
2. Via the Paragraph dialog box seen in Figure 4.17. (You can see the Indent settings in the figure; clicking the "Tabs" button at the bottom left would launch the Tabs dialog box to control the tab settings.)

Personally I prefer the Paragraph dialog box. I know the ruler is always there, and I've seen people work their magic with a mouse and a few deft strokes, but to be honest, I never quite seem to get the results I want from setting tabs on the ruler. After a few minutes of trying, I usu-

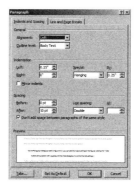

FIGURE 4.17

ally give up and fall back to the tried-and-true, well-understood, Paragraph dialog box. If you really want to use the ruler to set your tabs and indents, though, let's take a moment to look at how you do that.

Using the Ruler to Set Tabs and Indents

When you first look at the Word ruler, you won't see any defined tab stops, but you know (or you will after you finish reading this sentence) that the Normal template in Word includes default tab stops every .5 inches. And you can see that in action if you start at the beginning of a blank line and start pressing the TAB key . . . the cursor will advance to the right half an inch every time you press the button.

▼▼▼▼▼

There's a reason that tabs and indents are on the paragraph tab of the Page Layout group—they are assigned to paragraphs by default. If you set tabs on a paragraph and then continue typing the next paragraph, the tab settings will follow. If you select an existing paragraph in the middle of a bunch of paragraphs, your new tab settings will apply only to the selected paragraph. Want to apply the tabs to multiple paragraphs? Select them, then set the tab settings. Want to apply tabs to the entire document? Hit CTRL+A to select all, then set your tab settings.

The first step in setting up your tabs is to place your insertion point in the paragraph that you want these tabs to apply to. For simplicity we'll assume you're just going to set up some tabs to use in the current and future paragraphs.

The next step in setting up your tabs is to click the tab selector at the left end of the ruler, as you can see in Figure 4.18. It looks sort of like a capital "L."

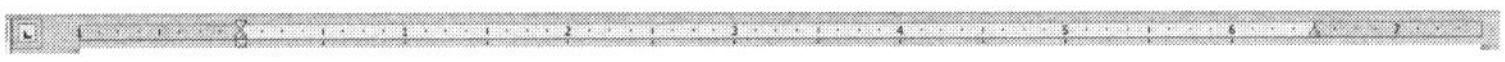

FIGURE 4.18

Each time you click it you'll get a different cryptic little symbol. The first three to be addressed are fairly standard types of tabs:

■ Left Tab: A left tab looks like an L, sensibly enough. If you set a left tab, then text that starts at that tab stop will continue, as you type, to the right. This is the sort of tab you're used to. You can see one in Figure 4.18.

■ Center Tab: A center tab looks like an upside-down T. If you set a center tab, the text you type will center off that point—in other words it will adjust left and right from that spot.

■ Right Tab: A right tab looks like a backwards L. When you set this tab, text will proceed from that point to the left as you type.

If you don't see the ruler at the top of your document, you probably have it turned off. Go to the View tab of the Ribbon and click the "Ruler" checkbox, or click the "View Ruler" button, which is at the top of the vertical scroll bar on the right side of your document.

The next two tabs are a little different.

■ Decimal Tab: The decimal tab character looks like the Center Tab character (the upside-down T) but with a decimal point to the right of it. When you set a decimal tab, the text (which is presumably numbers) will align along the decimal point. This is the way you can align a column of numbers with decimal places so that they align on the decimal just like what you see in Figure 4.19.

■ Bar Tab: (Pause for laughter.) This type of tab is different from the rest in that it's not designed to align text. It creates a vertical line on the page—the sort of thing you might use to create the vertical line in a pleading heading (if you didn't heed my advice to use the "line between" setting in columns). When you click the tab selector until

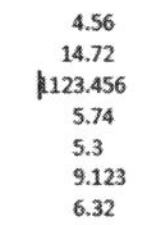

```
          4.56
         14.72
       1123.456
          5.74
          5.3
          9.123
          6.32
```

FIGURE 4.19

it looks like a vertical line, that's the bar tab. If your waitress starts to look like a vertical line, it's probably a good time to ask for your bar tab . . . and call a cab.

Tip

If you're not sure which kind of tab you're looking at in the Tab Selector, just hover your mouse over the top of it and you'll get a tool tip that tells you.

After you've clicked through the five kinds of tabs, the Tab Selector button will, curiously, offer you two types of Indent you can set up.

- First Line Indent: The first line indent does pretty much what you think it does—indents the first line of the paragraph the specified distance. The icon for this one looks like a downward pointing triangle.
- Hanging Indent: The hanging indent moves the entire paragraph over the specified amount. This icon looks like a small box.

Once you've selected the type of tab or indent that you want to create, click on the ruler where you'd like to place the tabs or indents. You can place as many tabs as you'd like (within reason), but only one indent per paragraph.

Tricks of the Pros

Want to quickly remove a tab you set manually? Just drag the tab indicator off the ribbon using your mouse.

Using the Tabs Dialog to Set Tabs

To get into the Tabs dialog box shown in Figure 4.20, press ALT+O, T (or go through the Paragraph dialog launcher and click "Tabs" as I mentioned previously). Here you can type in the placement of the tab stops you want, and you can select what type of tab alignment you want.

FIGURE 4.20

The other setting you can select here that's interesting is the Leader setting. By default there's none, but if you want the tab to be prefaced by dots, a dashed line, or an underline, you can select that here.

TRICKS OF THE PROS

One question I get asked sometimes is how to have some text on a line that's right-aligned and other text on the same line that's left aligned. We often see that in a header, for example. I've seen people muddle around trying to do it manually, but there's a *much* easier way. All you need to do is create a right-aligned tab and set it all the way against the right margin. To do that, click the tab selector to change it from Left tab to Right tab, and then click on the ruler near the right margin to place that Right tab. Now gently drag it from where you placed it to the right until it's directly on the right-margin. Now . . . just type your left aligned text on the line. It'll naturally line up left. Press Tab and your cursor will jump to the right margin where, as you type, your text will naturally right-align on that tab you created. Voilà: left-aligned and right-aligned text on the same line.

Want some centered text, too? Just add a center-aligned tab exactly in the middle of the line.

Reveal Codes

Want to start an excited conversation in a group of Word and WordPerfect enthusiasts? Utter the phrase "Reveal codes." WordPerfect users will hoist their swords and claim it's the killer feature that WordPerfect has and Word lacks. And . . . they're kind of right. But Word does have an analogue of sorts: Reveal Formatting. (See Figure 4.21.) Word doesn't really have

FIGURE 4.21

codes, so the best it can do is show you what formatting has been applied to the current paragraph section or selected text. The Reveal Formatting task pane can be launched by pressing SHIFT+F1, and it will show you everything you need to know about the formatting applied to the selected text, current paragraph, or current section.

If you want to make a change to one of the formatting elements, just click the hyperlinked title of the element. The appropriate dialog box will be opened so you can make the changes you want. Take some time to learn to use this tool—it's worth it.

Tables

One feature of Word 2010 that you'll probably use a lot is the Tables. They have a lot of utility and can help you add some nice formatting to otherwise rough content. Tables can contain all kinds of custom formatting and can even perform some basic calculations for you.

Creating a Table

Creating a table is a pretty simple matter. Go to the Insert tab and find the Tables gallery (Figure 4.22). The quick way is to just start at the top left corner with your mouse and drag down and over until you have the number of columns (up and down) and rows (left to right) you need. You can make a table of up to ten columns and up to eight rows that way. If you need something else, or you just can't get the hang of using the mouse for this task, you can click the Insert Table command to get the Insert Table dialog box you see in Figure 4.23, and then you can specify however many columns or rows you need. If you guess wrong, don't worry about it. It's not that hard to insert additional rows and/or columns later if you subsequently discover that you forgot one.

FIGURE 4.22　　**FIGURE 4.23**

There are two other useful features you'll find in the Insert Table window. The first is a way to control how AutoFit is going to work in this table. In other words, you're deciding whether Word will automatically adjust the width of the column to fit the content. By default, Word 2010 will try to make some intelligent guesses about how the table should be laid out and will auto-size the columns accordingly. Those intelligent guesses will be based solely on the number of columns and the width of available space, though—they won't have anything to do with the contents of the columns. If you'd like the columns to resize based upon their content, here's your chance: just click the radio button next to "AutoFit to contents." The columns will automatically size to accommodate the widest bit of content. Naturally there are limits; you can't have five columns that are each three inches wide on a letter-sized sheet of paper for instance.

The second handy tool here is that you can tell it to remember these dimensions for new tables. If you think you're going to make several tables of the same size, checking that box will save you a bit of time on the next few tables you create.

Quick Tables

Word 2010 provides you with some tools to help you create tables that are a little more than basic. When you go to the Insert tab on the Ribbon and click the drop-arrow on the "Table" button, you'll see "Quick Tables" listed at the bottom of the menu. Highlight it and the Quick Tables gallery, like in Figure 4.24, will appear. These are predefined tables you can insert—calendars, matrices, lists, and so forth. The colors schemes may

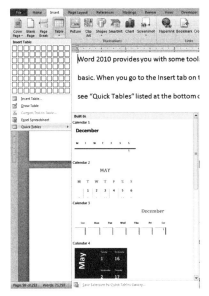

FIGURE 4.24

vary a bit because they depend upon which theme you have assigned to your document, but the basic content will always be there. If you want to create a fancy table, check here first to see if there is a predefined Quick Table for that. If so, you'll save yourself a lot of time trying to reinvent one.

The Table Tools Tabs on the Ribbon

What's this? New tabs? Yes, Word 2010 tries to keep the Ribbon a manageable size by offering contextual tabs. There are a lot of tools for working with tables in Microsoft Word, but you don't really need those tools if you don't have any tables in your document. So Word conveniently hides those tabs from you until you actually insert a table into your document. Create a table and place your cursor anywhere within it, and you'll magically be presented with two new tabs on the Ribbon under the heading "Table Tools."

> "Any sufficiently advanced technology is indistinguishable from magic."
> —*Arthur C. Clarke*

The Design Tab

The design tab (Figure 4.25) gives you tools to control the basic look and feel of your table: colors, lines, shadings, and so forth.

FIGURE 4.25

The first group of commands in the Design tab includes some checkboxes that let you specify if your table has special rows or columns in it. If you have a header row or first column that contains data labels, check the appropriate boxes. If you have a total row or a last column that contains sums or summary data, check those boxes. They will apply special formatting to set off those rows or columns a bit to make it clear that they're headings or summaries.

The checkboxes for banding just specify if you want the alternate rows to be shaded for easier reading.

The next group on this tab gives you a gallery of quick table styles (see Figure 4.26). By default you've got a

This is another example of Word 2010's live preview feature. Just by hovering your mouse over the sample tables in the gallery, Word will change your table to show you what it will look like if you select that option. No need to trial and error it, just move deliberately through the gallery until you find the look you like, and then click on it.

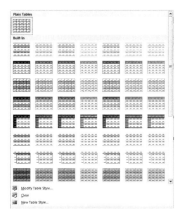

FIGURE 4.26

plain table (If you created your table with the Insert | Table tool), but you can pick from dozens of other choices in various styles, accents, and even colors just by selecting from the gallery.

You also have the ability to customize the shading and/or borders of your table from the Design tab. Click the drop arrow next to Borders and you'll see the image in Figure 4.27. Here you can do all sorts of tricky things with custom borders like adjust the thickness of the lines or have borders only along the sides or top and bottom of the cell.

FIGURE 4.27

The Layout Tab

The layout tab (Figure 4.28) is all about configuring the actual functionality of your table: adding rows and columns, splitting cells, sorting, or even inserting basic formulas. Let's take a moment to look at the most important features of the Layout tab.

FIGURE 4.28

Properties

The table properties dialog box seen in Figure 4.29 lets you format various settings for the table as well as the individual rows, columns, and cells. You can specify the width, alignment, and how you'd like the text to wrap around it. To give you some idea of text wrapping, Figure 4.29 is set for wrapping the text around . . . which is why you see this text alongside it. If text wrapping is set to None (which it is by default), then the table will stand alone and no text will appear alongside it.

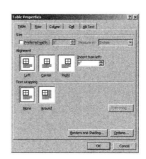

FIGURE 4.29

Rows and Columns

The Rows and Columns group contains commands for easily adding rows or columns to an existing table. If you underestimated how many you'd need, this is your solution. (You can also right-click your table and choose "Insert" to get at those commands.)

Merge

The merge group lets you merge or split cells, or even the entire table. You might want to merge cells, for example, to create a heading above two columns of cells that span both columns. You'd merge those top two cells and type your heading into it.

If you decide your table would be better as two tables, you can use Split Table to divide it in two.

Alignment

The Alignment group gives you some tools to adjust how your text will sit inside the cells—aligned to the top, bottom, left, right, middle . . . you get the idea. You can also control text direction here, in case you want your text inside the cell to rotate 90 degrees and appear landscaped, for example.

Data

The Data group contains some of the most interesting table features that Word has. First, the "Sort" tool lets you sort any column based upon the data. Sort alphabetically, numerically, or by date, depending upon the kind of data in the column. This is a great way to reorder data that you quickly input without having to worry about inputting it in a particular order to begin with.

Convert to Text lets you break down your table without deleting the data within it. Essentially, this command will take a table and convert it directly to text.

▼▼▼▼▼
Tricks of the Pros

Lots of folks don't realize that you can actually sort lists of text that aren't in tables in Word. Just select your list of terms and click "Sort" on the Home tab of the ribbon. You'll get the Sort Text dialog box you see in Figure 4.30. You can do a three-level sort if your data is that complex, but most of the time you'll probably just do a simple ascending or descending (A–Z or Z–A) sort.

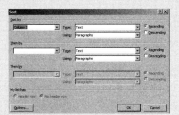

FIGURE 4.30

Notice the Header row options toward the bottom? That lets you tell Word if your list has a header row at the top that you don't want sorted into the text.

Tricks of the Pros

Most Microsoft Office pros wouldn't spend a lot of time creating a complex table, especially with a lot of formulas, in Microsoft Word. The tables feature just isn't that robust. Instead we would create the table in Excel and embed it into Word in the appropriate place. In Chapter 7 we'll dig into how to do that. Trust me; you'll like it.

The formula command gives Word limited, very limited, calculation capabilities. You can create formulas to do a lot of things, but don't get too carried away. Creating and maintaining more than a few simple formulas is a chore in Word.

Deleting a Table

Deleting a table is not quite as easy as you might think, but that's probably a good thing. If you took the time to create the table, you probably really wanted it and you wouldn't want to just blow it away casually. The best way to delete the table is to click somewhere in the table, then go to the Table Tools—Layout tab of the Ribbon (which appears only if you actually have a Table in your document and you are working with it), click the "Delete" button and select "Delete Table" as you can see in Figure 4.31.

That's also where you can delete individual rows, columns, or cells.

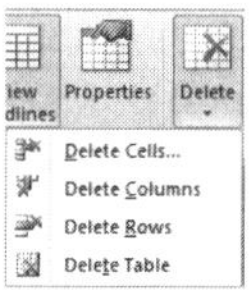

FIGURE 4.31

Introduction to Templates

A template is a starting point for a document. It generally includes formatting, layout (like margins and paper type), and even boilerplate text to get your document started. One simple example might be if you print on a sheet of custom mailing labels frequently, and you want to set up your page layout (margins, borders, etc.) to fit those labels and then save that as a template for later reuse. Or a more advanced example might be if you have a standard retention letter that you send to clients to acknowledge the attorney-client relationship, you could create the standard letter, minus the specifics like names, dates, and addresses, and save that as a template. Then in the future, when you want to send that letter, you just start from the template, fill in the variables for that particular client, and you're ready to go.

Word has been based upon templates for years. There are two kinds of templates that you should be familiar with in Word:

- Global—global templates are always open, regardless of what kind of template you based the document on. Normal.dotm, the default template in Word, is an example of a Global template.
- Document—a document template is the template that you base an individual document on. There are a couple of dozen of them that come with Word (faxes, memos, letters, etc.) and hundreds more available (generally for free) from Microsoft Office Online. Or you can build your own, as we'll talk about in Chapter 8. Document templates are probably what you're thinking of when you think about templates.

Summary

It's not just what you say; it's how you say it. Your content is critical, of course, but we all know that legal documents have very precise formatting requirements, and you have to make sure you have complete control of how the content is laid out. It does you no good to make a brilliant legal argument if the court rejects it because it's improperly formatted.

Word provides you with some great tools to control formatting—styles, tabs, tables, columns, and more. Mastering those tools will give you control over how your work is presented. If you only have time to master *one* of these concepts though . . . spend that time on Styles.

Stuff Lawyers Use

5

Recognizing that I have no way of knowing what jurisdiction you're in (or even what country!), I can't get overly specific in this chapter. Each of you may have different requirements for documents in your specific jurisdiction. What I will try to do is show some of the features that tend to appear in legal-specific documents and hope that you'll be able to evaluate these tips in the context of your own court rules and make any needed adjustments.

Pleadings

Word has, for quite some time, actually, had a template for pleadings. Unfortunately Microsoft didn't make it terribly easy to find, but once you have it, you can use it all you like. Your best bet for finding it is to go to File | New, and at the very top of the New Document window is a search box for searching the Microsoft Online site for a particular kind of document. Type in "Pleading" and press enter as shown in Figure 5.1.

FIGURE 5.1

What you'll get is a list of templates that match that keyword—as you can see in the figure, I've gotten seven hits that are types of pleadings. Since this is a Web search, by the time you do it you might see more (or fewer) pleading forms available. Select the pleading template you want—I picked the one with twenty-eight lines for my test, but you can select whatever fits your jurisdiction best.

▼

Note: You'll need to do this, at least the first time, from a computer that is connected to the Internet. If you're disconnected at the time, you'll have to wait. Once you've downloaded the template, you can save it to your local hard drive and you'll always have it.

These templates are provided free of charge, but the program will check your Microsoft Office first using the "Microsoft Genuine Advantage" tool to verify that you are using a legal and properly licensed copy of Microsoft Word 2010. Assuming you are, the download should take mere seconds, and you'll be ready to roll with your new pleading template.

Table of Authorities

Attorneys love to create tables of authorities. A table of authorities is a list of references in the document, along with the page number indicating where the reference can be found. Creating a table of authorities is pretty easy, actually. You simply insert your citation into the document where you want it, highlight it, and then go to the References tab on the Ribbon and click "Mark Citation" under the Table of Authorities group. Doing so will launch the dialog box you see in Figure 5.2. The Selected Text box shows how the citation will be listed in the table of authorities. You can also edit the short citation (it should match how you're going to reference the citation elsewhere in the document; e.g., "Carter v. Bruha") and change the category, if you'd like.

FIGURE 5.2

If none of the categories built into Word suit you, you can edit the list of categories by clicking the "Category" button on the right side of the dialog box. Add or change the categories to whatever you like.

Once you've got the category and short citation the way you want them, click "Mark." If you have multiple instances of this citation, click "Mark All" to flag every citation that matches either the selected text or the short citation. That will insert the field code that flags that item as a citation and will turn on "Show/Hide" so you can see that it's tagged as a cita-

Tips of the Pros

You can also press ALT+SHIFT+I to mark the citation.

tion. If you want to turn off that display—because if we're being honest, it's distracting, just click the Show/Hide button (¶) on the Ribbon (or press CTRL+SHIFT+8) to hide them again. You'll want to hide those marks before you insert your table of authorities (that's next; be patient) so that your document paginates correctly.

Once you've marked all your citations, you're ready to insert your table of authorities into the document. Just go to where you want it and click "Insert Table of Authorities" from the like-named group on the References tab of the Ribbon. That will open the Table of Authorities dialog box you see in Figure 5.3. You can select a specific category of citations you want to include or, more likely, just select "All" for the categories.

FIGURE 5.3

If you subsequently add authorities that you want included in the table, just go back to the References tab and click the "Update Table" button in the Table of Authorities group.

Make sure that you come back to the References tab and click "Update Table" to refresh your table of authorities before you finalize your document. This will ensure that the page numbers are correct and reflect any repagina-

 If you add additional citations of already-marked citations, go back to the original citation, open the Mark citation dialog box (ALT+SHIFT+I) and click "Mark All" to re-scan the document and mark the new instance(s) of that citation.

tion that might have occurred since you originally inserted or last updated the table.

Numbered and Bulleted Lists

Lists—both numbered and bulleted—are one feature that attorneys use quite often. The difference is fairly straightforward—a bulleted list is used when the order of the items isn't important. A numbered list is a way to create a list when you want to specify an order of events (like a set of step-by-step instructions) or when you want to create a list of items that are set off with unique identifiers so they can be more readily referred to later. Numbered lists are more common, for this last reason, in legal documents.

Word is pretty intelligent about recognizing when you want to create a bulleted or numbered list. If you start a new paragraph with a "1." Word will assume that you intend to create a numbered list and will apply the default style for that. This is also true if you start an outline with the classic Roman numerals ("I." etc.) or an alpha list with "A."

If you want to start a bulleted list instead, you can just preface your line with an asterisk (*) followed by a space, and Word will convert that automatically to the default bullet.

You can change the numbering format by clicking the drop-arrow to the right of the numbering button on the Ribbon, like in Figure 5.4. Here you can select an alternate format for your numbered list or define a new number format.

FIGURE 5.4

That's fine if you just want to do a very simple numbered list. The problem is, lawyers often want to do far more complicated numbered lists, numbering paragraphs and sub-paragraphs and sub-sub-paragraphs and . . . well, you get the idea. When you do those kinds of more complicated numbered lists, you've probably discovered that things in Word can go very wrong, very fast. That's why in a few pages I'm going to show you a better way to do those deep numbered paragraphs and lists.

▼▼▼▼▼

If you'd like to turn off Word 2010's proclivity to initiate numbered lists when you start a line with "1." or whatnot, you can do so by clicking File | Options | Proofing | AutoCorrect Options | AutoFormat as you Type, as you see in Figure 5.5.

FIGURE 5.5

Uncheck the box under "Apply as you type" for "Automatic numbered lists" and your worries are gone. Well, they are if your worries consist only of Word automatically creating numbered lists.

Understanding Numbering in Word

It's probably a good idea for me to give you a rudimentary understanding of how numbering works in Microsoft Word. We could do an extensive study of the subject, but if you're an attorney you've already had a lot of years of school, and you probably don't want to spend two more just trying to figure out Word's little complexities in the area of numbered lists. So let's try for the short-course version.

There are two basic kinds of lists in Word: simple lists and multilevel lists. (Yes, I'm oversimplifying just a bit, but just come with me on this.) The defining characteristic of a simple list is that it has only one level: 1., 2., 3., 4., etc.; A., B., C., etc.; or even bullets. Whatever the delineating character, the point is there's just the one level of list. Multilevel lists are outlines and similar lists that contain multiple levels with different symbols or numbers (typically) to delineate the levels. Like this:

1. This is the first level.
   a. This is a second level.

    b. This is another second-level item.
        i. You can have a third level.
       ii. Or more levels, but you get the idea. . . .
  2. And another first level item to finish my example.

WARNING: GEEK CONTENT AHEAD!

In reality, all lists are multilevel lists. Word always sees a list as having nine levels, no matter how many levels you actually use.

All of these lists are really a series of paragraphs (each line is a new paragraph) that have been formatted as List paragraphs. Where you can sometimes run into problems with lists is in using the List galleries to apply your list formatting.

There isn't any real difference between a bulleted and a numbered list, as far as Word is concerned. The only difference between them is the kind of character prefacing each paragraph.

You can create a numbered list from scratch, or you can convert existing text to a numbered list.

Tip

If you want extra space after an item or if you want to type another paragraph within your list without preceding that paragraph with a number, press SHIFT+ENTER instead of ENTER. When you press ENTER again, Word will resume your list.

To create a new list, just type the number you want to start with (such as "1.") and begin typing your list. At the end of each item, press enter to get the next number.

If you want to convert an existing set of text to a list, just select that text first, then use the Numbering or Bullets gallery to apply your list format. Each paragraph in your selected text will be formatted as a separate list item. Note: You may have to clean it up a bit by separating or recombining items, depending upon how diligent you were in using paragraphs to create the text to begin with. If you want to separate something as a new list item, just move your cursor to the beginning of that word or phrase and press ENTER to make it a new paragraph (and thus a new list item). If Word has made two list items out of something that should be a single list item, just go to the beginning of the second item and hit backspace to delete the paragraph definition and move it up onto the previous line.

Automatic Lists

Word will often create lists for you automatically, sometimes whether you want it to or not, if you start typing one. To start a numbered list automatically, just start a paragraph by typing "1." and pressing the space bar, as we did above to start our new list. Word will start a numbered list. "A." or "a." or "I." will have the same effect with different numbered list formats. To start a bulleted list, type an asterisk (*) then press the space bar.

If the automatic behavior annoys you and you would like to have more control over your lists (and non-lists), you can turn the feature off. Like a lot of the things Word does automatically, that capability is provided by AutoCorrect. To turn it off just click "File," go to Options | Proofing, and click the "AutoCorrect Options" button. Then go to the "AutoFormat As You Type" tab and under the "Apply as you type" group you'll find entries for "Automatic bulleted lists" and "Automatic numbered lists." Clear one, or both, of the checkboxes as you desire, and Word will stop making automatic lists for you.

Continuing a List

Maybe you've ended a numbered list and somewhere later in the document you want to resume that list, or maybe you got tired of pressing SHIFT+ENTER to insert un-numbered paragraphs and decided it would be easier to just end the list, type your additional paragraphs, and resume the list later. Either way, there is a fairly simple way to continue a previous list. Just type the next number in your sequence and Word will pick up where you left off and automatically join these new items to the previous list.

For example, if you had something like this:

1. An item
2. A second item
3. A third item

Then you added some un-numbered text like this, before adding . . .

4. A fourth item.
5. And a fifth item.

I simply had to type the "4." to have Word continue my previous list. And yes, if I were to go back up and add another item between 2 and 3, Word would automatically renumber the items below to account for that.

Restarting Numbering

If you want to restart your numbering back at 1, just type "1." in front of your first item and Word will create a new list for you starting at 1. When you're ready to end your list, just press ENTER twice.

Now, that's all well and good for relatively simple lists. But what about more complicated lists and paragraph numbering where you have multiple levels and sub-levels? For that we need to roll up our sleeves and do some work. What we're going to do is create a set of custom paragraph styles and a new paragraph list style to tie it all together.

Creating the Styles

First we need to create nine new custom styles. Why nine? Because, as we already learned, all multilevel lists (including numbered paragraphs) are actually nine levels deep, even if you're only using three of them in a given list.

Now I'm going to make some assumptions here, because I don't really want to write 200 pages on customizing numbered paragraph styles. The assumptions I'm going to make are as follows:

1. You want to number your paragraphs levels as "1", "1.1", "1.1.1", "1.2", "1.2.1," etc.
2. You want to use the same formatting on all of it. You don't want 1.1 to be bigger than 1.1.1 or different colors or any of that.
3. The formatting you want to use is basically the same as the "Normal" style in Word.

If any of these assumptions are wrong, you'll be able to make adjustments to the styles to compensate. I just don't have the time (or paper) to explain every possible scenario.

▼▼▼▼▼

Normally, when setting up paragraph styles for list numbering, we'd want to use the built-in "Header 1," "Header 2" styles. That comes with the associated formatting and the inclusion of those headers in the table of contents (if you have a table of contents). There are a bunch of good reasons to use the built-in header styles for regular numbered lists. But for numbered paragraphs, I think we're better off with the custom styles because we usually *don't* want them in the table of contents, and we *don't* want each level to have different formatting, etc.

To create your styles, type a bit of sample text in Normal style, then select that text, go to the Styles group on the Ribbon, and click the drop-down arrow to expand the gallery (see Figure 5.6). Click "Save Selection as a New Quick Style." Give your new style a name, as I have in Figure 5.7. I've chosen to name my style "ParaNum1" to indicate that it's a paragraph

FIGURE 5.6

FIGURE 5.7

numbering style for level 1. Repeat those steps for levels 2–9. When you're done you should have identical styles named "ParaNum1," "ParaNum2," "ParaNum3," etc. Once you get the hang of it, you should be able to create the whole set in about 30 seconds.

Next, we create a new List Style for our Paragraph Numbering.

Create the List Style

Click the drop arrow next to the multilevel list button on the Paragraph tab of the Ribbon (see Figure 5.8). Select "Define New List Style" and you'll get the dialog box you see in Figure 5.9. Give your new list style a name: I'll call mine "ParaNums." Click the "Format" button at the lower left and select "Numbering." Now you'll see the Modify Multilevel List dialog shown in Figure 5.10. This is where the work gets done. (Don't worry; we only have to do it once.)

If your Modify Multilevel List dialog box looks a little different from mine, click the "More" button at the bottom left. You'll need the options it reveals for this.

FIGURE 5.8   FIGURE 5.9   FIGURE 5.10

To start, click "Level 1" in the left hand column. Then follow these steps:

1. Link level to Style. Click that and set it to "ParaNum1."
2. Delete the text that appears under "Enter formatting for number" and then select "1, 2, 3" from the "Number style for this level" field. Click after the number that appears and type a period.
3. Under "Click level to modify," select level 2.
4. Repeat step 1 and assign "ParaNum2."
5. Click in the "Enter formatting for number" field, and where it reads "Include level number from," click the drop-down arrow and select "Level 1."
6. Type a period after the number that appears, and then in the "Number style for this level" select "1, 2, 3."

7. Type a period after the number that appears in the "Enter formatting for number" field. It should look like Figure 5.11.
8. Under "Click level to modify," select level 3.
9. Repeat step 1 and assign "ParaNum3." (Notice a pattern developing?)
10. Click in the "Enter formatting for number" field, and where it reads "Include level number from," click the drop-down arrow and select "Level 1." (Yes, Level 1.)
11. Type a period after the number that appears in the "Enter formatting for number" field.
12. Click in the "Enter formatting for number" field, and where it reads "Include level number from," click the drop-down arrow and select "Level 2."
13. Repeat step 6.

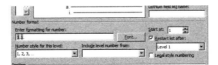

FIGURE 5.11

Rinse and repeat for all levels through level 9. Yes, it's a bit tedious and will take you some time to do it. Once you have it set up, though, you won't have to do it again. One key point . . . at each level you need to do steps 10 through 12 once for *each* preceding level. So for Level 9, you're going to select Level 1, type a period, then select Level 2, type a period, then select Level 3, type a period, then select Level 4 . . . you get the idea.

Once you have that all set, you can click "OK back out" to save your new list style.

Note: If you want to automatically indent any (or all) of the paragraph levels, you can set that up in the Modify Multilevel List while you're assigning number formats. The bottom section of that dialog box is all about text indents. Naturally, you can also turn off all of the indentation here, too.

> **TIPS OF THE PROS**
>
> If you'd like to precede your paragraph number with some text, such as "Section" or "Article" or "Paragraph," just type that text in the "Enter formatting for number" field, followed by a space, and then insert your numbers as described above.

Using the Paragraph Numbering

Using your new paragraph numbering is simplicity itself: just apply the appropriate style to your paragraphs. Apply ParaNum1, and watch your paragraph number magically appear. Apply ParaNum2 to the next style and voilà, your "1.1" paragraph number appears. ParaNum3? You guessed it . . . 1.1.1 will appear. The numbers will increase incrementally and should be stable.

Want to skip a paragraph? Just apply "Normal" style and it won't be numbered.

Ready to number another paragraph? Apply the proper ParaNum level and Word will automatically continue the numbering from where it left off. All that work setting it up was worthwhile.

Table of Contents

Building a table of contents is somewhat like creating a table of authorities. You mark text and then insert the table of contents, and Word will build the table for you and update it whenever you ask. Marking the text is actually a little more automatic with the table of contents than it is with the table of authorities because the table of contents builds with the predefined "Heading" styles in Word that you're probably already using. (Or at least you *should* be using.)

Whenever I create a long document I use the Heading 1, Heading 2, Heading 3, etc. styles to format section and sub-section headings. If I want to add a table of contents, it's thus quite easy to do; I just go to where I want the table of contents, switch to the References tab, and click the "Table of Contents" button to display the Table of Contents gallery of predefined styles. I can also create my own if I don't like any of the built-in tables. When you select a table of contents from the gallery, it will be inserted in the document at the current insertion point.

Maybe you want to add some body text to your table of contents, though, not text that's in a heading but rather text that's just . . . well, text. You can do that, but it's not quite as easy as it sounds. You might think it's going to be easy because the Table of Contents group on the References tab of the Ribbon (see Figure 5.12) contains a button called "Add Text," which, if you highlight it, claims that it will add your plain old body text to the table of contents. Except it doesn't. Well, that's not true, it *does* . . . but it does it by reformatting your text like a heading. I'm not entirely sure how that feature made it through quality control, but there it is. No, if we want to have proper body text in our table of contents, we need to make a custom new style . . . that doesn't look like a custom new style. Here's how:

1. Select the text you want to add to the table of contents.
2. Click the drop arrow on the Styles gallery to expand the Styles gallery.

3. Click "Save Selection as a New Quick Style."
4. Give your new style a name like . . . "TOCText."

FIGURE 5.12

OK, job done. Now whenever you want to flag some body text for the table of contents, just select that text and assign it the TOCText style.

Once you have all of your text flagged, we have to do one more thing. Go to the References tab of the Ribbon, click Table of Contents | Insert Table of Contents and then click the "Options" button. You'll get something like what you see in Figure 5.13. Scroll down until you find your TOC-Text (or whatever you named it) style and assign it to a TOC level. You can give it level 3, so it's on the same level with Heading 3 text, or you can give it level 4, so it's indented below. Click "OK back out."

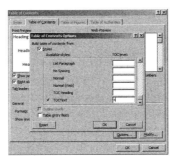

FIGURE 5.13

Next time you update your table of contents, your marked body text will be right there where you want it.

Electronic Filing

Electronic filing is rapidly becoming the rule rather than the exception, and Word 2010 is even more compatible than any version before with those e-filing rules. Though the specific requirements will vary slightly from jurisdiction to jurisdiction, virtually all of them will accept your e-filing in PDF/A format, which means that Word 2010's native PDF capability gets you to where you need to go to file electronically. Make sure to check one thing, though, before you create those PDF/A files: When you go Backstage by clicking File, then Save & Send and Create PDF/XPS Document, make sure to click the "Options" button before you publish the PDF file. On the Options dialog (see Figure 5.14), you'll notice an "ISO 19005-1 compliant (PDF/A)" checkbox. I circled it on the figure. Make sure that's checked so your PDF is created in the proper format.

FIGURE 5.14

If you're in a jurisdiction that accepts Word documents, it probably still requires the .DOC (Word 97-2003) format files, which you can also easily produce with Word 2010 by simply doing a Save As and changing the Save As Type to "Word 97-2003 Document" (see Figure 5.15).

FIGURE 5.15

Process Diagrams and Flow Charts

Sometimes you'll want to illustrate a flow or a relationship in Word using graphics. This can be an effective way of communicating a concept, an organizational chart, or a process to a client or even an opposing counsel. Word does have the ability to create those kinds of diagrams.

On the Insert tab, click "SmartArt" and you'll get a dialog box similar to what you see in Figure 5.16. Here you can choose from a variety of

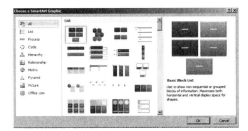

FIGURE 5.16

charts and diagrams to insert. Insert a diagram and you'll be able to type the appropriate text inside the shapes. Additionally, when you have the diagram selected, you'll now have two new tabs on the Ribbon.

Design

The SmartArt Design tab (Figure 5.17) has the tools you need to control the layout of the chart itself. You can add shapes above or below and left or right of existing shapes, promote or demote the shapes, and even change your mind about which layout to use. You can also adjust the colors or shading of the diagram. Finally, if you feel you've goofed up your diagram beyond easy repair . . . a simple click of "Reset Graphic" will put it back the way it was before you started messing with it.

FIGURE 5.17

Format

The SmartArt Format tab deals more with the text and the formatting of the individual shapes. You can change colors, fill (which means background), and other effects here.

Summary

Lawyers make heavy use of many pretty specific features of Microsoft Word to create the documents we use in our practices. Among those features, the Table of Authorities, Electronic Filing, and list formats have improved dramatically in Word 2010. Master those capabilities and you'll be more effective than ever before.

Collaboration

6

Microsoft approached Office 2010 with a very heavy emphasis on collaboration, and this plays nicely into how attorneys tend to use their tools. Partners, associates, co-counsel, clients, witnesses, paralegals . . . on any given document, there may one or many authors and editors. Effectively working together to produce a professional finished document is key to running a great law practice.

"I've always believed in writing without a collaborator, because where two people are writing the same book, each believes he gets all the worries and only half the royalties."
—*Agatha Christie*

SharePoint

SharePoint is Microsoft's browser-based collaboration portal. If you have Windows 2003 server (or later), then you already have a license for Windows SharePoint Services, which is all you need to create shared document libraries and a fair set of other collaboration tools. Creating and configuring SharePoint sites is a little beyond the scope of this book, but I'll try to offer you a few tips for working with SharePoint from a user's standpoint.

Want to know more about how to collaborate to produce documents in your practice? Visit the ABA Online Bookstore and pick up a copy of Dennis Kennedy and Tom Mighell's excellent book: *The Lawyer's Guide to Collaboration Tools and Technologies*.

Windows SharePoint Services (WSS)

Windows SharePoint Services (WSS) is the basic set of services that provide collaboration and a Web-based interface. Microsoft Office SharePoint Server (we'll talk about that next) is built on top of WSS. However, WSS is all you need for most collaboration. WSS installs right on top of any Windows 2003 or Windows 2008 server and runs there as a service. Check with your IT consultant or systems administrator—you may discover that you already have WSS installed and running in your firm. Did I mention that if you have a Windows 2003 (or 2008) server, then you already own the WSS license? Effectively, it's free.

Microsoft Office SharePoint Server 2010 (MOSS)

Microsoft Office SharePoint Server (MOSS) adds a lot of bells and whistles on top of WSS. Most of those bells and whistles involve search and personalized portals. For most firms, especially small firms, MOSS is overkill—especially because MOSS is not even remotely free. You'll have to buy it separately to install on your servers.

Using SharePoint

OK, so you've got SharePoint installed on your server. Now what? Before you start saving to your SharePoint site you should add it to your Network Places—that'll make it easier to save there. To do that, click "File" and "Save As." Toward the bottom of the Save As dialog box, click the "Tools" button to get the drop-list you see in Figure 6.1.

FIGURE 6.1

Select "Map Network Drive" to get the dialog box you see in Figure 6.2. (Note—this was done in Windows 7; your dialog box may look a little different if you're using another version of Windows, but the process is basically the same.) Once you get there, click the link that reads "Connect to a Web site that you can use to store your documents and pictures." That will start the "Add Network Location Wizard," which walks you through the process. Make sure to select "Choose a Custom Network Location" instead of "MSN Communities" if it asks you for that. When you get to the screen that asks for the location, type (or copy and paste from your browser) the address of your document library in SharePoint. If you're not sure what it is, ask your network administrator. After you specify the location you'll be asked to give it a name; just pick a friendly name that makes sense to you. "Our Share-Point Server" or something like that is fine. When you're finished, Word will add the location to your folders list so it will be able to save documents in the future without going through the mapping steps each time.

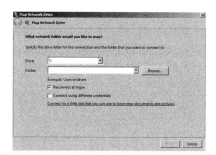

FIGURE 6.2

Uploading Existing Documents to SharePoint

If you want to upload documents you've already created, just go to your SharePoint site in your Web browser and click the Upload button on the document library's toolbar.

It will ask you where the document is and walk you through the upload. Easy enough for one document. If you want to copy a *bunch* of documents, however, you may want to use a slightly different technique. For that you'll want to use Explorer View.

Click "All Documents" and select Explorer View. That will open your document library in a view that looks just like Windows Explorer. Now open the real Windows Explorer (Windows Key+E will do it) alongside and navigate to the folder that contains the documents you want to upload. Select those documents and then drag and drop them to your SharePoint Explorer view.

Co-Authoring

One of the interesting new features in Word 2010 is the co-authoring capability. Basically, that allows multiple users to work in the same document at the same time.

As the other author makes changes to the document or adds content, that content is automatically highlighted on the screen in almost real time. The highlighting is color coded and shows the initials of the author/editor who created it. Word

Office 2010 offers co-authoring functionality for Word 2010, PowerPoint 2010, and OneNote 2010 documents as long as they're hosted on Microsoft SharePoint Server 2010.

2010's version support makes it easy to see when (and by whom) changes were made and gives you the ability to quickly see changes relative to an earlier version of the document.

Important to note: this functionality works *only* on documents stored on a SharePoint 2010 server.

SkyDrive

Microsoft's Office Live service, AKA "SkyDrive" (Figure 6.3) offers you 25 GB of free online storage for your documents and files. Recently Microsoft sweetened the deal with the release of Microsoft Office Web Apps—browser-based versions of Word, Excel, PowerPoint, and OneNote that let you not only view but edit your documents and files in the browser. Are the Web apps full-featured? No. But they're pretty good and it's hard to beat the price.

Don't have a SkyDrive account and want one? Just go to http://explore.live.com/windows-live-skydrive. If that link doesn't work (the Internet changes a lot faster than this book does), just Google or Bing for SkyDrive and you'll find it. SkyDrive accounts are free.

SkyDrive folders can be easily shared with one or more other users; in fact, I'm using a SkyDrive folder to share the chapters of this book with my editors as I get them done. You can control the permissions to a limited extent—detailing some users as "read-only" while others may have the permissions to create, edit, or even delete files.

FIGURE 6.3

Collaboration via E-mail

Over the last decade or so lawyers have gotten very comfortable collaborating via e-mail, by sending documents back and forth. This method is tried but not really true . . . and that's because it tends to generate an unwieldy number of document versions. Especially if you're working with more than one other party, it can become a nightmare of tracked changes and trying to merge different versions of the content into a single master document.

Tracking Changes

One of Word's most controversial features—if a word processor can be said to have "controversial features"—has got to be Track Changes. The reason is that if you're not careful, you can inadvertently transmit those tracked changes to other, potentially adverse, parties in your case. And that can be bad. Really, really bad. See Chapter 11's section on metadata for more on that. But here we're going to focus on using the powers of Track Changes for good and not evil.

Track Changes can be found on the Review tab of the Ribbon (see Figure 6.4).

FIGURE 6.4

If you're going to use it, the first thing you'll need to do is turn Track Changes on. Just click the "Track Changes" button to do that. On the status bar (see Figure 6.5) it should change from "Track Changes: Off" to "Track Changes: On."

FIGURE 6.5

There are also a number of options you can set or change for Track Changes. To get to those, click where it says "Track Changes" on the Ribbon to drop down the menu and select "Change Tracking Options" (Figure 6.6). That will display the "Track Changes Options" dialog box that you see in Figure 6.7.

Most of these options just have to do with how the changes will be displayed—which colors or font effects you want to apply—but a couple of them are especially useful. For instance, I find it hard to read a document that has too many highlighted changes, and I want any substantive changes that get made to really stand out. So I tend to turn off the ability to track formatting changes. Not many formatting changes are going to get made to a legal document anyhow (since the formats are fairly prescribed), and for the stuff

If you don't see the "Track Changes" status on your status bar at the bottom of Word then you really *do* want to turn that option on. Right-click the status bar and click where it says "Track Changes" to turn that on and add it to the status bar. Believe me . . . if Track Changes is on, you want to know it.

that I write, I don't care much about the formatting. To turn tracking of formatting changes off, just uncheck the box next to "Track formatting."

FIGURE 6.6   FIGURE 6.7

The other interesting settings here allow you to customize how the balloons (those are the pop-out colored text boxes that explain or display the change) are formatted. You can set little things like how wide they should be, and which margin you want them in. These are all personal preference settings, and I tend to leave them alone since the defaults are fine with me. If you'd rather have the balloons in the left margin instead of the right or 2 inches wide instead of 3 inches, then you can make those changes here.

One other configuration change I'll encourage you to make is to how the balloons work. If you click the Show Markup menu on the Ribbon you'll find a Balloons menu item that controls how the balloons are going to function. The default is to show all revisions in balloons, and if you like to work that way that's fine, but I think most attorneys are more comfortable with revisions being displayed inline—which means the affected text is struck out and the replacement text, in a different color, is inserted in its place. This has the "redline" effect that most attorneys are familiar with. I do like to see comments and formatting in balloons, as those can be easily set off to the side. But for actual text revisions, I like to see them inline, where the editor wanted them to go. So my setting would look like Figure 6.8.

FIGURE 6.8

The next field I want to point out in Track Changes is the Display for Review field (Figure 6.9), and it really is important. You want to make sure that if Track Changes is on, you either have one of the ". . . Showing Markup" options selected or are very aware of the fact that you don't. Again, Track Changes can be great, but it can also be seriously bad if you accidentally allow a document with tracked changes into the hands of another party who shouldn't see those changes. If you change your "Display for Review" to "Final" or "Original," Word will hide the tracked changes from you, even though they will still be embedded in your document. If you find editing a document with the markup displayed to be too distracting, it's OK to turn the markup display off . . . but be darned sure you turn it back on and give the document a look-over, plus run it through a metadata checker, before you send it along to anybody who isn't collaborating on its creation. That may include the client or court, as well as adverse parties.

FIGURE 6.9

Under the "Show Markup" button (Figure 6.10) you can control which markup is going to display. Again, with the possible exception of formatting, I think that you really should have all of it showing.

FIGURE 6.10

The Reviewers list lets you control which reviewers you want to display markup from and, cleverly, shows which color their edits will appear in. In my document, John Simek's comments are going to appear in purple; while mine will appear in red (and comments I make from my netbook appear in blue). (See Figure 6.11.) If you want to hide markup from a particular reviewer, you can turn it off (or back on) here. Usually you should leave this alone, though, so you can see all markup from all reviewers.

FIGURE 6.11

The other tool you're going to find handy, I predict, is the Reviewing Pane (Figure 6.12). When the Reviewing Pane is turned on, it shows a summary (either vertically along the left side of the document or horizontally at the bottom) of changes and lets you quickly navigate through them. I use this tool all the time when I'm dealing with the many comments and edits my editors come back with. When you have 71 edits in a 200-page document, it can be nice to have that tool to help you quickly address them.

FIGURE 6.12

Once you have changes in your document and you want to start merging (or rejecting) those changes, the next Ribbon group, appropriately titled "Changes," provides just the tools you need. When you select a particular change in your document, you can click "Accept" to make that change part of the final document or "Reject" to delete that change and leave the document as it was before the change was made.

Clicking the drop arrow on "Accept" (or "Reject") will give you a couple of tools that may speed up the process somewhat (Figure 6.13). Most notable is the ability to accept (or reject) *all* changes in the document in a single stroke (well . . . a couple of clicks anyhow). If you have supreme confidence in your editor, or if you've already reviewed and

> 66
> *"Carpe See-um"*
> Do it while you're looking at it!
> (Yes, I just made that up.)
> 99

FIGURE 6.13

agree with (or hate) all of the edits he or she has suggested, you can accept (or reject) them all at once. A huge time saver!

▼▼▼▼▼
Tips of the Pros

If you want to accept or reject all changes made by one particular reviewer, there *is* a way to do that in Word 2010. On the Reviewing Pane of the Ribbon, click "Show Markup," highlight "Reviewers," and uncheck "All Reviewers," which is the default. Annoyingly, Word will now make you again click "Show Markup" and highlight "Reviewers." Now you want to select only the reviewer (or reviewers) whose changes you want to work with. With that done, you can go back to the "Accept" button, hit the drop arrow (as we did above), and select "Accept all changes shown," and only the changes from that reviewer will be accepted en masse. Yes, you can also use this trick to reject all changes from that reviewer.

The "Previous" and "Next" buttons in the Changes group take you to the previous (or next) change in the document without doing anything to the current change. Handy if you're just reviewing changes without wanting to take any action on them. As a general rule, however, I recommend acting upon the changes while you're there—it's poor time management to touch the same change twice if you don't have.

Version Tracking

If you have "Save AutoRecover Information" and "Keep the last autosaved version if I close without saving" turned on in Word (see Chapter 9), Word will periodically save a version of your document that you can revert to if needed. With the current version of the document open, go to File | Info | Manage Versions and you'll see that Word offers you the last five auto-saved versions of the document.

If you open one of those files you'll be given the option to compare that version with the current version, highlighting the differences (see Figure 6.14). You'll then have the option to Restore the older version as the current version, or you can File | Save As to permanently save the older version with a new name.

FIGURE 6.14

If you need something a little more extensive, you're probably looking at document versioning in your document management system, if you have one, or fashioning something a little more manual.

When you're creating and/or collaborating on documents, it is often handy to have some way to track what version you're currently working with. Word provides a rudimentary way to do that automatically, in the advanced properties. Click File, then Properties (see Figure 6.15), and then "Advanced Properties." What you'll get is a dialog box similar to Figure 6.16, and on the Statistics tab you'll find the "Revision Number." All that really is, unfortunately, is a count of how many times the document has been modified and saved. If you press CTRL+S after every word, you'll increment the Revision Number awfully quickly.

FIGURE 6.15   FIGURE 6.16

If you're using a fancy third-party document management system, it will handle the version tracking for you.

There is also a simple, manual way to track versions and keep old versions around, and that's to simply always use Save As on your document and save it with a name that includes a version number—like "Smith Memo v1" or "Smith Memo v2." The new version won't overwrite the old version, and if you're faithful to this system you'll always be able to easily tell which version you're on. The downside to this is that your folders may fill up quickly with a bunch of outdated versions of your documents, and you may find yourself frequently needing to do some cleanup to get rid of them.

The key is to find a balance—using Save As for major revisions but a simple Save to reflect minor changes to the current version when you're going with the version number system.

Reviewing

An important element of collaborating is reviewing the results of that collaboration. Microsoft Word 2010 provides you with some tools to use in reviewing those documents. The Review tab of the Ribbon (see Figure 6.17) provides quick access to those tools.

FIGURE 6.17

Comments

When you're reviewing a document you can use Word's Comment feature to add your own comments to the document for review. Select the text you want to comment on and click "New Comment." Type your comment in the balloon that appears—it's that easy. Your comments will appear in one color, and comments by other reviewers will appear in different colors.

You can quickly navigate to the next (or previous) comment in the document with the buttons on the Ribbon.

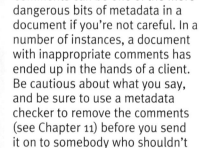

Tip

Comments can be one of the more dangerous bits of metadata in a document if you're not careful. In a number of instances, a document with inappropriate comments has ended up in the hands of a client. Be cautious about what you say, and be sure to use a metadata checker to remove the comments (see Chapter 11) before you send it on to somebody who shouldn't read those comments.

Compare Versions

One of the features that gets a good workout by law firms is the black lining feature (what we often call "red lining"), which is where you have the system compare two versions of a document and Word highlights the changes for you.

To use it, click the "Compare" button on the Ribbon and select "Compare Two Versions of a Document." You'll get the Compare Documents dialog box (see Figure 6.18), which lets you specify the documents to compare and set the options for the pending comparison. I usually just accept the defaults, but there are one or two settings here I want to spend a moment on.

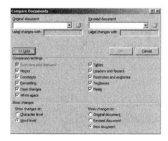

FIGURE 6.18

First of all, under Show Changes you should leave the "Show changes at" at "Word Level" instead of character level. Character level is OK, but it tends to be distracting since most character changes that don't also change the word aren't worth looking at. Any character change of significance also changes the word and would be flagged anyway.

The second setting you should be aware of is the "Show Changes in" setting. You can have the changes reflected in the Original or Revised documents, but I prefer to have a new document created showing the changes. The reason for that is that I like to leave the original documents unchanged, just in case I need to go back to one of them at some point.

> **Tip**
>
> If you don't want to see the source documents, you can close any of the four default windows by clicking the "X" in the top right corner of that window.

Once you're satisfied with your options, click "OK" and you'll get something that looks like Figure 6.19. The original document is at the top on the right side, the revised document is on the bottom on the right side, and the compared document (showing the changes) is in the middle. On the left side of the screen you'll see a list of the changes, and you can quickly navigate to a change by clicking it on that list.

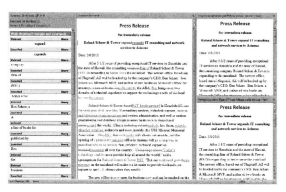

FIGURE 6.19

At the top of the revisions list is a summary of the revisions in the compared documents (see Figure 6.20). Here you can see the total number of revisions along with a breakdown of how many insertions, how many deletions, how many comments, etc.

FIGURE 6.20

When you're satisfied with the combined document (and yes, you can edit the combined document right there in that window), just click "Save" (or press CTRL+S) and you'll be prompted to give the new document a name and save it.

Third-Party Document Management Systems

I have to admit that I sort of resent third-party document management systems. They're an expensive crutch whose sole reason for existence is simple human weakness. With any modern computer, if you use an intelligent file naming convention in a disciplined fashion and a good file searching system—Copernic Desktop and Windows Desktop Search (WDS) are two such options that are also free—then you really won't need a third-party document management system. Document management exists to help you and your colleagues intelligently save, store, and find documents. You can accomplish the same thing by setting up a policy that reads "All memos will be saved to the client's folder, under the matter subfolder, with a file name in the format of 'Memo to [X] regarding [Y],'" and then adhering religiously to that policy. Everybody will be able to find a document they are looking for, and the search tool (like WDS) will help cover those scenarios where simple, good file names and directory structures don't fit the bill.

Unfortunately, in the real world people get rushed and corners get cut. Pretty soon the root folder of the structure starts to fill up with files named "Memo1," "Memo2," "Jonesmemo," and so forth as people cut the handful of steps required to save the file properly and just save it as quickly as they can with whatever name they can bang in fast and move on. Soon you have the filing equivalent of kindergarten, and nobody can remember which cubby they put their shoes in.

Document management systems solve this problem by automating some of the process (extracting keywords from the document itself and inserting the author and editor IDs) and by forcing other parts of it—requiring the user to type in a client or matter number, for example. They also generally include a search engine that can be used to search the document profiles as well as the document itself. In addition to the purpose-built document management tools I'm going to mention momentarily, many case management suites like ProLaw, Clio, or Client Profiles have the capability to do some document management. If you already have a full-featured case management suite deployed, you might want to check to see if it can suit your document management needs before you invest in a separate document management tool.

DocsOpen by Open Text (Formerly "Hummingbird")

The venerable DocsOpen system is one that just about any lawyer who has been around a decade or two has probably run across. It was, for a time, the most popular system among the AmLaw 100, and if it has fallen from that perch it is only because of cost, competition, and perhaps some disillusionment among firms with the product—which, to be honest, is probably inevitable with a product as complicated and ubiquitous as a document management system.

More information is available at http://www.opentext.com/2/global/sol-products/sol-pro-edocs-products2/pro-llecm-docsopen.htm. If the URL is any indication, you can already sense this is going to be complicated.

Interwoven WorkSite (Formerly Known as iManage)

Probably the other leading vendor in the AmLaw 100 for document and content management is Interwoven. Its WorkSite is extremely modular and can be customized for a particular firm.

More information is available at http://www.interwoven.com.

Worldox

Worldox has been around since the late 1980s and is widely deployed in small to mid-sized firms. Unlike its competitors, Worldox has always been Worldox and hasn't evolved through acquisition and change of ownership. It started out as a small, reasonably priced solution for smaller firms and has grown a bit from there. It's still pretty reasonably priced for what you get.

More information is available at http://www.worldox.com.

Protecting Your Documents

Office 2010 extends the Information Rights Management (IRM) features that not that many people used in Office 2003 or Office 2007. Basically it's a powerful file-level technology that lets you control who can access documents and what they can do with them. It's not without its limitations, of course, and while you can prevent individuals from printing or forwarding your document, you can't really prevent them from calling their friends over and showing them the document on the screen. You can prevent them from getting a screen capture of the document, but you can't prevent them from whipping out their camera phone and taking a photo of the screen. Basi-

---

▼

Don't see IRM? You might not have it. It's not included in the Office Starter, Home and Student, or Home and Business editions.

cally the old adage holds—try not to send sensitive documents to people you don't trust. But if you have to, then IRM can help make it a lot more difficult for your document to be misused or fall into the wrong hands.

What IRM CAN Do

■ Prevent an authorized recipient from copying, changing, printing, forwarding, faxing, or copying/pasting the content. It also blocks the Print Screen function in Windows and the screen clipping feature in OneNote. (However, it doesn't necessarily block *all* third-party screen capture applications.)

■ Lets you set an expiration date on a file so that the recipient can access the document only for a limited amount of time. It's sort of the "Mission Impossible" feature—except without as much smoke.

IRM in Office 2010 can protect a wide range of file types—not just .DOC and .DOCX files but also templates (.DOT and .DOTX), macro-enabled documents and templates (.DOCM & DOTM), and XPS files. As you might expect, IRM doesn't apply only to Word; Excel, PowerPoint, and Outlook all respect IRM settings, too.

> .XPS files are the "XML Paper Specification" format that is sort of Microsoft's version of an Adobe .PDF file.

To use IRM, you have to have the Windows Rights Management Services (RMS) Client with at least Service Pack 1 installed (as of this writing, Service Pack 2 for RMS Client is available, so you should get it if you don't already have it). If you're a Vista or Windows 7 user, then you already have the RMS client. If you're running Windows XP, then you'll have to download and install the RMS client. You can get it for free from Microsoft's Web site.

> If you're a Windows XP user, installing and configuring the RMS client isn't that difficult, but you might be more comfortable having your systems administrator or consultant help you with it. If you're going to use RMS, you want to make sure it works properly. Again, Windows 7 and Vista users don't have to install anything—it's already baked in.

Opening a Windows Rights Management Services–Protected Document

The first time that you try to open a document that's protected with RMS, the client software will try to connect to a licensing server to confirm your credentials and download what's called a "use license." That use license will define what level of access you're going to have to the requested file. The level of access determines if you'll be able to open it, edit it, print it, or whatever . . . and for how long. The sender of the file not only gets to determine what actions you're allowed to perform, but he or she can expire those actions as of a certain date as well.

This process has to be repeated for every RMS-protected file you receive. The good news is that it has to happen only once per file—so after you've obtained that use license you don't have to download it again on that computer.

▼▼▼▼▼

If you attempt to access the same protected document from multiple computers, you'll have to install the Rights Management client on each of those computers and it will have to obtain the use license for you on each computer. There's no cost to you to do that—you just have to make sure that each computer has Internet access for this process. Windows 7 and Vista users already have the Rights Management client but will still have to obtain the use license on each machine.

Another permission you can control is whether to allow the recipients to forward the document to a third party. If they try to, they'll get a dialog box that offers to contact the author for updated permissions. If you choose to, you can give individuals "Full Control" permissions, which allows them to do just about anything with the document, including forwarding it to others and assigning permissions to other people. Essentially, you give them the authority to specify what third parties can or can't do with it.

Rights management permissions are generally assigned on a per-user basis—you give Susan and David and Ashley permission to read but not edit, for example, but maybe J.D. has rights to read and edit. You can, in limited cases, give access on a per-group basis. As an example, you may want to give the Immigration department permission to edit the document for the next five days. The tricky bit with assigning permissions on a per-group basis is that it's really going to work only for users and groups inside your firm. That's because RMS requires access to your Active Directory (that's your network's authentication directory) to confirm who is actually a member of the group. If you send the document to another firm, then you won't have access to its Active Directory to select the group, and the group members won't have access to your Active Directory, either. Lots of things in computing and permissions get trickier when you have to travel between firms—when the document leaves the friendly confines of your own network.

Using Windows Live

If you don't have your own Rights Management Server, Microsoft provides that service for free if you have a Live ID (which is also free). To get a Live ID (which you should) just go to http://www.live.com and sign up. There are all sorts of benefits, including a free SkyDrive account.

Once you have the account . . . go to Review and click "Restrict Editing," and then at the bottom of the task pane click "Restrict Permission." You'll get the dialog box you see in Figure 6.21. Read the terms of service provided on the screen and, if they're acceptable to you, click "Yes" to indicate you want to sign up for the free service.

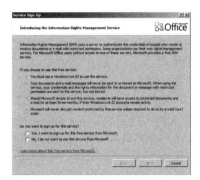

FIGURE 6.21

I shouldn't have to remind lawyers to read terms of service agreements, but I find that they skip them almost as often as laypeople do. The only part of these terms of service that might concern you is the last bit about Microsoft not decrypting content protected by the service unless required to do so by court order. Note that Microsoft doesn't actually *have* your document—encrypted or otherwise—it has only the decryption codes. So, if the government were to get its hands on the document, it could, in theory, get a court order requiring Microsoft to unlock it.

After selecting "Yes," click "Next." You'll get the dialog box shown in Figure 6.22. Here Windows Rights Management is asking if you have a Live ID or if you need one. If you already have one, select "Yes"; if not you can select "No" and get one.

FIGURE 6.22

Presuming you selected "Yes," The next screen will ask you to log in with your Windows Live ID. Then you'll get the dialog box you see in Figure 6.23. Most of the time you'll be using this on a private computer, so you can select that option and click "I accept." Now you'll get the Select User dialog box you see in Figure 6.24. If you have multiple Rights Management accounts or Live ID accounts, you can select which one you want to use for this document. I use only one Live ID account for Rights Management, so I select the only one I have and I check the "Always use this account" box. Word won't ask you again which account to use if you check that box. Click "OK."

FIGURE 6.23   **FIGURE 6.24**

Now you get to the meat of the issue . . . Figure 6.25 shows you the simple dialog. Here you can specify which users will have Read access and which will have Change access to the document. I actually like to work with the Advanced version of this dialog, so I click "More Options" and get what you see in Figure 6.26.

Here you can specify some detailed options. You can list the users who have access and what their access level is. You can set a date when the document expires, and allow or disallow printing and even content copying. Finally, you can set an e-mail account where a user can request

FIGURE 6.25   FIGURE 6.26

additional permissions—in case you restrict something like printing and the user needs to have that capability.

Click "OK," and the document is locked according to your settings.

Document Retention

One of the hottest topics in law technology, as evidenced by the volume of books and articles about it and the fact that it's one of the hottest tracks at ABA TECHSHOW, is eDiscovery. Now, I may not be an expert on eDiscovery, but I can tell you this . . . they can't discover what no longer exists. You may be required to keep certain documents for a certain length of time. Certainly if you're in a field that has to operate under HIPAA, Sarbanes-Oxley, FCRA, or any of a number of other regulatory and compliance instruments, then you're going to be required to keep certain documents for a certain period of time. If you're an OB/GYN, you know you're keeping your patient records for at least 18 years, for instance. But once you don't need to keep them anymore . . . don't keep them anymore. Rarely does anything good come from having outdated and expired documents in your files.

If for no other reason than efficient record keeping and tidiness, establish a document retention policy that specifies how long you need to keep documents, how long you want to keep documents, and what you're going to do with those documents once the periods have expired. Will they be shredded? Returned to the client? Figure it out now, get the policy in place, document it carefully, and start enforcing it immediately.

By the way, if you're not already familiar with it, you should also get friendly with the term "Litigation Hold."

Document retention is something you want to do *now*, not when you have an issue that arises. You want to learn to swim while it's dry and sunny out; not when the water is around your waist.

Electronic Media

Your document retention policy doesn't extend to just paper documents. It's not enough to toss that old client file in the fireplace and heat the lobby in the winter. If the documents were created on your computers, then there is a good chance that copies (yes, plural) of that document exist in your system. A few places you might want to grab a metaphorical flashlight and go looking:

- The Document Management system. Whatever you happen to have—whether it's Interwoven, WorldDox, some other commercial system, one you rolled yourself, or even just a fancy hierarchical directory structure on a simple file system—it's the first, and most obvious, place to find the document. Archive the document or delete it as appropriate when its time has come.

- Backups. It does you no good to shred the paper and delete the file from your document management system if that document is still sitting on a backup tape on the shelf above your server. Make sure you have a policy for how long to keep old backup tapes. Chances are that your document retention intervals will be measured in years anyhow, so any tapes that old aren't likely to be useful anymore—don't bother erasing them; in most cases you should just have those ancient tapes destroyed.

- E-mail. If the document went to the client, co-counsel, or opposing counsel or was collaborated on within the firm, there is a good chance that one or more drafts of the document (which could be far more damaging than the finalized—and sanitized—document) may exist in your Sent Items folder or other e-mail folders. It's probably a good idea to clean those out; in fact, you may not be required to keep e-mailed drafts of the documents for any specific period of time, especially if you have a copy of the final document in your document management system. So it may pay to be especially aggressive about cleaning out attached document drafts from your e-mail.

- Home computers. Lots of lawyers like to work from home these days, and you may have a system setup that lets them do so. If so . . . might they have copies of documents they've worked on stored on their local hard drives at home? What about that brief they slaved over all weekend and stored a copy of in their My Documents folder at home?

- Personal e-mail. Attorneys want to work from home or while on vacation (defeats the purpose of "vacation," no?), so they e-mail certain documents they're currently working on to their RoadRunner, Yahoo, Hotmail, Gmail, or other personal e-mail accounts.

Scenario

Lawyer works at home occasionally on his trusty but aging desktop computer. He brings home files on a flash drive or maybe even e-mails them to his personal e-mail account so he can access them at home and saves them in his My Documents folder. He copies the finished product back to the USB flash drive to take back to the office on Monday to finalize, print, or send to the client. A couple of years go by, and the lawyer decides it's time for a new home computer. Good dad that he is, he donates his old trusty desktop to his kid's school. Not knowing any better, he also just donated 2.5 years of client work product to his kid's school. *Uh-oh.*

Even when the case is long over, they never think to delete the e-mails with the attached documents from their personal e-mail. No, they didn't delete it from the Outlook Express Inbox on their home computer either.

- Mobile devices. These days a lot of lawyers are carrying BlackBerries, iPhones, Treos, and other mobile devices on which they can get their e-mail. Any documents e-mailed to them are probably on their mobile devices too, as attachments, unless they have cleaned those messages out. Don't forget about USB flash drives, iPods, and other USB storage devices the attorneys might have used to transport documents to and fro.

- In the Cloud. There are few topics hotter in technology than Cloud computing these days. Many firms have signed up for cloud-based services like Clio or Rocket Matter. Many others are using online backup services like Mozy or Carbonite. If you've uploaded your documents to any of those services, you need to make sure that service is respecting your document retention policies, too. And don't forget *their* backups. You may have deleted the document from Rocket Matter, but did Rocket Matter delete your document from *its* backups?

Don't think your folks would ever e-mail documents to their home accounts or use their iPod to transport documents here and there? If you don't have some system in place to easily allow them to work on documents from home or on the road, then you can almost guarantee that even the most vaguely savvy among them have already improvised systems of their own. Google "free document sharing service" and be prepared for more than 3.5 *million* hits. Google and Microsoft are just two of the companies that as of this writing offer more than 1GB of free file sharing space to anybody who can fill out a short registration screen and click "OK." Don't be surprised if some of your people are using it. And that's not the sort of thing your firm wants to find out about when it is compelled to produce documents it thought were long-since expired.

Collaborating with Other Word Processors

As much as Microsoft would like to make it so, the reality is that not everybody is using Microsoft Word 2010. You may have to interoperate with people who are using older versions of Microsoft Word or even, Bill, forgive me for saying so, products from other vendors like Corel's WordPerfect.

Older Versions of Word

Operating with older versions of Word is actually fairly easy. The Office 2010 OpenXML file formats were all new to Office 2007, and the older versions of Word don't understand them natively. Microsoft has found a great way to accommodate users of the older versions, however. It has created "file converters" that you can install on older versions of Microsoft Office (Office 2000 or later) that enable those versions of Office to read *and* write the newer file formats natively! How cool is that?! Better still, these file converters are free. I won't try to post the cryptic URL for them here; just Google for "Office 2010 File Converters" and you will quickly find the site to obtain and download them, along with simple instructions. Most, but not quite all, of the document features will be available to users after installing the file converters.

Even if you're *not* interacting with Office 2010 users, the file converters convey the benefits of the new file formats to the older software—such as the smaller file sizes.

▼

OK, you dragged it out of me. An example of what might not be available to a Word 2003 user running the file converters is equations created using the new Word equation editor. When the Word 2003 user opens a 2010 document with equations in it, they will be converted to images—the equations will be; not the Word 2003 user.

If the other party isn't interested in installing the file converters, all is not lost. You can still click File, do a Save As, and choose Office 97-2003 Document (see Figure 6.27) to save the document in the old, binary .DOC format. It shouldn't surprise you that if you do that you lose all of the benefits of saving in the new OpenXML formats. You've simply created a classic .DOC file that can be opened and edited by any application capable of working with those documents (such as Word 2002, aka Word XP).

FIGURE 6.27

When you save a document in the older file formats, you're saving in what Word calls "Compatibility Mode." Word will caution you that certain elements of your document might not translate properly in compatibility mode. Luckily, those things usually are not elements that lawyers care about—mostly it's about themes and SmartArt, for example.

Microsoft Word for Mac

If you happen to be collaborating with one of that small, but vocal, contingent of users who believe that putting an "i" in front of anything and painting it white makes it cool, then you're in luck—Microsoft Office 2008 and 2011 for Mac supports the Office OpenXML format (.DOCX) natively. There are file converters for older versions of Office for Mac, just like the PC versions.

WordPerfect

Amazing how times change. When I first started in legal technology, about two decades ago, WordPerfect (for DOS back then) was easily the dominant word processor in law firms. Today you still find it here and there, but for the most part it's a distant second to Microsoft Word. You obviously know what I mean, since you

In It for the Short Term

If you have to collaborate with somebody who has an obscure, or rather old, word processor and it's only going to be a short-term collaboration (a few weeks perhaps), then maybe you can persuade him or her to download and install the trial version of Microsoft Office 2010. It's fully functional and free; it just stops allowing you to edit documents after about sixty days. Great solution? No. But it may be better than beating your head against the wall trying to share documents with somebody who uses StarOffice 5.2.

bought this book. Unless you're my mother and just bought a copy to give to my Aunt Susan, I suppose.

That said, if your colleagues are using Corel WordPerfect Office X4 or X5, then they can already read and write the Word Open XML format files. No special hoops to jump through for you. The Corel users, however, should save their documents in Office OpenXML format (.DOCX) before they send them to you so that you can read them.

Corel's WordPerfect X3 support for Office OpenXML is a little more uncertain. A number of vague statements implied that X3 would support Office OpenXML, but X3 didn't support it when the product was new. There are a lot of documented instances where working between X3 and Office 2010 (and even older versions of Word, for that matter) resulted in some fairly frustrating issues, particularly around the way fonts were translated between the two products. Your best bet, if you have to work between these two products, is to use a format that is more common to both products. You could try saving the documents as Word 97-2003 format, but again, be prepared for possible formatting inconsistencies.

OpenOffice

OpenOffice is the open source productivity suite that is nominally authored by Sun Microsystems. At the time of this writing it's at version 3.2, but like all things open source, that could change at any time. Working with Open Office users is relatively easy since OpenOffice supports OpenXML natively and Word 2010 supports the OpenOffice formats natively, too.

Working on the Road

We're an increasingly mobile bunch, and the technology has evolved to the point where we don't have to be sitting at our desks to access and edit our documents. A number of technologies have emerged (and continue to emerge and impress) that allow you to work from anywhere at any time.

Mobile Devices

Just about everybody is carrying a mobile device these days—many of you are carrying phones that function as personal information devices. Windows Mobile 7, for example, includes a version of what we used to call "Pocket Word" or "Word Mobile" (depends a bit upon which version you have). It's a mobile-enhanced version of Microsoft Word that you can use to read, edit, or even compose documents . . . if you're really desperate. Let's be honest—working on a document of any size on a 2-inch diagonal screen with a thumb keyboard is not exactly an optimal experience. You can create bulleted lists, use primitive fonts, add and edit text, and even send your completed document via e-mail when you're done (assuming your device is configured for e-mail).

To use Word Mobile, just transfer the document to your mobile device via the USB Sync cable, Bluetooth, wireless, SD card, or whatever other file transfer mechanism may be available to you. Once it's on your device, just go to Start | Programs and look for either "Pocket Word" or "Office Mobile" | "Word Mobile," and when the program opens you'll be able to navigate to your document and open it.

I think I can safely say that this is not something you'll choose to do if you have other options, but it's nice to know that in a pinch, if you really have to review or edit a document while you're stuck in traffic somewhere and can't get access to a real computer, this option can get the job done if you're patient enough.

That applies to DataViz's "Documents to Go" (for Android devices), too.

The increasing popularity of tablet devices like the iPad and Motorola Xoom means that mobile users are getting larger screens (but still no physical keyboard) to work with. The iPad can read Word documents natively (assuming you can get them on your iPad to begin with), but if you want to edit them you have to get an additional application. As of this writing, the best solution is probably Pages for the iPad ($10).

Another option would be to use Google Docs to read documents (as long as they're under 500K). For perspective, this book manuscript is currently almost 7MB. Be careful with the free version of Google Apps, though; their terms of service give Google generous access and rights to your content—including the right to republish or "perform" (whatever that means) your documents.

By the time this book is in print and in your hands, there's a good chance that some newer and better solutions for working with Word documents on your tablet device will be available.

Telecommuting

Technology is increasingly enabling the ability to work from anywhere at any time, and this can be a blessing and a curse. There are three main technologies for telecommuting—which you use is up to you and your IT department or consultant.

Remote Node

Remote node computing is the "VPN" or "Virtual Private Network" solution where you connect to your office via the Internet and establish a secure "tunnel" across the Internet that lets you join your local computer (home computer or laptop, typically) to your office network. Then you work on your local computer just as if you were sitting in your office. You have access to all of the files and resources of the office network, just as you do from your desk—albeit probably a little slower since you're limited to an Internet connection.

If you have Microsoft Word 2010 installed on your local computer, then you can use it just as you would Word 2010 on your desk at the office. It's as easy as that. All of the processing occurs on your local computer. One advantage of remote node is that it's not too hard to work off-line (which means disconnected from the office) because your local computer is a stand-alone machine with Word 2010 installed. You can simply copy or check out documents to your local hard drive, disconnect from the office, and work on those documents locally. Later, when you connect back up, you just copy or check in those documents back to the office.

This is pretty handy if you're taking a laptop on an airplane and want to work rather than watch the movie.

Remote Control

Remote Control is the old "pcAnywhere" or "GoToMyPC" solution. With this solution you connect to the office, again, across the Internet typically, and with an application on your local computer you take control of a remote PC sitting idly at the office—usually your office computer. As the name sort of implies, you are remotely controlling your office computer, and that means you quite literally have everything you have at the office. The office computer is transmitting to you images of the screen, and you are transmitting to it keystrokes and mouse movements. All of the processing occurs on the office computer.

Remote control is fairly easy to set up but does have one big drawback . . . if you don't have an Internet connection, you're out of luck. You *have* to be able to connect to the office to use it, which means that you sometimes can't do it from airplanes (aerial WiFi is here but not ubiquitous quite yet) or other disconnected areas. It also means you probably have to remember to leave the machine you're remotely controlling turned on when you leave the office, which may introduce other security issues. Also, if the office machine is shared with other users it won't be accessible to you while another user is logged in to it, either remotely or locally (sitting at the keyboard).

With remote control you're literally using the same machine you use when you're sitting at the office, so you are using the same copy of Microsoft Word 2010 (complete with any customization) that you are used to.

Remote Host

The third basic technology you'll find is remote host. This is the "Citrix" or "terminal server" solution, where a server at your office hosts some number of simultaneous users who connect in remotely with virtual Windows desktops. The advantage to this is that you don't need to leave your office computer turned on—you're connecting to a server that is always on. Also, if you have a number of remote users, you don't need to provide office machines for each of them; they can remote into the terminal server from their home machines or laptops and work from there. It may be a little pricier to set up and configure than "GoToMyPC," but the results are a tad more professional, especially in an office where you may have a lot of simultaneous remote users.

With remote host you can install and run Microsoft Word 2010 on the terminal server or Citrix server, and all of the functionality we've described in this book would still apply.

Note: If you have a remote host server and you want to install Word 2010 on it, you have to make sure you get the volume license version of Word 2010. You can't install the Word 2010 that came with your PC (known as the "OEM" or "Original Equipment Manufacturer" version) or a retail version of Word that you bought at the computer store or from Amazon.com. Volume license versions are actually less expensive than the retail version, and, contrary to popular belief, you don't have to have fifty machines to qualify. You need only buy five (or more) licenses to get volume licensing.

In "the Cloud"

The newest player in the telecommuting market is actually an old concept (ASPs) brought back to life. Software as a Service (SaaS) is what you've got when a outside provider is hosting your software on its servers, across the Internet, usually for a monthly subscription fee. Google Apps (free and paid) are examples of SaaS products. Microsoft's new Office 365, which provides stripped-down Web versions of Word, PowerPoint, Excel, and OneNote across the Web, is another. Every week it seems like new SaaS products are popping up. SaaS can be a great solution for the mobile legal professional—you can access it from anywhere, you don't need to maintain your own servers, and it's constantly updated and monitored. But there are some downsides, too:

- Cost. It seems like SaaS would be cheaper than having your own software, and often it is, but sometimes it's not. If you're paying $30 a month to use that suite of apps that cost you $499 to buy . . . in 18 months you'll have spent more on the SaaS than the purchase price of the product. It pays to do the math.
- Security. Google's free apps have a very liberal terms of service agreement that gives the company the right to reproduce and republish any content you submit to their service (i.e., documents

you're storing there). Will it ever do that? I don't know, but are you comfortable agreeing to a contract that gives it the right to? (Note: Its *paid* version of apps does not suffer from this same shortcoming.)

Additionally, almost all SaaS services are in what's called a "Shared Tenant Environment." That's how they keep the price down—economy of scale. You're on a server with dozens or hundreds of other users and customers. The chances of that server getting compromised (or seized by authorities) have to be weighed.

- Access. If your Internet connection goes down or is otherwise unavailable, so is your data. If you're going to be dependent upon SaaS applications, it's wise to have redundant Internet connections and a plan for what to do in case of a total outage.

  Also, make sure your SaaS provider lets you have a local copy of your data. You don't want the provider to have all of the control over your critical data—heaven-forbid you ever have a billing dispute or mistake and the company cuts off your access to the data while you're under deadline.

- Geolocation. When your data is hosted somewhere else, you don't always know where that somewhere else is. Make sure to ask. If your data is being hosted in Iowa or Seattle, that's probably OK. If your data is being hosted in Canada or Scotland . . . that might be OK. If your data is being hosted in China or North Korea . . . that's probably *not* OK. Don't forget to ask where the host's backups are, too.

Summary

Collaborating and working remotely help to maximize your productivity, and Microsoft Word 2010 has been designed with these benefits in mind. The Office OpenXML format is the most open and portable format yet for Microsoft Office, and increasingly other word processing products, such as Corel's X5 and OpenOffice 3.2, will be able to comfortably support it natively. Additionally, Word 2010 now supports the OpenOffice formats natively as well.

Working with Other Programs 7

One of the advantages of purchasing the Microsoft Office Suite is that the applications in the suite tend to work well together. Office 2010 takes this idea further than ever.

Outlook

Outlook is the application that is open the longest during the day for most users of Microsoft Office, and it's the place where a lot of information that is useful to Word documents (names and addresses, for instance) are stored. Naturally, people want to be able to use that information in Word as seamlessly as possible.

Mail Merge

Commonly, attorneys and firms keep a list of clients in Outlook in the form of a Contacts folder. You can leverage that list of information to create mailing labels or form letters in Word. The way you do that is called a "mail merge," and it basically involves creating a document template with fields where your variable data goes—things like "Name," "Address,"and "City."

You can start your mail merge from either Word or Outlook, but I generally recommend you start from the Outlook side because Outlook offers better filtering capabilities than Word does.

Tricks of the Pros

Mail merge is a great reason to use categories in your Contacts. Categorize your contacts as "Clients" or "Holiday Card" or whatever, and then filter your view either with the Search Contacts tool at the top right or by setting an actual Filter on the view with View | View Settings | Filter | More Choices. Once your Contacts folder is displaying only the contacts in the category you wish to merge from then you can proceed with step 2 of the merge.

1. To begin, you'll want to switch to your Contacts folder in Outlook and select the contact items you want to use for your merge. If there are only a handful of them, just hold down the CTRL key and click on each one to select it, or, if they are contiguous, hold down SHIFT and click the first and then last one in the group. If you want to select *all* of the contacts in the current view, then you can skip to the next step.

2. Click the "Mail Merge" button on the Home tab in Outlook. You'll get the "Mail Merge Contacts" dialog box, like you see in Figure 7.1. If you're sending to *all* of the displayed contacts, then check the "All contacts in current view" radio button. If you've selected specific contacts and want to merge only those, then select the "Only selected contacts" radio button. Leave "Fields to merge" as "All contact fields" if you have the option.

FIGURE 7.1

3. Select the Document you want to merge to. Usually it will be a new document, but there may be times when you have a preexisting main document (that's what Word calls the document that contains the text and information you're merging into) that you want to use.

4. If you plan to do this merge repeatedly with the same, unchanging group of contacts, you can save this contact data to a permanent file. I discourage this except in *one* scenario: you want to keep a snapshot of the merge data for reference—to show who you sent the newsletter to or what address you had on file for the recipients at the time. The rest of the time your merge data will likely change from month to month and year to year as new contacts are added and old contacts are removed (not to mention address changes).

5. Under Merge options select the Document Type. Normally, it will be either Form Letters, Mailing Labels, or Envelopes. A "Catalog" is essentially a directory. I've yet to find a practical use for that option in a law firm setting.

6. Under Merge options you can change the "Merge to" setting from "New Document" to either "Printer" or "E-mail." I discourage using "Printer" because that's going to perform your merge to the printer, and if something isn't right with the merge, you might blow through fifty pages of paper before you realize it. I always merge to a "New Document" so I can preview my results *before* I send them to the printer or out via e-mail.

7. Click "OK." Word will open with what looks like a blank document (assuming you chose "New Document" in step 3), but there is a key difference . . . the Ribbon will open to the Mailings tab and a number of the buttons will be active.

8. Create your document as you would like it to appear. Type the text that isn't going to change, and in those places where you want to insert data from the merge (like Full Name or Mailing Address), click the "Insert Merge Field" button to get the gallery of possible fields from your data set to merge (see Figure 7.2). Select the field or fields you want to insert there. For example: "Dear «Title»«Last_Name»."

FIGURE 7.2

9. When you have the document completed, with fields in those places that will be replaced with Outlook contact data, you can preview your results by using the "Preview Results" button. Click that button and Word will perform the sample merge.

10. Use the forward and back arrows on the Go To Record command to move forward and backward through your previewed results and make sure everything looks the way it should.

11. When you're happy with the results, click the "Finish & Merge" button, and then you can print (or e-mail) the results.

Tricks of the Pros

When merging addresses from Outlook, rather than use the "Home Address" or "Business Address," use the "Mailing Address." That's because some of your contacts may want their mail sent to their home address and some to the business. It could be a nightmare figuring out which is which and doing two merges, so just use the "Mailing Address" option. Mailing Address is controlled by a checkbox in Outlook that lets you specify which of multiple addresses is the mailing address.

One-Off Envelopes

One of the features I've liked since the days of WordPerfect 5.1 for DOS (remember that one?) is the ability to print envelopes. It just looks a lot more professional to have a printed envelope, and it's a pain to have to load your envelope into a typewriter and type the address on. Especially since I don't even own a typewriter anymore. If you don't want to have to do a whole mail merge just to print a single envelope then Word's Envelopes feature is for you.

To print an envelope with Word, just go to the Mailings tab and click the Envelopes button. That will give you the Envelopes and Labels dialog box you see in Figure 7.3. You can type your delivery (destination) address in the provided field or click the address book icon just above it to the right to access your Outlook address book and have Word pull the address from there. If you click the down-arrow NEXT to the address book (as I have in the figure), you'll see the last few addresses you've selected so you can reinsert a common address if you need to.

▼

I've always liked being able to print a barcode on the envelope for the destination address. Word 2007 does away with that feature. The reason it was pulled was that the POSTNET codes that the Barcode field in Word produced were no longer compliant with USPS regulations. It could be argued that Microsoft could have fixed the POSTNET codes but to be honest the US Postal Service is using high-speed scanners on all mail now and they are perfectly capable of reading a printed address on an envelope. So there really isn't any advantage to printing the barcodes on the envelopes anymore.

FIGURE 7.3

You can add your return address or check the "Omit" button if you have preprinted envelopes or if you're going to use a sticker for it. When you're ready to print the envelope, just load it into your printer and click the "Print" button. Voilà: a lovely envelope.

Labels

You can create labels with addresses from your Outlook address book the

Tricks of the Pros

If you have your destination address in the document, such as in an address block at the top of a letter, just select that address first, then click the Envelopes command in the Mailings tab. When the Envelopes and Labels dialog opens, that selected text will already appear in the Delivery Address field.

same way you created envelopes. You can print a whole sheet of the same label or just a single label—and even use a partial sheet of labels! Word will let you specify which column or row you want to print the single label on.

Excel

Word and Excel make it easy to embed Excel data into a Word document—either as a static table or as a live link that updates as the data in Excel updates. There are a few different ways to do it, but let's start with the easiest way. Create your spreadsheet in Excel, select the cell/cells that you want to embed in your Word document, and click "Copy." Switch to your Word document, place the insertion point where you want the data, and click "Paste." There's your data (see Figure 7.4), easy as that!

FIGURE 7.4

Of course, that's a static representation of the data. If it changes on the Excel spreadsheet, it won't change in the Word document. If that's what you want, great. If, on the other hand, you were hoping for something more dynamic, then you need to take one more step. See the little clipboard at the bottom right corner of Figure 7.4? That's a tool that gives you paste options, and in this case it's pretty useful. If you click, it'll get the options you find in Figure 7.5. The six basic options relate to how the table of data will appear. Keep Source Formatting means that any formats in Excel (including colors and lines) will transfer over. Match Destination Table Style will bring the data but replace those formats with a table style from your document.

FIGURE 7.5

The default is to paste the data in as a table, but Paste as Picture will paste it as a static image instead. That's a good one to use if you want to maintain the source formatting and make sure the data can't be easily edited.

Keep Text Only doesn't paste the data as a table, but rather as plain text. This is good for simple content, but not very good if you have a lot of data to paste.

All of those options differ in how the data is presented, but they're the same in one very important way: they're all going to paste the data statically. In other words, the data is the data and that's it—there's no link back to the source Excel workbook. If the data changes in the source workbook, it won't be updated in the Word document.

The two middle options in Figure 7.5 address that shortcoming. Basically, you're just going to choose if you want to keep the Source Formatting (i.e., have the data look like it does in Excel) or if you're going to match the Destination Formatting (i.e., have the data look like a default Word table), but either way the data *will* be linked back to the Excel workbook. If the data in the workbook changes, then the data in the Word document will change as well.

The converse is not true, by the way. If you change the data in Word, it

I guess I should point out that this works only as long as the Excel workbook is available. If you e-mail this Word document to a colleague at another firm, then the link will be broken since your colleague doesn't have the source workbook. He or she will see the Excel data as of the last update, but any subsequent updates won't be reflected. If you move the Excel file to another location in your organization, Word will cleverly update the link to reflect the new location . . . so future changes will still be reflected, as long as you can access the Excel file from that computer.

will *not* update the data in the Excel spreadsheet. In fact, the next time you make a change in Excel, any changes you made to the Word version of the data will be lost—overwritten with the current version of the Excel data.

This is a pretty useful feature for documents that are a work in progress—for example, if you have a complicated purchase offer and you're still running all the "what-ifs" and scenarios in Excel. You can link the relevant Excel data to your Word document, and Word will always reflect the latest numbers for you until you're ready to send or print. When you've got what you want, just print it or PDF it and send it off. When you PDF the document, you essentially affix the numbers as they are—they won't change in the PDF no matter what happens to the Excel workbook.

The other place this feature is really handy is in recurring reports. You can set up your report in the Word document and link in relevant data from Excel workbooks. For each period, your Word document will already have the relevant numbers from your Excel workbooks—making much shorter work of preparing the report.

If you'd like to break the link so that Word no longer automatically updates the data, just right-click the table in Word and choose Linked Worksheet Object and then Links, as I have in Figure 7.6.

FIGURE 7.6

The Links dialog box (Figure 7.7) includes a number of clever tools for working with the linked data, including a "Break Link" dialog that will effectively convert your linked table to a static table. If you only want to prevent the link from updating temporarily, click the "Locked" checkbox

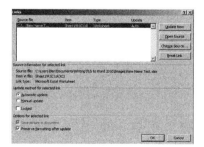

FIGURE 7.7

under Update Method on the Links dialog box instead of the "Break Link" button. Later, when you want to resume updating, just go back in and uncheck "Locked."

OneNote

OneNote is Microsoft's free-form note-taking software. It's an application that should be extremely popular with attorneys because it is essentially an electronic version of the yellow legal pad but with a lot more power. OneNote is exceptionally good at serving as a starting point for Word documents. When I start to write a long memo (or a book, for that matter), I'll often start it as an outline in OneNote. I can do my Internet research, collaborate with colleagues, and reorganize things until I'm ready to write the actual detailed content. In OneNote (pictured in Figure 7.8) you can create your outlines and other content, and when you're ready to send it over to Word for finishing and formatting, you just click File | Send | Send to Word, as you see in Figure 7.9. When you do that you'll get a fresh new Word document with your outline ready for content.

FIGURE 7.8   FIGURE 7.9

You can also readily copy and paste content, images, diagrams, and other items from OneNote to Word.

Linked Notes

OneNote and Word have another interesting integration trick. You can click the Linked Notes icon in the OneNote group of the Review tab in Word (Figure 7.10). That will open OneNote and dock it to the right side of your screen. OneNote will ask you what section you want to put the linked notes in, similar to what you see in Figure 7.11. Pick a section to locate the linked notes in, and OneNote will give you a blank page where you can start taking notes. At the top right corner of the OneNote page you'll see a little chain link icon, shown in Figure 7.12. That's your cue that these notes are linked to a document.

FIGURE 7.10   **FIGURE 7.11**   **FIGURE 7.12**

Now here's where the fun begins. You keep working in your document. As you go, you can take notes on the document in the OneNote window docked to the side. You can see that I'm doing that with some sample content in Figure 7.13. "So what?" you might be thinking? Well, this is OneNote's party piece . . . if you click on one of your linked notes in

> **Tip** OneNote linked notes also work for PowerPoint and Web pages, too!

OneNote, you'll get a little Word icon appearing to the side, just like in Figure 7.14. If you click that icon, you'll be taken to the place in the Word document you were working on when you took those notes.

OneNote becomes a powerful repository for you to take notes and do document review. None of the OneNote notes appear in the Word document, so you don't have to worry about any metadata from them.

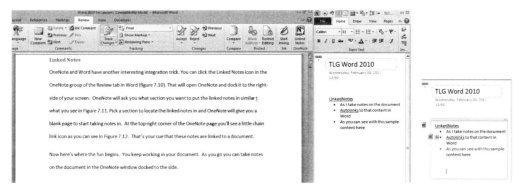

FIGURE 7.13   **FIGURE 7.14**

PowerPoint

Microsoft PowerPoint is a tool for taking information and presenting it to a live audience. Word integrates with PowerPoint in two ways that are interesting to us.

Send to PowerPoint

If you have a document that you want to present to an audience, you can use it as the basis for a presentation. The first trick to doing that successfully is to properly format the document you're sending.

PowerPoint decides what text goes where based upon the styles you're using in the document (as if you needed another reason to use styles). Heading 1 text becomes slide titles. Heading 2 is the first-level bullet point. Heading 3 is the second-level bullet point. And so on. If you've properly formatted your document, every major heading becomes a new slide, and the sub-headings under them are the bullet points.

Body text that doesn't have a heading applied won't appear on your slides.

> *"Waiter, taste my soup."*
> *"What's wrong with the soup?"*
> *"Just taste the soup."*
> *"OK, where's the spoon?"*
> *"Aha!"*

Now that you've got a properly formatted document, you're ready to send it to PowerPoint. Great! How do we send it? There's no button on the Ribbon, nothing Backstage under the File menu.

No, we have to add the button. You could add it to the Ribbon, but that would require adding a custom tab, and it seems silly to add a whole tab just for this one command. If you already have a custom tab, go ahead and add this to it if you want to. If you've created a custom tab before, you already know how to add this button. For the rest of you . . .

Click the drop-down on the end of the Quick Access Toolbar and choose "More Commands" from the menu that appears. On the left-hand column set "Choose commands from" to "All Commands" and then scroll down to "Send to Microsoft PowerPoint" (see Figure 7.15). Add

FIGURE 7.15

that to the Quick Access Toolbar and then click "OK" to go back out to your document.

Now, ready to send to PowerPoint? Just click the new button for that on the QAT and Word will start the process.

Word for Handouts

The other handy integration between Word and PowerPoint comes when you already have a PowerPoint slide deck and you want to make a set of handouts to give to the audience. In PowerPoint just go to File | Save & Send | Create Handouts, and click the "Create Handouts" button. PowerPoint will ask you how you want to lay out your handouts (notes next to slides, blank lines below slides, outline only, etc.). Select the style you like, then click "OK" and a Word Document will be created for you with your PowerPoint content. Ready to print and present!

> **Tricks of the Pros**
>
> That's not a bad way to create speaker notes to have at the podium during your presentation, too—in case you're not using PowerPoint's Presenter View for some reason.

Pictures and Diagrams

They say a picture is worth a thousand words, and there may well be times in your documents when you'll want to include a picture, diagram, or graphic. Word 2010 makes it pretty easy to do so. Go to the Insert tab, click "Picture," and use the Insert Picture dialog box to navigate to the picture you want to insert. When you've found it, click once to select it and then click "Insert."

Once you have the image inserted in your document, you can resize it by pointing at one of the tiny squares around the edge (called "handles") with your cursor and drag the handle to resize it. If you need to be more precise in your image sizing, just right-click the image to get the context menu you see in Figure 7.17 and choose "Size and Position. . . ." In the size dialog box, you can not only specify the size of the image, but you can also rotate the image or change the way that text wraps around it.

> **Tricks of the Pros**
>
> If you're working with an image that you might change in the future, consider inserting the picture as a link to the file by clicking the drop-down arrow on the "Insert" button. Later, if you want to change or update the image, simply replace the image file on your hard drive with the new file, using the same name.

FIGURE 7.17

As long as I'm on the subject . . . there are a couple of other items on the context menu in Figure 7.17 that you should be interested in. The "Change Picture . . ." command lets you select a different image—handy if you realize that you inserted a picture of what was supposed to be a photo of a disputed property line but is actually a shot of your family at the Grand Canyon.

"Hyperlink" is handy in electronic documents if you want to be able to click on the picture and open a file or Web site. It doesn't do anything for paper documents, of course.

"Insert Caption" brings up Word's captioning tool (Figure 7.18), which I happen to find a bit inflexible and primitive. But it can be handy if your needs align with what it does.

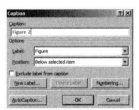

FIGURE 7.18

Scanned Documents

Just like inserting pictures, there may be times when you'll want to insert a scanned document. There are two basic ways you might want to do that:

1. As an image. You want the other person to see and probably be able to read the document, but not edit it. Perhaps it's just an exhibit that you're including in your document.
2. As editable text. You've received the document in paper form and now you want to be able to edit the text like any other word document. To do that you'll have to scan the document and run it through an OCR (Optical Character Recognition) program.

When you first scan in a file, or receive an image of a document via e-mail or other electronic transfer, the computer just sees a picture. It doesn't know a document from a building or an elephant; it's all just pixels to the computer. When you run the OCR program, it will look at the image and try to recognize the text so that it can be converted into As and Bs and Cs and so forth. The results are saved as a document file that you can then edit.

When it comes to OCR, the cleaner your original, the better your results. If your original is clearly printed, in a nice clean font, with black text on white paper, then you'll probably get very good results. If your original is a little wrinkled, with colored text, highlighters, handwritten notes scrawled in the margins, and so forth, then your results may be somewhat unpredictable. Either way, be sure to carefully proofread the results before you trust them. Especially in legal documents, a single word or number that's wrong could have serious consequences.

The best OCR programs include spell checkers and some context-sensitive capabilities that make good guesses at what a word should be—but even so, they're not perfect. Even the best tend to average only about 99 percent accuracy.

Summary

Word is part of a suite of applications that are designed to work together. Over the years, this statement has garnered chuckles or snarls from users who have tried to make them do that without much success, but Word 2010 and the Office 2010 suite go further than ever before to try to help the applications work together more smoothly. Whether you're doing mail merges from Outlook or embedding data from Excel, Microsoft Word 2010 can help you be more productive, more effective, and generally happier.

Automating Word

8

Microsoft Word 2010 offers some very powerful tools for automating your document creation and editing—reducing repetitive tasks and giving you better quality control while reducing errors.

Power Corrupts. Absolute power is really kinda cool.

Document Assembly

Document assembly is the usage of tools like macros, scripts, or applications to automate the building of standardized documents. Mail merge is a form of document assembly, too. There are a lot of third-party tools that can do it, as well as some tools built right into Word. The key to document assembly is to create a library of reusable parts (phrases, images, and even entire pages of boilerplate text) so that you don't have to create them from scratch every time.

HotDocs (and others)

HotDocs (owned by LexisNexis) is an example of a third-party document assembly application. The premise is pretty straightforward—you create a model document that is going to be the basis for all of the future documents of this type. In the document you identify those bits that are going to vary from document to document—the client's name, dates, amounts, locations, and so forth. Once you have your model document completely built, you run the document assembly software, and it performs an "interview" where it asks you for the variable information you previously specified for the document.

The assembly software will take your answers, plug them into the places you specified in the model document, and create a fully built document.

Kiiac

Kiiac takes a slightly different approach from HotDocs. You show Kiiac a library of documents, and it analyzes them to find the documents that are similar and identifies the most common clauses. Later, when you need to build a new document, Kiiac presents you with the most common or successful clauses for you to choose from and helps you to build a document that most closely resembles the model documents you've identified. Kiiac helps you build and maintain clause libraries and document templates. It's not cheap, but especially if you're creating a lot of documents on a value-based billing system, it could be worth it.

Building Blocks

A popular feature among attorneys in earlier versions of Word was Auto-Text. Commonly, attorneys and staff would create custom AutoText entries with often-used phrases or paragraphs, and then use the AutoText to quickly and easily insert those bits where they needed them. In Word 2010, Building Blocks have replaced the AutoText feature, making it simultaneously more powerful and more difficult to use. Building Blocks let you create and save snippets of a document that you expect to reuse often. One way Building Blocks improve on AutoText is that they're not just limited to text. You can make a Building Block out of just about any element of a document. For attorneys, that will still usually mean text, but it could just as easily mean an image like a logo or scanned signature file.

To create a Building Block you just select the element—highlight the text, for example—you want to add to the Building Blocks gallery and then go to the Insert tab, "Quick Parts," and "Save Selection to Quick Parts Gallery." What you'll get is what you see in Figure 8.1.

FIGURE 8.1

Give the Building Block a name. In Figure 8.1 I've named my Building Block "CrtBldBlk," because the name you have needs to be descriptive but fairly quick and easy type. (I'll explain why in a moment.)

Pick a gallery to add your new part to—you'll see several of the known galleries like "Cover Pages" listed. Generally speaking, you'll want to choose either AutoText or "Quick Parts" if you're just adding text or maybe a scanned signature image, as most attorneys will. Choosing "Quick Parts" has the added benefit that your new block will appear on the Quick Parts gallery under the button on the Ribbon.

The next field is for Category, and this one is purely up to you. You don't have to use Categories if you don't want to—put everything in General instead. But if you're going to use a lot of custom blocks, you might want to organize them by creating custom categories. Click the drop arrow for Category and you'll see that "Create new category" is a choice.

Give your new block an optional description and then choose which template to save the block in. For the most part, you'll want to save in the Building Blocks template. The one exception I can think of that many of you may encounter is if you were going to create a Building Block to share with others. In that case, you might create a custom template and save to that—then you can send that template to those you want to share with and they can open it.

▼▼▼▼▼

To share Building Blocks with others, create a new template by saving a new document (create a Word document with a brief description of your intended Building Blocks, for example) as a template. Click the File | Save As | Change the File Type to Template, and give it a name. Save your Building Blocks to that template and send the template to the people you want to share with. They can save the template to Word's Startup folder (C:\Users*USERNAME*\AppData\Roaming\Microsoft\Word\STARTUP is the default in Vista and Windows 7), and the next time they start Word the custom Building Blocks will be available to them.

Finally, you have an Options field that lets you configure how your block should be inserted into the document you're working on.

- "Insert Content Only" inserts the contents of the block at the current cursor point. This is what I usually use, as most of my Building Blocks are just bits of boilerplate text that I save as Building Blocks to keep from having to retype it or having to search it out and copy and paste it from another document.
- "Insert Content in its own Paragraph" sets off your block as a paragraph of its own. Useful for signatures or if your block is . . . well . . . a paragraph.
- "Insert Content on its own Page" creates page breaks before and after your block. This is a nice option if you have an entire page of boilerplate that you want to be able to quickly add to your

Tricks of the Pros

If you have pages of text that change only a bit, create Building Blocks from them that are their own pages. When you need to build that document, insert the pages and then go back and make the subtle changes to each of those pages. Building Blocks, once inserted, are edited as easily as any other bit of text. This way you can quickly build a several-page document with the benefits of, but not the hazards of, document reuse.

documents. For example, you may have a biography page or one or more pages of standard contract language that you don't change often.

With the old AutoText feature, you'd type the name of your AutoText entry and it would offer to replace your AutoText name with the actual text. With Building Blocks, you have to type the name of your Building Block (which is why we want it to be something easy to type) and then press "F3" to activate it (i.e., replace the name with the actual block).

To organize your Building Blocks, go to the Insert tab and click on the "Quick Parts" button. You'll find the "Building Blocks Organizer" pictured in Figure 8.2.

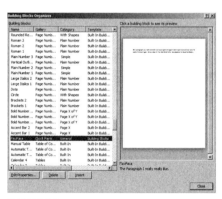

FIGURE 8.2

The Building Blocks Organizer is how you can edit the properties of a Building Block after the fact—for example, if you decide to change the category you assigned the block to or what gallery it appears in. You can also preview and insert your Building Blocks from the organizer.

If you want to edit an existing Building Block, however, that's a bit of a different matter. There isn't an easy way to do it—the best I can offer you is that you can insert the Building Block you want to edit into a blank document and make the changes there. Then highlight and save the edited text as a new Building Block with the same name as the old one. Word will prompt you if you want to "redefine" the existing Building Block. Click "Yes" to replace the old one with the new version. If Word doesn't prompt you to redefine, then double-check to make sure you used the same name and saved the new version of the Building Block to the same gallery or template as the old one.

Macros

Word's macro language is amazingly powerful. So powerful, in fact, that it became the basis for a number of Word macro viruses a few years ago. The macro language that Word uses is Visual Basic for Applications (VBA). Entire books far thicker than this are devoted to the subject, so I won't attempt to cover it in detail here. Besides, the reality is that most of you will never do any VBA coding. What I'll do instead is show you how to use the Macro Recorder to create simple macros yourself, and then later in this chapter I'll give you a taste of what VBA is capable of, walk you through a couple of things that are especially useful for attorneys, and point you toward some resources if you want to know more.

Insert Text from File

One way to build a document is to assemble it from a collection of other documents. If you'd like to insert the entire text of another file into a Word document, you have a couple of ways to do that:

1. Open the file you want to paste into in Word.
2. Open the file you want to paste from.
3. Select all of the text in the donor document.
4. Copy that text.
5. Switch to the recipient document.
6. Find the spot you want to put that text and paste it.

Or, you could just go to the document you're trying to create, place the cursor where you want to insert the other document's contents, go to the Insert tab of the Ribbon and click the drop-arrow next to "Object" and select "Text from File." Word will let you browse for the file you want to insert. Select it and click "Insert." Done.

Quick Parts—Fields

Some content in your document may be dynamic—either metadata or calculated. You don't have to type (and update) that data manually. Word has a long list of fields you can insert that will dynamically update as you need.

To access the list go to the Insert tab on the Ribbon and click "Quick Parts" and then "Field." You'll get the Field dialog box like you see in Figure 8.3. From here you can insert any number of things from a formula that will automatically calculate and present the result, to various dates, author names, numbers, page count . . . a vast array of things. By placing

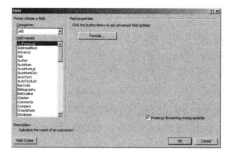

FIGURE 8.3

the appropriate field code you can save yourself some time and effort and let Word insert the appropriate data for you.

Recording Macros

The easiest way to create a new macro is simply to record it, and Word provides a capable facility to do just that. To access the Macro Recorder, you can go to the View tab of the Ribbon, to the Macros group on the far right end, and click the drop-arrow on the button (see Figure 8.4) to find "Record Macro."

FIGURE 8.4

So, let's say for our example that you'd like to create a macro that prints only the current page of your document. All we need to do is start recording, name our macro, step through the actions we want to record, and then stop the recording and save it as a macro. So let's give it a go. . . .

1. Go to the View Tab, Macros, and Record Macro. The Record Macro dialog box (Figure 8.5) will appear. Give your macro a name—I called mine "CurPrint" for "Current Page Print."
2. You can assign the macro to a button that you might put on the QAT (Quick Access Toolbar), which we covered in Chapter 2, or you can give it a keyboard shortcut. If it's not a macro you'll run often or if you want to invoke it using something like AutoHot-Key, then you can do neither and just save it by name. I chose to assign it to CTRL+ALT+P, replacing "InsertPageField," which I rarely do.
3. If you only want this macro to be part of a custom template, you can change the "Store In" field, but realistically you'll almost always

leave that alone. If you're sophisticated enough to want finite control of which template the macro gets saved in, then you've probably skipped these simple step-by-step instructions anyhow.

4. You may want to give a description for what your macro does, especially if you have a lot of them and may not remember later, or if you're going to share it with other users and want to make sure they know what it does.

5. Click "OK." You'll be returned to your document, and your mouse pointer will have a small "cassette tape" (remember those?) icon attached to it, which indicates that recording is currently on.

6. Perform the actions you wish to record. In our example, we're going to click "File," then "Print," and then click "Print all Pages" and change that to "Print Current Page." Then we'll click the "Print" button.

FIGURE 8.5

Your document should print, and you should find yourself returned to the editing screen. Since clicking "Print" was the last step of your macro, you can go back to the View Tab | Macros button and click "Stop Recording." Recording will stop and your macro will be saved for future use. The next time you invoke that Macro—via View | Macros or the button or keyboard shortcut you selected—the *exact* same set of steps will be repeated. Those steps can do anything in Word that you can do—including type entire documents of text, perform a series of actions, order a pizza . . . well, ordering pizza requires somewhat more advanced programming skills.

When recording macro actions, the speed with which you perform the tasks is irrelevant. The macro will be replayed much faster than it was recorded. I tend to move very deliberately when I'm recording so that I don't record mistakes. Plan ahead, click on things deliberately, pause to make sure you know what your next action is, and then take that action. You'd rather not record mistakes or have to stop and start over.

What Can VBA Do?

VBA can do just about anything you want it to do, and even a few things you don't. You can manipulate data or files, automate repetitive tasks, or even roll your own more advanced application extension. In the previous section we used the Macro Recorder to record a macro, but what that really did was create some VBA code for us. We could have written that code manually, but in that example we used the recorder to automate the process of creating the code.

Creating a Form Template

At times, you may want to create a form in Word that has some custom controls to enable more professional data entry. I can't account for every possible form scenario you might have, but let me introduce you to the controls at your disposal and let your creative juices flow.

The first step is to create your sample form. In Figure 8.6 I've created an oversimplified New Client Intake form. Now that you have the form, you need to add controls that will let the user fill out the form.

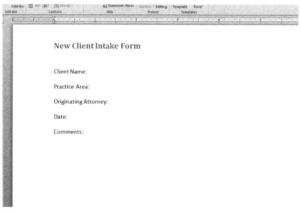

FIGURE 8.6

Controls

On the Developer tab, there is a group called "Controls" that contains a number of tools for creating professional-looking forms.

To start, we need a field to enter the client's name. The first control in the group is the "Rich Text Content" control. Click to insert one of those. If your cursor isn't at the place in the document where you want the control, just use your mouse to drag and drop it where you want it. In our sample, I'll put it next to the "Client Name:" label.

Don't see the Developer tab? Right-click the Ribbon, choose "Customize the Ribbon," and check the box in front of "Developer" in the right-hand column.

The next field is "Practice Area," and I'll use a drop-down list control for that. Click "Drop-Down List Content Control" in the Controls group and insert it where you want it—in this case next to Practice Area. You now have a lovely field that lets you choose a Practice Area . . . but you haven't told it what practice areas you have.

To do that, just click once on the control on your form, then click "Properties" in the Controls group on the Ribbon. You'll get the dialog box you see in Figure 8.7—and I've taken the liberty of naming our control and entering some sample options.

Note in Figure 8.7 that I've also checked the box to prevent the user from deleting the content control—just a little extra precaution to keep somebody from messing up your form.

FIGURE 8.7 **FIGURE 8.8**

The next field we want to fill in is the Retainer Received field. And we're going to use a checkbox for that. This control is pretty simple—just add it where you want it, and it inserts a clickable box.

Next we have a Date field to enter. Click the "Date Picker Content Control" from the Controls group and place that next to Date. The user can enter a date or click the drop-arrow on the right end to get a Date Picker, as you see in Figure 8.9.

Unfortunately there isn't an easy way to default the date picker to today's date, but the user can just click the "Today" button at the bottom of the date picker to easily insert it.

FIGURE 8.9

Finally, for the Comments field, we're going to do it a little differently; we're just going to draw a text box to provide a place for the user to write optional comments. To do that, go to the Insert tab of the Ribbon, click the drop-down under "Text Box," and choose "Draw Text Box." Using your mouse, draw a nice big rectangle next to Comments.

The end result of our sample form looks like Figure 8.10.

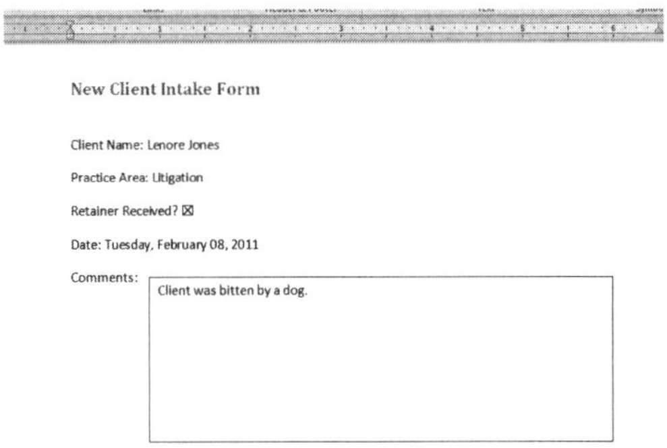

FIGURE 8.10

Obviously, this was just a very simple sample form. You can make far more complex and detailed forms, if you like. Once your form is done, save it, mark it Read-Only, and then you can make it available to your users. When they fill it out and click "Save," it will force them to give it a new name (since the original is read-only).

Other Tools

VBA isn't the only way to do macro and scripting in Microsoft Office. There are tools both built-in and from third parties that can help you with that as well.

AutoCorrect

Word's built-in AutoCorrect can be found Backstage by clicking File | Options | Proofing | AutoCorrect Options, which launches the dialog box you see in Figure 8.11.

AutoCorrect is a handy tool to fix typos as you go. If you accidentally type "teh," Word's AutoCorrect will fix it to "the" on the fly. In fact, I had to undo an AutoCorrect to type that example! That's the typical usage of AutoCorrect, but it can also be customized to replace any text with any other text. Leaving aside the potential for clever practical jokes, this gives

FIGURE 8.11

you a tool for replacing short strings of text with much longer ones. For instance, perhaps you work for "Jones, Smith, Jones, Smith, Jones, and Rumpelstiltskin." Naturally you don't want to have to type that out very often. It would be easy to add an AutoCorrect entry so that if you type "JSJSJR" (or even just "JSJ"), Word would replace it with the full firm name (which I don't feel like retyping here).

> If you're typing away and Word has auto-corrected something for you that you didn't want it to, you can press CTRL+Z to undo that auto-correction and it will restore your originally typed text this time.

I hope you're seeing a lot of possibilities here. Have certain clients you work with a lot? You can put their name in and have Word replace their initials with the full name. Use it for addresses, location names, court names, or other words and phrases you type a lot. It'll save you a lot of time and reduce the chances that you inadvertently send out a document in which you refer to your firm as "Jones, Smith, Jones, Smith, Jones, and Rumpledsuitman."

That's great for working in Word, but what if you want those same replacements to work in other apps? Keep reading . . . our next tool gives you a universal AutoCorrect capability.

AutoHotKey

One of my all-time favorite free tools, AutoHotKey (http://www.autohotkey .com), is an all-around scripting language that, with a bit of effort, you can use to automate tasks not only in Word but in the entire Office suite and, in fact, any application in Windows. You can launch programs with it, you can script installations in it, you can create blocks of text that will be inserted with a short string of characters, you can create mouse gestures . . . you can do a lot of really cool things.

For example, I have a little script set up in AutoHotKey so that whenever I type "bwa" and press the spacebar, it replaces that with "Best wishes and aloha," which is my typical e-mail sign-off. That's an easy way to insert a signature block.

▼▼▼▼▼
What's a Mouse Gesture?

A mouse gesture is an action with the mouse that triggers another action. For example, if you hold down the right mouse button and move the mouse to the left, you could have that action tell your Web browser to go "Back." Or hold down the right mouse button and draw a clockwise circle to make your browser refresh. With a little effort you can create just about any gesture and have AutoHotKey do whatever you'd like it to do in response.

Coding something like that in AutoHotKey is quite easy. You just open the AutoHotKey script in any text editor (like Notepad) and add lines that say this:

::bwa::Best wishes and aloha,
return

The first bit defines what keystrokes you're going to type—"bwa," in my case. The second bit indicates what it's going to replace that with—"Best wishes and aloha," in my case. (In fact, I just used my bwa tool to put that in!) The "Return" just tells AutoHotKey that you're done with what that action does.

While AutoHotKey is a good way to insert text quickly and consistently, it can also be used to automate any repetitive series of keystrokes or mouse clicks, and since it's not tied to any one application, scripts you create in AutoHotKey are available everywhere. I use it to launch applications, too.

Did I mention it's free?

Customize Word's Hotkeys

Most people don't realize that they can customize the hotkeys that Word 2010 uses. Don't want to use CTRL+B for boldface? You can change it. To get to the Customize Keyboard dialog box like the one you see in Figure 8.12, just go to the File ⏐ Options ⏐ Customize Ribbon (yes, I know) and at the bottom left, next to the label "Keyboard Shortcuts" you'll find a button for "Customize."

Let's try a useful exercise. One of the symbols that attorneys commonly use is the section symbol: §. So let's assign it to a keyboard short-

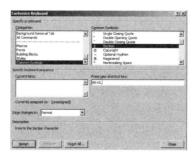

FIGURE 8.12

cut to make it easier to access. Go to the Customize Keyboard dialog box (instructions are still on the previous page if you need a refresher), and on the left side where it says "Categories" scroll all the way down to where it says "Common Symbols." It's the very last thing on that list. Then, in the box on the right that now says "Common Symbols," scroll down until you find the section symbol. Select that one and you'll notice that under "Current Keys" the box is empty. There aren't any keys assigned to it yet. On the right, click where it says "Press new shortcut key" and press "ALT+S." You'll notice that when you enter that in the box you get a message below the "Current Keys" box that tells you what that hotkey is currently assigned to (as far as Word knows). By default, it's available. Well, it's sort of available. By default, ALT+S will open the references tab on the Ribbon. But you can still get to the References tab by pressing and releasing ALT, then pressing S. So you can assign ALT+S to the section symbol and just use ALT, then S, to get to the References tab.

> Word can tell you only about hotkeys it knows about. If some other program, like AutoHotKey, has ALT+S for something, there's no way Word can know that and warn you about it. The other limitation here is that any hotkey you set up in here is going to work only in Word.

To finish assigning ALT+S to your section symbol, click the "Assign" button. Then you can exit back out to your Word document and give it a try. ALT+S should immediately put a § at your insertion point. Nice, eh?

The Roland Schorr 10-Most Method

If you're a fairly quick typist, I want to encourage you to use keyboard shortcuts and automation to make your Word experience substantially more efficient. Here's the way you do it:

1. Put some kind of notepad next to your keyboard. You can use an online thing like Vista's Notes sidebar gadget or OneNote's docked

page if you want to, but I really think it'll be easier to just have a piece of paper and a pencil.

2. Use Word in the course of your normal workday.

3. Each time you grab the mouse to click an icon or launch a command (like print, save or boldface) quickly note what it was. The first time you do it make a note, and each additional time you do the same thing put a checkmark next to the first note to indicate a repeat.

4. After you have enough of a sample size—perhaps a day or two—go back and try to identify the ten most common tasks for which you used the mouse.

5. Learn, or create if necessary, the keyboard shortcuts for those tasks. If the shortcut takes more than two or three keystrokes to do it, then use AutoHotKey or Word's Macro Recorder to automate the task down to a single keystroke. It may be too much to try to master all ten in a single day, so it's OK to break it down into chunks. Start with the most common tasks and learn two or three a day.

> **Tip**
>
> This is also a great use of Building Blocks. If you can identify bits of text that you type often and can convert to Building Blocks, you can save time. Bonus . . . use AutoHotKey to insert a Building Block and then perform some common action on it, like applying a style.

If you can get to the point where your five, ten, or fifteen most common non-editing tasks (e.g., formatting, printing, or launching applications) can be done with a just one or a few keystrokes or hotkey combinations, you can save yourself a lot of time in the course of your normal day.

Resources

Like all URLs ("Uniform Resource Locators," aka Web addresses) you see in print, these could change between the time that I type them here and you read them there. In those instances . . . Google is your friend.

- http://msdn.microsoft.com/en-us/vbasic/default—this is Microsoft's MSDN site for Visual Basic for Applications. It has a lot of useful resources and tools for people doing development with VBA.
- http://en.wikipedia.org/wiki/Visual_Basic_for_Applications—Wikipedia's article on Visual Basic for Applications. It's a good starting point with some general background. It also includes a nice collection of references and links to more information.

Summary

Microsoft Word is an application that requires a high degree of user inter-action—by that I mean that unlike some applications where you start a pro-cess and just let it run, Word is an application where virtually everything that happens occurs because the user presses a button or clicks a mouse. A lot of those interactions are repetitive, so learning to automate Word will make those interactions easier and faster. Attorneys and legal staff, in par-ticular, tend to create a lot of repetitive documents—documents that don't vary greatly from one to the other. Using tools for document assembly and automation can help make the law office operate more efficiently and with fewer mistakes.

A number of tools are available to help in that process.

Document assembly lets you automate the process of building stan-dardized documents. By asking only for the variables (i.e., the stuff that changes: names, dates, places) and placing them in the document where you need them, document assembly software can significantly reduce the time it takes to build standard documents and ensure consistent quality and accurate content.

Visual Basic for Applications is a very powerful macro language. In fact, I daresay it's the most powerful macro language ever implemented in an office productivity suite like Microsoft Office. It can manipulate data, run various functions of the application, and even interact with the operat-ing system in powerful and potentially dangerous ways.

AutoHotKey is a free utility that can help you create powerful scripts that not only automate tasks in Word but in any other Windows applica-tion as well.

AutoCorrect and hotkeys are built-in Word tools that can be extended by the user to help automate tasks or simplify how things are initiated.

With just a bit of thought and practice, you can easily find a lot of new efficiencies. Especially as law firms and in-house legal departments move increasingly toward value-based billing, it's important to find new and pow-erful ways to streamline the process of practicing law and creating docu-ments while improving accuracy and quality.

Managing and Maintaining Word 2010

9

In this chapter we'll take a look at some of the configuration options of Microsoft Word. To get to these options click "File" and toward the bottom of the Backstage menu you'll find a button labeled "Options."

General

The General group used to be named "Popular" (Figure 9.1), and it contains a few of the most commonly used options in the program. If you find the Mini Toolbar more annoying than useful, you can turn it off right here. Likewise, the Live Preview (galleries) may be a burden to a slower system, though if they're not causing you problems I would leave them on. They'll save you more time than they could cost.

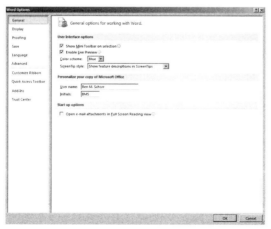

FIGURE 9.1

Another setting on this tab you should be concerned with is whether you want e-mail attachments to open in Full Screen Reading view. This is a feature I get a lot of questions on—attorneys receive e-mailed document attachments, and when they double-click them to open them (after acknowledging all of the "Are you sure you want to open this?" prompts) they expect the documents to just open in Word the way they're used to seeing it. Instead, the documents open in this curious "Reading View" that looks a bit odd and can be unsettling. That view *is* useful in many ways, but if you'd rather that Word just do what you expect it to, uncheck the "Open e-mail attachments in Full Screen Reading View" box, and Word will just skip that screen and open normally for you.

▼

"Skin" is the term used to describe the color and layout of the interface in software. Some programs let you do a lot of creative things with the skin; others (like older versions of Office) gave you almost no control over it. With Office 2010, you can change the color scheme, but that's about it.

The next option we're interested in debuted in Office 2007, and that's the Color Scheme option. Here you can change the "skin" of Office to a different color scheme.

The three options are "Blue," "Silver," and "Black." Blue is the Office default, and it's what most people use (in part because most people don't realize you can change it). Silver is a pleasant look and the one that I tend to use. Black is a dark skin, which I have tried but personally found to be just a little too dark for my tastes. Whatever you choose is personal to your user profile, and you can change it every few minutes if you want to, so feel free to play around and figure out which of the three schemes is the most pleasing to you.

The last settings on this page that interest us allow you to customize how Word identifies you. It lets you tell Word what your initials and full name are. These are used in instances like inserting comments, metadata about last editor and author, and signature blocks and such where this information can be automatically inserted for you. If you inherited this copy of Word and user profile from a previous user, and his or her name and initials are still appearing in the product, this is one place you should go to change it.

Display

The Display group (see Figure 9.2) lets you control how Word will display applications.

The first option is "Show white space between pages in Print Layout view." That option basically shows the top and bottom margins, just like you'd see on the printed page. If you want to save a bit of screen real estate, you can turn that option off or just edit your documents in draft mode.

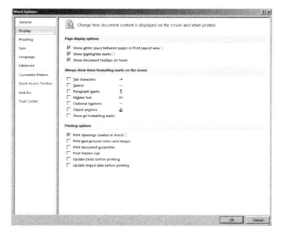

FIGURE 9.2

This option will also show the headers and footers on a page. If you want to quickly turn it off (or back on), just point to the top or bottom edge of the page and double-click.

If you've used any highlighter marks in your document, which is a pretty common action when reviewing and collaborating on documents (you did read Chapter 6, right?), you may want to turn off the display of highlighter marks. Turning them off here not only suppresses their display on the screen but also keeps them from printing.

"Show document tooltips on hover" turns off (or on) the display of balloons detailing the changes made to the text when Track Changes is turned on. Essentially, if you make a change to the text and then later hover over that text with your mouse, the change will be displayed in a tooltip that will "magically" appear above your cursor. If those balloons annoy you, here's where you turn them off.

The problem with Draft mode is that you lose a lot of the layout features, especially any embedded images. Most people work in Print Layout mode because that's the default. I work in it because, as you may have noticed, I have a lot of screen shots and figures in the book and the figures don't display in Draft mode.

The next section of the dialog box is where you control the display of formatting marks. I may occasionally have Word display paragraph marks because those can be significant in document formatting, but unless I'm troubleshooting document formatting issues (we'll talk about that in Chapter 10), I tend to leave them all off. It's just a much cleaner look to the document.

If you want to turn all of the formatting marks on (or off) at once, you can just press CTRL+SHIFT+8 from within the document or click the button on the Home tab of the Ribbon that looks like a paragraph mark (¶).

There is one option in this section that I do tend to turn on, and that's the option to display hidden text. "What's hidden text?" Glad you asked. If you open the font panel (click the dialog launcher at the bottom right of the Font group on the Ribbon), you may notice that among the font effects (strikethrough, subscript, emboss, etc.) is "Hidden." Apply that effect to text on your page and . . . it disappears—unless you have Display Hidden Text turned on in the Display Options. So why would you use that? It's handy if you want to create a document with annotations, notes, or answers that you don't want to print. You type the questions and you type your notes. You mark your notes as "Hidden," however, and when you go to print the document, the hidden text doesn't print (unless you've changed another setting that I'm going to explain in the next page or two). But you can still see the hidden text on your screen—and you can choose to print the document *with* the hidden text for your own copy. Keep reading.

The last section of the Display group controls printing options. The first option lets you speed up your printing. The description is a little misleading—it implies that only drawings created in Word (how many drawings do you actually create in Word?) are affected. Actually, unchecking that box will suppress printing any graphics or text boxes—just a blank box will be printed in their place. It's fine for printing quick drafts, I guess, but in reality I don't know anybody who changes that setting. You probably *do* want to see your graphics, even on the drafts.

The next option enables the printing of background colors and images. I've never seen a legal document that had a background color or an image, but maybe you're creating marketing materials and want to print those things. Here's where you'd turn it on.

If you want to print a copy of your document with the document properties (author, created date, etc.), you can enable that here as well.

If you used the hidden text trick we talked about a few paragraphs back, you can change the setting here to have that hidden text print.

The last two options on this screen are actually pretty handy. "Update fields before printing" and "Update linked fields before printing" will ensure that your tables of contents, linked Excel data, and other dynamic content is up-to-date before you click print. It's a bad feeling to realize, as pages 35, 36, and 37 are rolling off the printer, that you forgot to update your table of contents and it's a few pages off.

Proofing

The proofing group (see Figure 9.3) contains tools that are essential to your document assembly (see Chapter 8). It handles how Word will take care of spell-checking, grammar checking, and AutoCorrect.

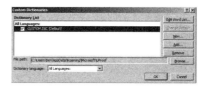

FIGURE 9.3   FIGURE 9.4

We already talked in Chapter 8 about configuring the AutoCorrect options, so here we'll talk about some of the other settings on the Auto-Correct Options dialog box.

AutoFormat as You Type

These settings are, as you might have guessed, primarily concerned with automatically applying some stylish tweaks to your documents. For example—changing straight quotes to "smart quotes," which are the curly quotes, and changing fractions to the fraction characters. (See Figure 9.5)

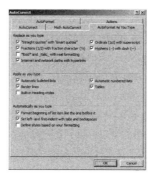

FIGURE 9.5

The fractions character option is a lot more limited than it may seem. There are "hidden" ASCII characters for three of the common fractions: 1/4, 1/2, 3/4. If you type one of those three fractions, Word will automatically replace it with the ASCII character for that: ¼, ½, ¾

> (assuming you have the setting enabled in AutoFormat as You Type, which it is by default). Type any other fraction and you'll just get what you typed since Word has nothing to change it to.

One of the options on this dialog box that we do get asked about is automatically starting a numbered list when you start an item with 1. or a bulleted list when you start a line with *. Those are handy features, but they do annoy some people . . . so here's how you can turn them off.

The sharp-eyed among you may have noticed that there are both "AutoFormat" and "AutoFormat as You Type" tabs in the AutoCorrect options. And they have many of the same options! So what's the difference? Word has a carefully hidden feature called "AutoFormat" that allows you to apply these settings to a document that has already been typed.

FIGURE 9.6

Don't remember that feature from our extensive Chapter 2 review of the Ribbon? That's because it's not on the Ribbon. In fact, to use it you'll have to add it to either the Ribbon or the QAT. To customize the Ribbon (or QAT), change the left-hand column to show "All Commands" and locate "AutoFormat Now" . . . that's what you need to add to use the feature.

Never used that feature before? Neither have I. Moving on. . . .

Actions

The Actions tab of AutoCorrect gives you a few custom actions that Word can take if it recognizes particular kinds of text in your document. They're like tags. Really intelligent tags. You might even call them Smart Tags. Well, that's what Word 2007 called them.

Smart Tags are a feature that debuted with Microsoft Office XP (aka Office 2002), in which Office applications can recognize certain bits of text, like a date or a phone number or an address, and then give you some options for what you can do with them. For example: if you have a street address typed in your document, you can select that text, right-click it, and choose "Additional Actions" (see Figure 9.7) to get a list of other things you can do with that data.

FIGURE 9.7

Note that this functionality has been deprecated in Word 2010. In earlier versions of Office, a Smart Tag might recognize that you've typed in a street address and underline that address with a purple dotted underline. Word 2010 no longer automatically recognizes and underlines your tags—you have to select the text and right-click to access that functionality.

Additional Actions can be useful however. . . .

They do take up a bit of additional resources, so many people have them disabled by default.

1. They're useful only on the electronic copies of the document. A printed document obviously has no use for the actions.
2. Powerful though they may be, you might not have much use for them yourself. They're often a solution in search of a problem. I've never asked Word to give me driving directions to an address I had in a Word document.

The "More Actions" button should take you to a useful place to add additional Actions, but in reality it just takes you to a Microsoft Web site that vaguely promises a collection of Actions developed by Microsoft and third parties but makes it rather difficult to find any actual Tags.

Math AutoCorrect

The Math AutoCorrect settings do the same thing the text AutoCorrect settings do . . . but they're specifically for replacing text with mathematical symbols and formulas. For most attorneys this isn't that useful.

A few of the default settings are worth noticing—for example, "Ignore words that are in UPPERCASE" or "Ignore words that contain numbers." In those cases, Word is going to assume that you're typing an acronym or a custom word/formula for which traditional spell-checking is likely to be of limited value. If you're in the habit of typing regular words in ALL UPPERCASE, then that's a habit I strongly suggest you break. Type in ALL CAPS is rather hard to read and looks like you're shouting. However, if you really insist upon shouting, then you might want to have Word not ignore those words, and you can make that happen by unchecking the box here.

Tip

One Math AutoCorrect function you might find useful is \inc, which inserts the △ symbol most attorneys like to use. Didn't work for you? Go into the Math AutoCorrect settings and make sure "Use Math AutoCorrect rules outside of math regions" is checked.

Another interesting option that appears on the main proofing page is the option to have custom dictionaries in Word. Click the Custom Dictionaries button to launch the dialog box you see in Figure 9.8. Here you can see the custom dictionaries that Word is going to use—the CUSTOM.DIC file is there by default and contains all of the words that you've added to the dictionary yourself. You can add new custom dictionaries, remove dictionaries, enable or disable them, edit the word lists, and do all sorts of other tricky things.

FIGURE 9.8

You may be tempted to add or buy—or even create—a "legal" custom dictionary for Word, but in my experience it's rarely needed. Most legal words ("abatement," "jurisprudence," even "venire") are already in the Word 2010 dictionary, and for the ones that remain ("voir dire" may trip your red, squiggly lines) you can easily right-click the misrecognized word and select Add to Dictionary to add it to your main dictionary.

Medical dictionaries are a little more useful, as the words are somewhat more complex and esoteric.

The next section on the Proofing tab offers a few useful choices.

- *Check spelling as you type* lets you turn off the live spell-checking. I recommend you leave this on, but if the red, squiggly lines distract you too much, you can turn it off.

■ *Use contextual spelling* will make intelligent guesses about how words are supposed to be spelled based upon the context. This is a new feature in Word 2010—it's supposed to help you figure out word choices like "than" versus "then."

One option that may have caught your eye is the Readability Statistics. Enabling that will let you check to see how complex your writing style is—at least according to a few computer algorithms. To use it, enable it in the proofing options, then go to your document and run a spell check from the Review tab of the Ribbon. Unfortunately, you'll have to go through the entire document before it will give you the readability results, a minor pain when you're working on a 257-page book and just want to do a quick Readability check so you can grab a screen shot. But if you were to lose

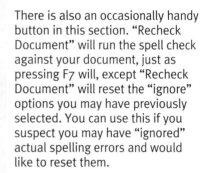

> **Tip**
>
> There is also an occasionally handy button in this section. "Recheck Document" will run the spell check against your document, just as pressing F7 will, except "Recheck Document" will reset the "ignore" options you may have previously selected. You can use this if you suspect you may have "ignored" actual spelling errors and would like to reset them.

patience with that process and choose, instead, to check a much shorter document, you might get a result that looks like Figure 9.9. Note, you *do* have to let Word check your grammar, too, for the readability statistics to appear.

FIGURE 9.9

Tired of the spell checker or grammar checker getting on your back in that particular document, but you don't want to turn them off completely? The last settings on the Proofing dialog let you tell Word to just ignore spelling and grammatical errors in this document only.

Save

The Save section of the Word Options helps you control options with how (and when) Word will save things.

First, you can control the default document format. You'll probably want to leave that set to "Word Document (*.docx)," which lets you take advantage of the new document formats. But if you have to share a lot of documents with users of older versions of Word, who refuse to install the File Converters, you can change the default here. Even if you change the default to .DOC you can still manually save a new document as a .DOCX file; you'll just have to manually set that each time you save.

Some of you may remember the days when computers crashed fairly often (no Vista or Windows ME jokes, please!), and losing the document you'd been working on was a real possibility. A lot of old-timers (like me) are in the habit of saving quite often, specifically so if the machine reboots suddenly you aren't going to lose your work. Word is, and has been for quite some time, smarter than that, however. It saves AutoRecover information on a regular schedule. What's AutoRecover information? It's what enables Word to offer to recover your work for you when you restart Word after a crash. By default, Word will save this information, quietly in the background, every 10 minutes. If you're paranoid or have a machine that crashes a lot, you can set that to be a little more often—every 5 minutes perhaps. If you're supremely confident, you can set it to a longer interval, though there isn't much reason to unless your machine is so underpowered that saving AutoRecover information slows it down, or if you're trying to milk every ounce of battery life out of that laptop and want to reduce disk activity.

The Default File location is where Word is going to save documents by default. Usually that's set to your own "My Documents" folder. You can change it to be anything you like—including a server location, if you have one.

The only other setting in this section I want to point out is under the "Preserve fidelity when sharing this document" section, and it lets you embed fonts in the file. Usually that's a waste of space, but it can be handy if you're using a non-standard font in your document and you're sharing the document with a user who doesn't have that font installed or for whom the document doesn't look quite right. Embedding the fonts in the file does just that—saves a copy of the fonts you used within the document file so that when the other party opens the document, he or she gets the fonts, too. The upside to this is that it helps the person you're sharing the document with see the document as you intended it. The downside is that it inflates your document size somewhat, using more storage space. If you're e-mailing this file to your collaborator, the extra file size may also slow down (or even prevent) the transfer.

Language

Figure 9.11 shows the new Language dialog in Word options. Office 2010 is a lot better at letting you work in multiple (or just different) languages than earlier versions of Office were.

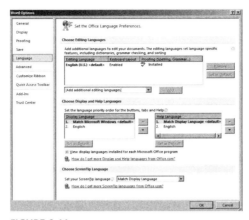

FIGURE 9.11

You can configure your editing languages, including keyboard layout and spell checker. Note that even though you can pick from an enormous list of additional languages (including Hawaiian), that doesn't mean that those languages support spell-checking and other proofing tools right out of the box. Some languages are listed but not included. Selecting them will simply tell you that the keyboard layout and proofing options are "Not installed." In some cases you can download a language pack for that particular language in other cases . . . *a'e* (no.)

If you want to change the languages for the buttons and help system, you can also configure that here.

Advanced

The Advanced page has a lot of sections and options in it. We'll take it section by section, but I'm only going to spend time on those options that I think you're going to care about.

Figure 9.12 shows the Editing options section where you can control how Word 2010 is going to behave while you're editing. The first option is "Typing replaces selected text." I'll explain it, so you know what it does, but I don't recommend you change it. Basically, if you select some text and then start typing, Word will delete the selection and replace it with whatever you

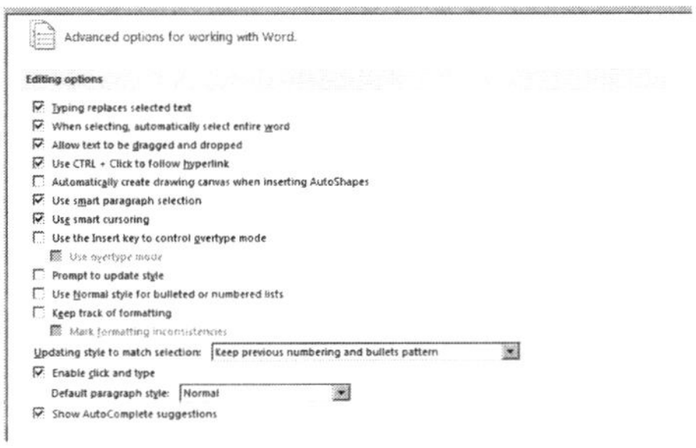

FIGURE 9.12

type. That's the default behavior and what most people expect to happen. If you clear that checkbox, Word will instead *insert* what you're typing before the selected text. In which case, forgive me for saying it, there's no point in selecting the text to begin with. Just place your insertion point where you want to insert the text and type away.

The second option is a little more helpful if you often find yourself wanting to select parts of a word and being frustrated that Word tries to be overly helpful and select the entire word. Clear that checkbox and your word selections will be a little more precise, but a little less efficient. I more often want to select entire words, rather than parts of words, so I leave it checked.

Word 2010 is increasingly smart in little ways. Smart paragraph selection makes sure that when you select a paragraph that the hidden paragraph mark (which is what holds the paragraph's formatting) is selected with it. That's good because if you select the paragraph to cut or copy it to somewhere else, you'll probably want to cut or copy its formatting too.

Smart cursoring means that when you scroll through a document, for example by dragging the vertical scrollbar up and down, the insertion point (i.e., the vertical bar that marks where you're typing) will jump to the page you're viewing if you touch an arrow key. To illustrate—if you drag the scroll bar several pages up or down, you will no longer see the insertion point. That's because it's still back at the last place you were editing. But if you press the left or right arrow key, the insertion point will suddenly jump to the page you're looking at. This saves you the extremely difficult task of using the mouse and actually clicking on the page you're looking at.

Wondering why the Insert key on your keyboard seems dead in Word? Probably because you have the "Use the Insert key to control overtype mode" option unchecked. That option was added because some users would inadvertently toggle on Overtype mode by hitting the Insert key on their keyboard accidentally.

If you change the formatting of text that has been formatted with a particular style, Word can ask you if you want to update the style to match that new bit of formatting—the assumption being that maybe you want *all* of the text in that style to have this new formatting. The checkbox "Prompt to update style" is what you check if you want Word to ask you about that. It can be a quick way to update your styles with custom formatting, but I find it fairly annoying to be asked every time I apply a little direct formatting (remember Chapter 4?), and so I leave it turned off.

Speaking of formatting and styles, the next options of interest are the "Keep Track of Formatting" and "Mark formatting inconsistencies" options. If you apply a style to some text in your document, let's say you use Heading 2, and then later you use direct formatting (font size, font attributes like bold, etc.) to format some other text in a similar way, Word will underscore that text with a blue, wavy line to indicate that you appear to be formatting two pieces of text in a similar way but with inconsistent methods. That's to suggest that you should use the same style for both. The idea is to help you create documents where you're using styles consistently throughout, rather than formatting different paragraphs with different methods—which can lead to some interesting issues later.

The final Editing option is the rather handy: "Enable click and type." The default is "enable" and that's the right way to go. This is what lets you basically click anywhere on the page with your mouse and just start typing. Gone are the days of having to manually insert a bunch of tabs or spaces if you want to start typing one-third of the way across a page.

The next set of options is for "Cut, copy and paste," as you can see in Figure 9.13. They let you configure how Word will behave when you use the clipboard.

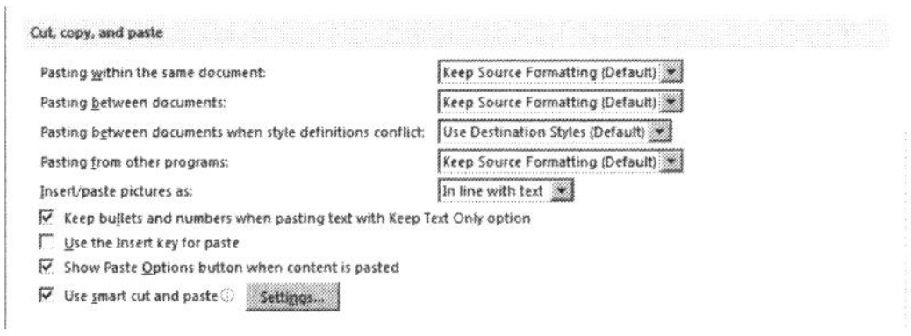

FIGURE 9.13

The first four settings let you configure the default behavior for various kinds of copy and paste operations, and for those you have three basic choices:

- Keep Source Formatting—this will paste the text and whatever formatting came with it. If the original text in the other document was 24 point and green, then it will be 24 point and green when you paste it, regardless of what the document you're pasting it into looks like.
- Use Destination Styles—this will bring over the text and any style definition associated with it, but it will apply the characteristics of the matching style (if there is one) in the destination document. For example: Let's say you copy some text formatted for Heading 3 in a source document, and in that document Heading 3 text is bold, italics, and red. You paste it into your destination document where Heading 3 is formatted as bold, underline, and blue. The text will come over, but the formatting will be changed to bold, underline, and blue. If the original text had no style definition applied, then the text will be assigned the style of the paragraph you're pasting it to (which will usually just be "Normal").

■ Keep Text Only—this is sort of similar to the last option except that *no* formatting information will be brought over. It'll just be the pure text. If you're having problems with formatting after pasting in some text, try using this option to eliminate any odd formatting elements that might have been brought over in the paste operation.

One exception to this is found in the first of the four checkboxes at the bottom of this group: *Keep bullets and numbers when pasting text with Keep Text Only option.* The description is fairly self-explanatory. Word won't bring over formatting; *however*, if the source text was in a bulleted or numbered list, Word will preserve that formatting element.

The next checkbox is actually pretty nifty if you do a lot of pasting and don't often change the insert/overwrite status. With the "Use the Insert key for paste" option selected, anytime you want to paste, instead of pressing CTRL+V you can just press the "Insert" key on your keyboard. You can still use CTRL+V if you want to, but Insert will do the same thing.

The next checkbox I want to mention is the "Show Paste Options" checkbox. Have you ever pasted something into an Office application, like Word, and seen the little clipboard icon that appears immediately alongside your freshly pasted content? That's the Paste Options icon. It has a drop-down menu that gives you a few options (mostly what I've described above about keeping source formatting, etc.) for how you want that pasted text handled. It lets you override the defaults you specified above on a case-by-case basis.

Finally, you have a checkbox that asks if you want to "Use smart cut and paste" followed by a Settings button that lets you specify a myriad of granular configuration options for how cut and paste will work. Honestly . . . stick with the defaults here. These settings mostly concern merging lists, spacing, and alignment of pasted items, and the defaults generally work just fine. If you're really having problems with how pasted items space or align, then you might want to tweak these settings. I have yet to meet an attorney who did.

If you're running Word 2010 on an old workhorse of a computer that is really gasping and wheezing to get the job done . . . well, then you probably need to buy a better machine. Until your new machine arrives, however, you might disable the Smart Cut and Paste and Show Paste Options features. That might get you a barely perceptible performance improvement.

The next section is a new one—Image Size and Quality (Figure 9.14). Not a lot here that excites us, although if you find that pictures you insert into your Word documents don't look very good, then you can either come in here and check "Do not compress images in file" or set the default target output to a higher resolution than 220 ppi . . . or get a better photographer.

FIGURE 9.14

The next section, Show document content (Figure 9.15), lets you control how Word displays certain bits of custom document content. There isn't really much here that is of interest to us, but do be aware of the "Font Substitution" settings. If you receive a document that was created with a font you don't have, then Font Substitution is how Word tries to imitate the original font using a font that you *do* have. This is usually not an issue but when it *is* an issue . . . it really is an issue. Font substitution can be one of the bigger headaches in troubleshooting why documents don't look right when transferred between machines.

FIGURE 9.15

One setting in here that might interest you, if you plan to use the Draft and/or Outline views you can change the font being used in those views to make it something a little more pleasing.

The next section is the Display section and that controls some of the more general display elements of Word (see Figure 9.16).

FIGURE 9.16

The first option lets you control how many Recent Documents will appear when you click the File. Twenty-five is the default, but you can set it as high as fifty. Of course, your screen size and resolution may not support *displaying* fifty files in that area, but you can give it a try if you really want to.

If you prefer to work metrically rather than imperially, you can change from displaying measurements in inches to centimeters (or millimeters). You could also choose points or picas, if you are so graphically inclined.

If you have more than one Word document open at a time, you may notice that you end up with multiple "instances" of Word on your Windows Taskbar. This is handy for switching between them, but if you're uncomfortable with the amount of Taskbar real estate it occupies, you can uncheck the "Show all windows in the Taskbar" option and that will consolidate all of your Word documents into a single window. It's a little harder to switch between them that way (you need to go to View | Switch Windows), but it does make Windows look a little cleaner, I suppose. Windows 7 does a much better job of handling (stacking) multiple application windows, so there's even less reason to uncheck that option if you're running Windows 7.

The only other setting in this group I think is worth mentioning is the ability to turn on or off the scroll bars.

The Print group (Figure 9.17) offers a couple of useful options, too.

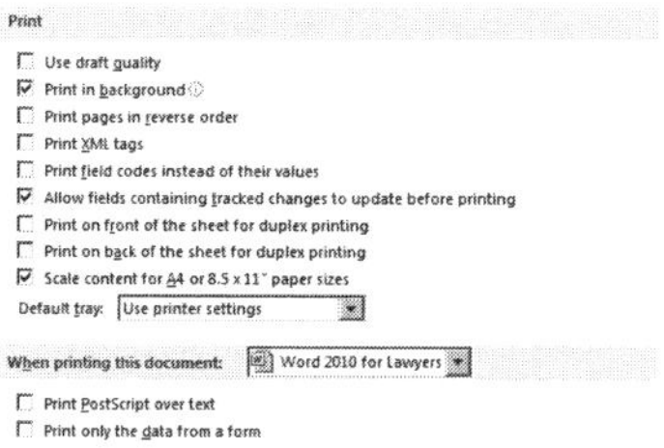

Print
☐ Use draft quality
☑ Print in background ⓘ
☐ Print pages in reverse order
☐ Print XML tags
☐ Print field codes instead of their values
☑ Allow fields containing tracked changes to update before printing
☐ Print on front of the sheet for duplex printing
☐ Print on back of the sheet for duplex printing
☑ Scale content for A4 or 8.5 x 11' paper sizes
Default tray: [Use printer settings ▾]

When printing this document: [🔲] [Word 2010 for Lawyers ▾]
☐ Print PostScript over text
☐ Print only the data from a form

FIGURE 9.17

"Use draft quality" is handy on slower printers or if you're printing large documents and want to reduce the amount of ink/toner you're using. It's great for documents you're printing for internal use and don't intend to show a client.

"Print in background" speeds your "RTA" (Return to Application) time by letting Word return to editing while the printing occurs in the background. If your machine is low on resources, this may not work that well, but most modern systems can handle printing in the background while you get back to editing.

The last settings I'll mention here, but won't go into detail on, control printing pages in reverse order (in other words, printing the last page first) and printing on the front/back for duplex printing. Those are little-used but occasionally handy options for dealing with certain kinds of printers. If your pages come out of your printer face up instead of face down, you may want to have Word print in reverse order so that they are already in order when you take them off the printer.

In the Save group (see Figure 9.18) there are some options we should look at.

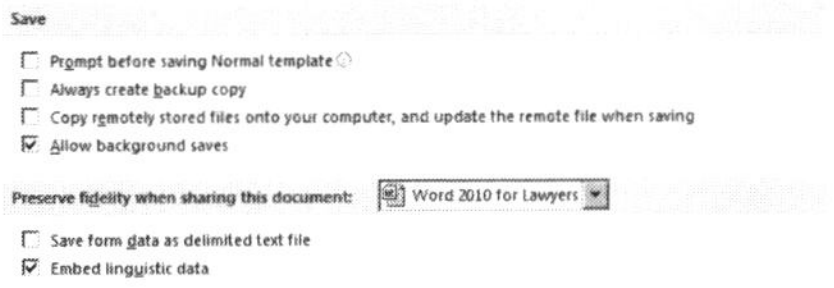

Save

☐ P̲rompt before saving Normal template ⊙
☐ Always create b̲ackup copy
☐ Copy r̲emotely stored files onto your computer, and update the remote file when saving
☑ A̲llow background saves

Preserve fi̲delity when sharing this document: 📄 Word 2010 for Lawyers ▾

☐ Save form d̲ata as delimited text file
☑ Embed linguistic data

FIGURE 9.18

"Prompt before saving Normal template" is a safety feature. A lot of Word malware attempts to infect the Normal template. Prompting before saving causes Word to warn you that changes have been made to Normal. dotm, which might alert you to something unfortunate before it can cause any problems. If you get prompted to save changes to the Normal template but didn't intend to make any, you should click "No" just as a precaution.

"Always create backup copy" will give you primitive document versioning. When you save your document, the prior version that was saved is renamed to "Backup copy of *filename*.wbk" and saved in the same folder as the document you're saving. That way, if you realize you made a bad change, it's easy to restore the backup copy. Each time you save the document the backup is replaced with the most recent prior save so you only have one version back.

To restore a backup, just click File | Open, set the "File of Type" field to "All files," and then locate and open the appropriate .wbk file. Once it's open you can File | Save As to save it as a regular Word document again—including re-saving it over the bad copy of the document (which will then get saved as a backup itself).

The "Copy remotely stored files onto your computer, and update the remote file when saving" option is not only long-winded but also sort of useful. With this option enabled, if you open a document from a network location, Word will create a temporary copy of the document on your local hard drive and work from that temporary copy. That gives you better performance than trying to work off the original remote copy of the document and protects you in case you lose network connectivity in the middle of editing the document. When you save the document, Word will save your changes to the remote location.

"Allow background saves" is another performance enhancing effort—when you do a Save, Word 2010 will do it in the background so that you can continue editing. If you're saving a five-page document, it probably doesn't matter. When you're saving a 205-page document, it can matter a lot in terms of your RTA time. With this option turned off, Word will stop to save the document and not let you do anything else (in Word) until the save is complete.

The General group contains a few options Microsoft couldn't fit anywhere else (Figure 9.19):

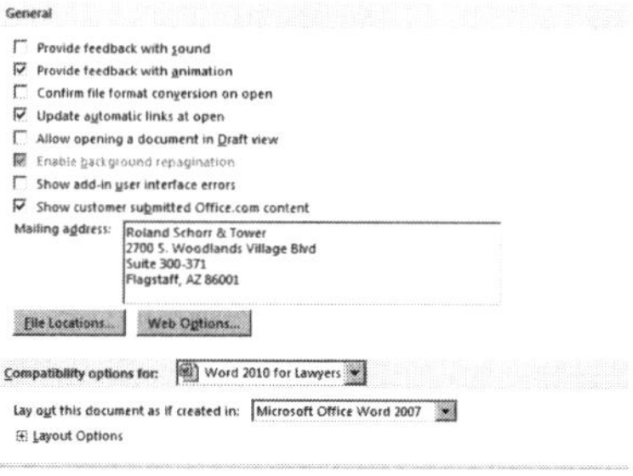

FIGURE 9.19

I always uncheck "Provide Feedback with Sound" because I get tired of Word chirping at me as I work to notify me of things.

I do like to let Word "Update automatic links at open"—that way if I've embedded some Excel data for example (remember Chapter 7?), and that data has changed, Word will get the latest data automatically. It's handy because I don't always remember to manually update. The only other option in here that I think you may care about is the one that lets you enter your mailing address. That's the address Word is going to use, by default, in places like the envelopes where it asks for your mailing address.

Near the bottom of the General tab are two buttons. Web Options you probably don't care about. Web Options are used if you're creating Web documents with Word 2010, which I generally discourage.

The "File Locations" button, on the other hand, is occasionally useful. Click that button to get the File Locations dialog you see in Figure 9.20. Here you can specify the locations of key Word directories—from where User templates are located to where AutoRecover files will be stored to where the Startup folder is. Most of this you don't need to change, but if you want to find (or change) them, here's where you can do that.

FIGURE 9.20

Customize Ribbon

Next in Word Options you'll find the Customize Ribbon page (Figure 9.21). This page is primarily about customizing the Ribbon—which you may want to do. It's fairly self explanatory: you select commands from the left side, and then click "Add" to add them to the Ribbon. Note that you can't add commands to the predefined groups on the Ribbon. You have to create a custom group—which you can do on any of the Ribbon tabs—and add commands to that.

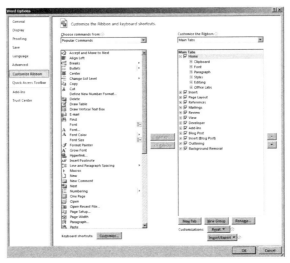

FIGURE 9.21

Quietly hidden on this page is the button to customize the keyboard shortcuts. Click it and you'll get the dialog box you see in Figure 9.22. We talked about it a bit in the last chapter. You can choose a category from the field on the left, then a command from that category from the field on the right. If there is already a keyboard shortcut for that command it will appear in the "Current keys" window once you have the command selected. Otherwise (or even so), you can click in the "Press New Shortcut Key" field and press a hotkey combination that you would like to assign to that command.

FIGURE 9.22

If the combination you select is already assigned to something, it will show up under the Current Keys field on the left. Otherwise it will say "[unassigned]," which means it's available for use. If you select something that is already assigned and click the "Assign" button, it will reassign it to your new command. That means you can remap the current Word hotkeys if you want to.

> **Tricks of the Pros**
>
> A lot of hotkey combinations are already taken. Things like CTRL+B or ALT+P are well used already. But combinations involving the symbol keys like ALT+; are often unassigned.

When you have the shortcut key you want, just click "Assign" to make it so.

If you later decide you'd like to undo those custom assignments (and restore the default assignments), you can do that in one move with the "Reset All" button at the bottom.

Quick Access Toolbar

The next group (see Figure 9.23) is very much like the previous group. This one lets you customize the Quick Access Toolbar though. Again, it's something you probably do want to do. It works the same as the previous group, too—except it's simpler. Select commands from the left side and click "Add" to add them to the QAT. Click them on the right side and select "Remove" to remove them from the QAT. Simple. Moving on. . . .

FIGURE 9.23

Add-ins

The Add-ins group (Figure 9.24) lets you control the helper programs that are running with Word. Honestly, not only will you rarely need to use this, but you really shouldn't mess around in here too much if you don't know what you're doing. The most common things you would do here are disable certain add-ins for the purpose of troubleshooting issues or use the "Manage" tool at the bottom of the window to do things like add or remove Smart Tags (see above).

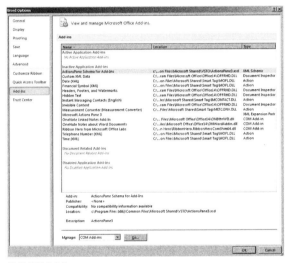

FIGURE 9.24

The initial screen you see in Figure 9.24 displays only the add-ins. To actually manage them, you need to click the "Go" button at the bottom of the page.

Trust Center

The Trust Center (Figure 9.25) is where you control the security settings of the application, and in Microsoft Word 2010 it's pretty basic—primarily concerned with privacy and how macros are handled. I wouldn't change any of the settings in here unless you know exactly what you're doing or you have the guidance of a good technical support person. The welcome screen has a lot of "administrivia" on it—privacy policies and such. There is a link here to let you opt in (or opt out) of the Customer Experience Improvement Program. I encourage you to opt in, but it's up to you. To explore further in the Trust Center, click the "Trust Center Settings" button.

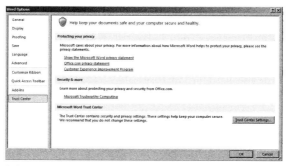

FIGURE 9.25

Again, most of what you see in Figure 9.25 you should leave alone. There are a few features of the Trust Center that I do want to highlight for you though. . . .

Trusted Locations

One common complaint with Office has been the security features added to the more recent versions. You open a document and have to click through a variety of warnings just to open your own documents! Well, Office 2010 gives you a way around that—you can specify folders on your computer (or on your network) that are automatically trusted (Figure 9.26). Documents you open from those locations won't prompt you. If you add a trusted location on your network you'll need to check the box that says "Allow trusted locations on my network" in order for it to work. If you're particularly paranoid you can disable all trusted locations. Unless you're particularly fond of dialog boxes I wouldn't do that as you'll be prompted nearly every time you open any kind of document.

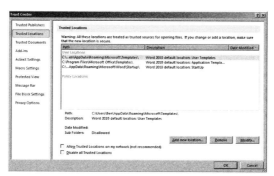

FIGURE 9.26

Trusted Documents

Sometimes you'll open a document and Word will warn you that it contains macros or other content and will ask you if you want to trust this document. If you click "Trust Document," then Word will shut up and let you use the document in all its glory—macros and all. The options you see in Figure 9.27 deal with that feature. You can decide if you want to let documents on a network to be trusted (as opposed to only documents on your own computer), and you can even disable the feature entirely so that *no* documents are trusted. Word remembers when you trust a document, so you don't have to re-trust it every time. You can clear that cache of trusted documents with the "Clear" button.

FIGURE 9.27

Protected View

A new feature in Office 2010 is Protected View (Figure 9.28), which opens documents from e-mails or the Internet in a restricted mode that doesn't allow macros or other active content. (It also doesn't allow you to edit.) Word will prompt you to trust those documents and enable those features, but if you really want to you can actually turn off protected view here. I strongly discourage that—Protected View is a very nice safety feature, but on rare occasions we've seen problems with opening e-mailed documents, and disabling protected view for Outlook attachments has fixed the problem. Again, I'd leave it alone unless you're having a problem.

FIGURE 9.28

File Block Settings

Another safety feature—Word 2010 lets you choose to block (or open in protected view) certain types of files. In Figure 9.29 you'll see the settings that you can control with regards to what kinds of files Word will treat that way. Can you guess what I'm going to say now? Yep, it's best to leave these alone unless you have a special need.

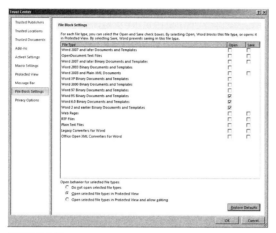

FIGURE 9.29

Privacy Options

In the Privacy Options window (see Figure 9.30) you can tell Word how paranoid you want to be. If you don't want Word to search Office Online for help content when you're connected, you can turn that off here (though, honestly, you really should use it; it's good).

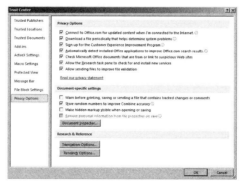

FIGURE 9.30

If you've decided that you don't want to participate in the Customer Experience Improvement Program, you can opt back out (since you had to opt-in to begin with) here. Again, this is a really useful program, so I encourage you to participate and assure you that there's no good privacy reason not to . . . but if you'd really rather not, then here's one place you can say so.

There are a couple of settings here that let Office check for and download updates and new features and services. I've never seen any problems as a result of these settings.

The final setting in here that I want to point out is the "Warn before printing, saving or sending a file that contains tracked changes or comments." It's probably a good idea to turn this option *on,* just to minimize the chances that you might inadvertently distribute a document with embarrassing metadata in it. See Chapter 11 for more on that subject.

At the bottom of the screen there are two buttons: "Translation Options" and "Research Options."

Translation Options

The Translation Options dialog (Figure 9.31) lets you control how Word's multilingual translation features are going to work. There are two kinds of translation available:

- Bilingual dictionary: This is what you use to translate individual words or phrases within Word. Unless you tell it otherwise, Word will try to use its installed dictionary first, then fall back to an online dictionary to perform the translation if it has to.
- Machine translation: This is what you use when you translate an entire document. Word will send the document to the online service listed, and the translation will appear in a Web page. Be careful with machine translation—*sometimes consequences unpredictable can be resulted.*

FIGURE 9.31

Research Options

The research options dialog (Figure 9.32) lets you configure what reference books you want to have available on the Research pane in Word. You can add or remove services, enable or disable services, update them, or even turn on Parental Controls to block certain reference sources from your kids. To be fair, I don't think I've ever seen a service on the Research panel that should give parents any pause.

FIGURE 9.32

But, if you really want that level of control, here's where you can find it.

Summary

For such a simple seeming product, Microsoft Word 2010 can be configured and personalized in a lot of different ways. Some of these features are really useful to tweak; most of them you're better off leaving alone.

Among the features that you'll probably want to pay some attention to are the proofing tools and the way Word is going to display the documents you enter. It can make a big difference if the proofing tools are working for you, rather than against you, and if you're comfortable with how the document editor actually looks.

Troubleshooting | 10

Word 2010 is probably the most robust and resilient version of Word Microsoft has ever created. That doesn't mean that nothing ever goes wrong with it, though, so in this chapter we'll take a look at a few of the common problems and how to resolve them.

Getting Help

Microsoft Word 2010 is a remarkably well understood and well documented application. There are a plethora of forums, Web sites, books, classes, and other resources out there to help you get the most out of Word 2010.

In the old days you used to get a big, thick manual with your software—it explained all of the features and capabilities in language that was rather dry but made up for it by being poorly organized. Software publishers quickly found out, mostly via calls to their support lines, that most users didn't bother to read the printed documentation. So these days, they save a lot of money on printing, paper, and shipping and just include that content, occasionally better written, as either online or digital content in the help system. Office 2010 is no different. On the right end of the Ribbon, on the same row with the Ribbon tabs, you'll find a small blue question mark in a circle, like what you see in Figure 10.1.

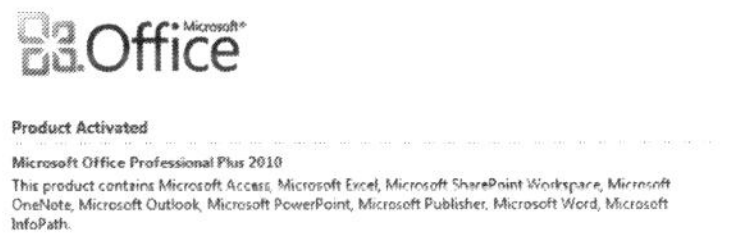

Office

Product Activated

Microsoft Office Professional Plus 2010
This product contains Microsoft Access, Microsoft Excel, Microsoft SharePoint Workspace, Microsoft OneNote, Microsoft Outlook, Microsoft PowerPoint, Microsoft Publisher, Microsoft Word, Microsoft InfoPath.

FIGURE 10.1

Clicking that will launch Word help. If you're lucky, and connected to the Internet, it can be a powerful and rich tool. Without Internet connectivity you still get the off-line help, but that system is not quite as robust.

At the bottom of each help topic in Word 2010 (when you're connected), you'll find something surprising . . . comments, left by other users! These are tips and tricks that other users have chosen to add to the help system, and sometimes you find some real gems in there. Just pick a help topic and scroll to the bottom to read the comments. You'll also get the chance to leave your own comment if you want to.

The other thing I encourage you to do is to use the "Was this information helpful" feedback. The Microsoft Office documentation teams *do* look at that feedback, and it really helps them to craft better articles for you. So please, take a moment to click "Yes," "No," or "I don't know" to express your opinion on the article.

Activating

If you find that certain features of the product don't seem to be available, or if you get an error message telling you that a certain selection is "blocked," it may be that you either haven't activated the product yet or that you're using a trial version of the product that has expired. A lot of computers come from the manufacturer with only trial versions of Office installed, and those expire in approximately sixty days. If you then go out and buy the full version, you can install it over your trial and all of your data and documents will be just fine. It's easy.

If you're sure you have a full version, just go to File and click the Help group. If the product is already activated, you'll see what you see in Figure 10.1. If the product isn't activated, you'll see a link to activate it.

If for some reason it refuses to activate over the Internet, try again and select "Telephone Activation." When you call the number provided, explain the situation and the staff should be able to help you out.

Safe Mode

Word 2010, like (almost) all Office 2010 applications, has a safe mode it can start in. Safe mode basically means that the program opens without any add-ins, customizations, or advanced features running—it's a quick way to find out if a problem is the result of a faulty add-in or something else. To start Word 2010 in safe mode, just hold down the CTRL key when you start Microsoft Word (or any other Office 2010 app, for that matter).

When Word starts up it will prompt you to confirm that you want to start in safe mode (Figure 10.2). Click "Yes," and Word will start.

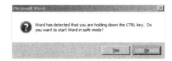

FIGURE 10.2

If the problem you're troubleshooting doesn't occur when Word is in safe mode, then try disabling add-ins by going to the File | Options | Add-ins section, as shown in Figure 10.3. As I mentioned in the previous chapter, the Add-ins tool can help you manage Word Add-ins. Click the "Go" button at the bottom of the screen to get into the tool that lets you enable or disable add-ins.

FIGURE 10.3

Repair Installations

In Word 2007 one of the steps we'd take to diagnose issues was to run Office Diagnostics. Well, Office Diagnostics has been removed from Office 2010. Instead, the recommendation is to do a Repair Installation of Office. It's really quite easy to do, although the exact steps vary slightly, depending upon the operating system you're using.

In a nutshell . . . go to Control Panel, Add/Remove Programs (or "Uninstall a Program" in Windows 7). Find Office 2010 on the list of programs, select it, and click "Change." The Office Setup program will start and present you with some options, as you can see in Figure 10.4. Choose "Repair," and the setup wizard will take over, check all of your Office files for corrupted or missing files, and reinstall any that need it.

It's a fairly harmless thing to do; you won't lose any settings or data. At worst, you lose a few minutes of your time.

FIGURE 10.4

Recovering from Word Crashes

If just starting Microsoft Word 2010 with a blank document causes it to crash or behave oddly, it could be caused by corruption in your normal .dotm, which is the standard template Word 2010 loads when it first starts up. Luckily, this is very easy to recover from. With Word 2010 closed, find the normal.dotm file (which should be located under C:\Users\[*your profile name*]\AppData\Roaming\Microsoft in Vista or Windows 7,or C:\Documents and Settings\[*Your profile name*]\Application Data\Microsoft\Templates in Windows XP), and rename it to something like "normal.old." Then start Word 2010 normally. Word will detect that it can't find the normal.dotm file as it expected and will automatically create a new one for you. If Word starts and runs normally, then you can be pretty sure the problem was some kind of corruption in your old normal.dotm file.

If that doesn't resolve the issue, then you may need to get down and dirty with your registry. This is the time when I need to offer you the standard disclaimer that editing the registry is not something I encourage regular users to do. If you change the wrong item in the registry you can do really bad things to your computer, so before you embark on this you should make sure that you have a good backup of your system and that you *really* want to do this yourself rather than asking a computer professional to take on this task for you. Assuming you really do want to proceed, and I have to make that assumption to continue this chapter, exit all Microsoft Office programs (including Outlook), and then click Start, click Run, and type REGEDIT in the provided command box. Click OK or press ENTER.

Within the registry find this subkey:

HKEY_CURRENT_USER\Software\Microsoft Office\14.0\Word\Data

With that subkey selected, click the File menu in Regedit and choose Export. Save the file to your desktop with a name something like "Word Data Key.reg." The reason we're doing this is because most of the Word customizations found Backstage are saved in the Data key of the registry (yes, that includes the Recently Used Files list). What we're about to do will wipe out those customizations, and if that doesn't fix the problem, you may want to be able to restore them—hence the exported .reg file.

Once you've exported your Data key to the .reg file for safekeeping, delete the Data key from the registry. Exit the Registry Editor and start Word. When Word 2010 starts up, it will notice that the Data key is gone and will automatically create a new one for you using the factory default settings. If your problem is solved, then you're good to go from there. If not, you can either continue with this new setup or you can close Word, go to your Windows desktop, and double-click that "Word Data Key.reg" file we made. This will put your customizations back in.

Corrupted Documents

Occasionally, Word documents will get corrupted or otherwise damaged. That can happen for a number of reasons—malware, hardware problems, power failures . . . or just darned bad luck. Corruption in a document isn't always obvious either—like a document that won't load or text that is completely ruined (though that would do it too). Sometimes it's more subtle, like odd behavior in the document such as page breaks moving around on their own or strange page renumbering. If that happens, the first thing to do is confirm that the strange behavior is limited to that one document. Open another document and see if the problem exists there as well. If it does, then you have some other issue with your system that you need to address—then the aforementioned Office Repair Installation or Safe Mode may come in handy.

If the problem is limited to the document, then the first thing to do is find out which template is used by the document. With the document open in Word, click File and then Options. Click Add-Ins. Click the drop arrow on the Manage box (see Figure 10.5), and then click Templates from that list.

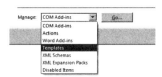

FIGURE 10.5

Finally, click "Go" to launch the Templates and Add-ins dialog box you see in Figure 10.6.

FIGURE 10.6

From this dialog box you can quickly see what the Document template is. In Figure 10.6 you can see that the current document template is "Normal," which is the default Word Template. That's good news for your troubleshooting because you can rename (or delete, if you're feeling brave) the normal.dotm global template, and the next time you start Word 2010 it will automatically re-create it for you (without the corruption that caused your problems, we hope). The only downside to deleting normal.dotm, honestly, is if you've customized the Normal template in some way and you don't want to lose those customizations. Chances are good that, like most attorneys, you haven't customized normal.dotm (at least not intentionally), so deleting it is just fine. Again, Word 2010 will quietly re-create it for you the next time you start up.

> NOTE: If you have the Developer Tab showing on your Ribbon, you can also get to the Templates and Add-ins dialog box by clicking the "Document Template" button on the Developer tab.

You Can't Edit the Document

Sometimes you'll open a document and you won't be able to edit the document. The title bar may even say "Read-only" in it. Usually Word 2010 is pretty good about warning you about that in the information bar at the top of the screen, but in case you didn't notice that it's possible that the document in question has been "Marked as Final." Assuming you're the author, you can turn that off again by going to File | Protect Document (on the Info group) and unselecting "Mark as Final."

It's also possible that the file itself or the directory it resides in has been marked as "Read-Only" in Windows. Go to File | Open, find the file, right-click it, and choose "Properties" to see if Read-Only is checked. You can do the same for the directory it resides in.

Beyond that, you're getting into territory that you may need your IT support people to help with.

Finding and Fixing Formatting Mysteries

One of the more perplexing issues lawyers and law firms have to deal with tends to be formatting problems. "Why the heck is that italicized?!" is a common refrain. In the good ol' days of Word Perfect we'd just open the Reveal Codes pane, track down the offending code, and remove it. But Word doesn't use codes that way so, tracking down an errant bit of formatting can be a little more challenging. (That's why you want to use styles as often as possible and as little direct formatting as you can.)

There are two common scenarios where you may have to trouble-shoot some curious formatting. . . .

Documents You Created

If it's a document that you created, the chances are good that you have an unfortunate combination of direct and indirect formatting. You may want to re-read Chapter 4 and pay particular attention to the information on Styles. The other thing you might want to do is go into File | Options (review Chapter 9) | Advanced and make sure that the "Keep Track of Formatting" and "Mark formatting inconsistencies" checkboxes are enabled. Then Word will help you to locate, and fix, places where you may have inconsistent use of styles and direct formatting.

Generally, when I see formatting issues in a document I created, I'll select the offending text and press CTRL+SPACEBAR to remove any direct formatting. Then I'll ensure that I have the correct style applied. That fixes it almost every time.

Documents from Somebody Else

Sometimes if you receive a document from somebody else there may be formatting issues, especially if that person is using a different word processor, or even a different version of Word. A common cause of that issue is the fonts that installed on the other person's machine versus the fonts you have installed. For example, the other machine may be using Word for Mac and have older, non-unicode, fonts that you don't have installed on your machine. Generally, if the differences are minor, you can solve them by just reformatting the text with your own font and minimal disruption. If, on the other hand, the differences are substantial and the formatting is unusable on your machine, you may have to go back to the originator of the document and ask for a reformatted document using a more common, or updated, font.

Of course they are just as likely (or more likely, if they haven't read this book!) to have made the mistake of using direct formatting instead of indirect formatting (styles), so it may be that the same tactic of selecting the offending text, pressing CTRL+SPACEBAR to remove the direct formatting, and then making sure the proper style is applied to the text will resolve it for you.

Printing Issues

There are two basic kinds of printing issues with Word: documents that don't print the way you expect them to and documents that don't print at all. The first kind is a little harder to troubleshoot because there are so many variables.

Document Doesn't Print as Expected

The first thing to check if a document doesn't print the way you expect it to is to run a Print Preview and see if it looks correct on screen. If it looks fine on the screen but doesn't look the same when the print actually hits the paper, then the problem may be with your printer.

The next thing to check is the font you've used in the document. If the text that doesn't print right is in an unusual font, it may be that you've chosen a font your printer doesn't support. In some cases you can add the font to the printer, but in most cases it's a lot easier to just select a more standard font. There are a lot of PostScript fonts available, and all modern printers should support PostScript. In some really unusual cases you may be able to have your printer print the font as an image instead of text, or download the font from the computer to use. You'll just have to decide how committed to that esoteric font you really are, I guess, to determine how much effort you're willing to put in to make it work.

Next, check to make sure you have the latest and correct print driver installed for your printer. Especially if you've upgraded the machine to a new operating system (Windows 7, most likely), it's possible that the printer is still using drivers from the old operating system. Make sure you've got the right drivers for your printer and that they're up to date.

> **Tricks of the Pros**
>
> One trick I sometimes use if I have a document/printer combination that doesn't want to print correctly is to save the document as an Adobe PDF file. If it looks right there, then I can print the PDF file.

Document Doesn't Print at All

Not surprisingly, most non-printing issues are the result of problems with the printer. Before you get involved in any complex troubleshooting, try a few basics: make sure the printer has paper and toner (or ink, as the case may be), is turned on, and is connected to the computer (or network) that it's supposed to be connected to.

If that all checks out OK, try powering the printer off and powering it back on. That will clear the printer memory and cause it to try to reestablish connection with your computer and/or the network.

The final thing to try, before seeking professional assistance, is to reboot your computer in case your print queue is jammed up.

If none of those remedies get the printer to work, then your problem is more than casual and you should contact your tech support person for further guidance.

▼▼▼▼▼
WARNING: GEEK CONTENT AHEAD

The Print Spooler. Put simply, the print spooler is a software process that resides on both the client computer (i.e., the workstation you're using) and the print server (which may also be the workstation you're using if the printer is directly attached) and processes the print jobs. The spooler handles the final rendering of those jobs. If the print spooler stops for any reason, your print jobs will back up and never make it to the printer. You can restart the service if you know how, but it's probably easier to just restart the computer. If the problem persists, then you should contact your tech support person. If it stops once, that could be a fluke. If it keeps stopping, that's a problem.

An Extra Page Prints at the End

Another common printing issue is that a blank page may print at the end of your document. Usually that's because you actually have a few extra lines at the end of the document you didn't know about and couldn't see. Go to the end of your document and turn on "Show Paragraph Marks" by clicking the "Show/Hide Paragraph Marks" button in the Paragraph group of the home tab (it looks like this: ¶) or press

▼

The ¶ symbol is called a "pilcrow" mark. It is also sometimes referred to as the "alinea" from the Latin meaning "off the line."

CTRL+SHIFT+8. You'll probably discover a couple of extra paragraph marks at the end of your document . . . delete them, then check Print Preview to make sure that your blank page is gone.

Word May Seem to Hang When You Try to Insert a Building Block

Sometimes when you go to insert a Building Block, Word might appear to freeze up, and the problem seems to get worse when you add more and more items to your Building Blocks list. That seems sort of obvious when you think about it, but the issue really is with how long it takes Word to build the Building Blocks gallery. Word isn't really frozen; it's just struggling to get the galleries populated. The faster and more powerful your machine is, the less of a problem you'll have with this. So there are two basic solutions: either upgrade your computer or remove some unneeded Building Blocks from the template so that Word doesn't have to work so hard to get those galleries built.

Not surprisingly, this problem is less and less common as people upgrade to faster machines with more RAM and 64-bit Windows 7.

You're Seeing a Lot of Oddly Named Files

If your folders are filling up with files whose names start with a tilde (~) you may have a problem with Word not shutting down properly. Those files are temporary files that Word should clean up when it shuts down normally; while Word is running you'll see those files from time to time, and that's fine. If Word is closed or if you're seeing growing numbers of those files, that may indicate a faulty add-in or another problem that is preventing Word from shutting down normally. If you're sure Word is closed and that all of the files you need are correctly saved, you can generally delete those files.

You See a Lot of Odd Text in Brackets

What you're seeing are field codes and they are often used in complex documents, especially documents that use document assembly. Word is supposed to substitute data for the field code, such as the path name to the document, author name, current date or time, merge data, and so forth. If you're seeing the codes instead of the data, chances are you have "Display Field Codes" turned on. To turn it off, press ALT+F9.

You See a Lot of Curious Marks In Your Document

. . . like dots where the spaces should be and pilcrows at the end of every paragraph? You've just got the formatting marks displayed. You have several options to turn that off (and back on), but the easy ways are to either click the "Show/Hide" button (looks like a pilcrow) on the Home tab of the Ribbon or press CTRL+SHIFT+8 on your keyboard. If you want to display some of the formatting marks but not all of them, you can configure that Backstage: File | Options | Display.

Performance Problems

If Word 2010 isn't performing very well, you can do to improve it in ways besides adding more RAM to your system, which is almost always a good idea.

1. User fewer fonts in your document. If you have a lot of fonts, that can suck up system resources.
2. Store your documents on a local hard drive. You may not be able to do this due to policy issues at your firm, but if you *are* able to, you may find that Word operates faster on documents that are located on a local hard drive instead of a network drive. This is a good example of where enabling "Copy remotely stored files onto your computer, and update the remote file when saving" can really help. Go back to Chapter 9 if you don't recall how to enable it. Go ahead; we'll wait.

   > ▼
   > If you're among the dwindling percentage of folks who still have a floppy drive in your computer, *never* edit Word documents that are located on the floppy drive. Copy the document to the hard drive first, edit it there, and then copy it back. You're welcome.

3. Disable the automatic spelling and grammar checks. These features require a little bit of system attention to operate; turning them off can help optimize Word performance. See Chapter 9 for details on how to turn them off.

Some Features Don't Seem to Exist?!

If you're trying to use certain features but can't, it's possible that your version of Word 2010 isn't activated (see the beginning of the chapter), or it's possible that you actually have Word Starter (a common pre-installed option on new PCs). Word Starter doesn't support a lot of features Word 2010 supports, such as:

- Macros. Can't create, edit, or run them in Starter.
- Add-ins. No Office add-ins run in Starter. That means it probably won't integrate with your document management or case management system.
- No tables of contents or footnotes.
- No Track Changes.

More Resources

- Office For Lawyers—http://www.officeforlawyers.com. A site I created to post supplementary information and articles for these books. It's free; no registration required.
- Microsoft Support Forums—http://social.answers.microsoft.com/ forums. Free peer-support forums hosted by Microsoft and frequented by Microsoft MVPs. There are forums for Windows, Office, and other Microsoft products. Ask and answer questions for free.
- Shauna Kelly's Word site: http://www.shaunakelly.com/word. Great site created by a Microsoft Word MVP with answers and information about Word.
- Adriana Linares' site for Word for Lawyers: http://www.lawtech partners.com/WordforLawyers.htm.

▼▼▼▼▼
What's a Microsoft MVP?

A Microsoft MVP, or "Most Valuable Professional," is a volunteer who has been recognized by Microsoft as an expert in one or more particular products. Anybody can be an MVP if they demonstrate a level of expertise and a willingness to help support that product. MVPs are not Microsoft employees and aren't paid for their efforts. For more information visit http://support.microsoft.com/mvp.

Summary

Microsoft Word 2010 is the most robust and recoverable version of Microsoft Word yet. But that doesn't mean you'll never have problems with it.

Office Repair installs will fix most things that go wrong with the program itself, but often the problem in Word may be a corrupted template or a misbehaving add-in. Be very reluctant to add even more add-ins to Word, especially if you're not sure what they are or why you should add them. More add-ins are not better—the best installation of Word is tight and fast with only the add-ins you actually need and use.

Mistakes Lawyers Make with Microsoft Word   **11**

Over the last twenty years I've seen lawyers make a lot of mistakes with word processors—as the systems have gotten more powerful and easier to use, the mistakes have become easier to make. Let's take a few minutes to look at some of the most common mistakes and how you can avoid them. Remember: the first step to recovery is admitting it!

> "I never make stupid mistakes. Only very, very clever ones."
> —*John Peel*

Licensing

One big mistake firms make with Microsoft Office is they buy it from their hardware vendor with their computers. They just call Dell or HP, and as part of the spec for the machine they include Microsoft Office, thinking that they're saving money that way. They're not! The software version you get that way is called an OEM version. The software itself is identical to the retail or volume license versions, but the *license* is different. Specifically:

- OEM software is locked to the machine it came on. If you ever replace that machine, you cannot move the Microsoft Office license to the new machine. You have to buy a new license. If the machine dies in fifteen months and you have to replace it, you'll need to buy a new copy of Office too.

■ OEM software can be installed only on that single machine—no additional machines.

The better play for almost any law office, certainly any office with five or more machines, is to buy a volume license of Microsoft Office. The volume license can be installed on *any* X machines (where X = the number of licenses you buy), but additionally you can install the *same* license on a portable device. Let me explain that:

Let's say Joe Attorney has a desktop computer. You install one of your Office 2010 licenses, obtained via volume license, on that desktop computer. But Joe also has a laptop that he uses when he travels or visits clients. You can install the same Office 2010 license that you used on Joe's desktop . . . on his laptop. The key is that the second machine has to be a portable machine with the same primary user (i.e., Joe).

But wait, there's more: volume licenses are extremely price competitive with retail and OEM licenses, and often cheaper.

So why not just walk into Best Buy and pick up five Microsoft Office 2010 boxes? Those aren't tied to any specific machine, so you can move them when the machine gets replaced. And with the retail license you *can* install on the desktop and a portable for the same primary user! But, with retail licenses you have to keep track of the licenses. You have to know which license you installed on which machine, and if you ever have to reinstall . . . heaven help you if you got them mixed up.

With volume licensing you get *one* product key to keep track of, and it's tied to X number of licenses that you've purchased. You just use that one product key for all of your installs. And if you later need to add licenses, you just call up your vendor and buy however many (or few) additional licenses you need—no need to keep track of multiple product keys. That will save you money in administration and management.

If you want to keep up to date on Microsoft Office, you can purchase your volume license with Software Assurance—that gives you free upgrades to the current version of Office within the period of the subscription. If you know a new version of Office is due within the next eighteen months and you're confident you'll want it, then it's probably cost effective to get your volume license with two years of Software Assurance.

"But darn, we only have *four* users!" That's OK. The five license minimum for volume licensing only has to be five licenses . . . it doesn't have to be five licenses of the same thing! You can buy four licenses of Microsoft Office 2010 Professional Plus and one license of something cheap like "Microsoft Math" or "Microsoft Streets and Trips." That extra license is just a placeholder to fill out the five license pack . . . but it counts.

Inconsistent Use of Styles

Styles are a powerful tool to standardize how paragraphs and text are formatted in Word. Sadly, most lawyers don't take advantage of their full potential. Too many attorneys rely on direct formatting instead of a well-thought-out set of styles. In Chapter 4 we explored styles in more detail—if you read only one chapter in this book, well then you've spent a lot of money for just one chapter. To get the most for your money, choose Chapter 4.

Document Naming

As discussed in Chapter 6, lawyers and their staffs are often in a hurry when they create documents—so much so that when it comes time to save and exit the document they occasionally name the document "Memo" or "Letter" or some other quick thing they can type without thinking about it. The problem is that with a title like that, it's almost impossible to find this document later or figure out what it's supposed to be. Worse yet, if you don't have a good document management system, you could end up with a folder full of documents called "Memo.docx," "Memo1.docx," "Memo2.docx," and that just doesn't help anybody. Word supports long file names like "Memo to Dr Sanders regarding Bruha claim.docx." Take the time to really name your documents, and you'll be a lot happier and save a lot of time in the long run.

Saving Over Old Documents

One thing most lawyers do is reuse old documents. The Smith will was so good that when Mr. Jones needs a will, you just open the Smith will, make the necessary changes, and save as Mr. Jones's will. One problem with that arises when you open the Smith will, make your changes, and then just click "Save" . . . and you've just saved over Mr. Smith's will with Mr. Jones's will. Oops.

▼▼▼▼▼

We get two to four calls per month from law firms that need us to help them retrieve a previous version of a document because somebody saved over the old one with an incorrect version. Fortunately, most of them have backup systems that allow us to retrieve the old version. In case that happens to you, however, don't delay. Backups are in a constant state of change. Every night a new backup is done—or at least it should be—and in many cases it overwrites a previous backup. If you wait too long to request a restoral, the correct file may be overwritten by the erroneously edited one. Let your IT staff know as soon as you realize the error—that will maximize your chances of getting it fixed.

There are a couple of ways to prevent this. One is that when you open Mr. Smith's will, but before you make any changes to it, click File and do a Save As to save a copy of the document with a new filename. (If you prefer the keyboard, press F12.) Then you're working with that new document, and Mr. Smith's original will is untouched.

A second way, and we'll talk about it in more detail a little later in this chapter, is that after you open Mr. Smith's will, you select all of the text by pressing CTRL+A, copy that text to the clipboard with a deft CTRL+C, then hit CTRL+N to start a new, blank document. CTRL+V pastes that text into the blank, new document, and CTRL+S lets you save that now not-so-blank new document with a new filename and location, if desired. You may then tap the CTRL key however many times you'd like to make yourself grin at how clever you were to not only preserve Mr. Smith's will but probably significantly reduce your metadata issues in one (well, four or five) swift strokes.

Not Saving Documents

Saving over old documents is one mistake. Another mistake is not saving often enough. I can't tell you how many times I've gotten calls from folks who lost a document (or at least part of one) because something bad happened and they'd forgotten to save during the last one or two hours.

▼▼▼▼▼
Tales from the field . . .
A few years ago I got a call from a client late on a Thursday afternoon. She had spent the better part of the day working on a brief for a case she was involved in, and at the end of the day she went to close her

word processor. (In fairness, it wasn't Microsoft Word, but for our purposes the story is the same.) It asked her if she wanted to save the document. In her haste, she accidentally clicked "No," and her word processor quickly and dutifully closed down . . . discarding hours of her work in the process. She immediately realized her mistake and grabbed her phone to call me. After she explained her predicament, the call went something like this:

Me: OK, well, how long ago did you last save the document?

Her: <long pause> I didn't.

Me: You didn't save it *at all* today?

Her: I know, I know. <sigh>

Me: OK, well, did you e-mail a copy of it to anybody?

Her: No.

Me: Did you print a copy?

Her: No. Is it gone?

Me: <long pause> Maybe not. I'll be there in 10 minutes. *Don't touch anything!*

Pondering her problem, I remembered that her word processor, like Microsoft Word, makes automatic backup copies every few minutes in the background. Those are there in the event that your computer (or even just your word processor) has an unexpected shutdown. These can be due to power failure, system error, foot/dog/cat/child/spouse brushing up against the power switch . . . you name it. If that kind of unexpected shutdown happens, the next time the word processor starts it detects that the backup files are there and offers to let you recover them. That can be quite a relief in those instances when you really need them.

However, when you close the document normally (such as by closing the word processor and answering "No" to the "Do you want to save?" question), the word processor is a good computer citizen and cleans up after itself, which includes deleting all of those apparently unnecessary backup copies. It occurred to me in pondering her problem that perhaps there was a way to recover one of those deleted files.

A computer deleting files is not really as thorough as you might imagine. All the computer really does in those instances is mark that space as available. It doesn't actually clean off the bits on the hard drive that previously stored that file. It leaves them as is, but just indicates that the space is available to be used by the next piece of data that needs to be stored. If I could get to her computer before any further data was written to that space on the hard drive, I just might be able to get the file back.

When I arrived at her office she was in a bad way . . . she was sure that all was lost and she was going to have to spend all night re-creating hours' worth of work. "It's impossible, isn't it?" she said with a pained voice. "It's unlikely," I responded. "But don't give up just yet."

I fired up my handy undelete program (there are a number of them available from various vendors) and set to work browsing to see if I could find the deleted backup files. Sure enough, I found several files that were of the type we were seeking, and by comparing the date and time stamps I identified one or two likely suspects. I restored them to her hard drive and started her word processor, which correctly recognized the presence of the backup files, assumed it had crashed, and offered to recover them. She jumped up and down with glee when she recognized the first page of her lost document. Sure enough, she had lost only about the last five minutes of her work, which amounted to a couple of minor edits she was able to easily redo. To say she was happy is an understatement, and our firm earned our unofficial slogan: "We Make the Impossible Unlikely."

Fortunately, modern technology has largely, but not entirely, mini-mized this problem. I have my computer plugged into an uninterruptible power supply so that if my electricity blinks momentarily, my computer won't notice. AutoRecover means that Word has frequent backup files so that if Word happens to crash for some reason, I have a good shot at being presented with a recovery file the next time I start Word, and I'll lose only a couple minutes' worth of work.

And, now with Word 2010, you can recover an unsaved document— even if you closed without saving. Just open Word 2010, click File | Recent, and at the bottom right of the screen you'll find "Recover Unsaved Documents." Click that and you'll see the Saved Drafts folder, which should contain your document.

Note . . . these documents are saved for only four days. If you've waited longer than that to recover them, you're probably out of luck.

But, honestly, how hard is it to press CTRL+S to save your document? Watch, I'll do it right now. There, wasn't that satisfying? Even though I know intellectually that the odds of losing my document (currently well into the eleventh chapter of it) are increasingly slim, I've been in this business long enough to remember when it was a regular occurrence. And I'm in the good habit of frequently saving my work as I go, so that just in case the cat jumps on my keyboard at the wrong moment, I still have a recently saved copy I can reopen. Right after I figure out whose cat that is.

Is it annoying or difficult to press CTRL+S every few minutes? Not at all. Look, I'll do it again.

Metadata

Metadata is data about data. Simple as that. The text of your document is data. The *title* of your document is metadata. The date the document was created, the name of the author, the number of words or characters within the document, any comments or tracked changes within the document . . . these are all metadata.

It's a popular misconception that metadata is strictly a Microsoft problem. In fact, virtually all office productivity applications, including Corel's Word Perfect, use metadata and face potential issues with it. That's why Corel included a metadata checker/cleaner in WordPerfect X3 and all subsequent versions.

What's the Matta with Metadata?

Other than being a sort of cheesy section heading, the "matta with metadata" is that there may very well be information contained therein that would be damaging to your case, your client, and perhaps your career if it should be leaked outside your firm.

For example, let's say you have a Word document and you have Track Changes turned on. (Go back to Chapter 6 if you're not sure what Track Changes does.) This Word document is going to be a settlement offer to opposing counsel. You decide that you will offer the other party $500,000 to settle the matter. Before sending the offer, and after discussion with your client, you decide to reduce the offer to $350,000. So you open your Word document, change "$500,000" to "350,000," save the document, and promptly e-mail it to opposing counsel. Opposing counsel opens the document in Word, makes sure he or she has Track Changes turned on as well, clicks the Review tab on the Ribbon, and changes the view to "Final Showing Markup." At this point, opposing counsel discovers that you had originally intended to offer $500,000 but later revised that figure. Do you suppose that might affect your negotiating position?

Does it make your situation better or worse if you and the client collaborated on the document and used the comments feature of the document to discuss your settlement strategy as you prepared the offer letter?

Another scenario: You're assisting a client with a press release for a pending acquisition. It's all very hush-hush and not finalized yet, so you're just holding onto the draft of the release. In the meantime, that client also wants your help with a press release for a new bond offer. Since you like the press release you did for the acquisition, and it already has all of the client's contact information in it, you decide to reuse the pending acquisition release and just change the relevant bits. You've already read the bit I wrote about not saving over old documents, so you know that you should open your original document and do a "Save As" to save the new version with a new name. You change the names, dates, and amounts to reflect the bond offer, and once you're satisfied that's all done, you helpfully send it off to the local business press. The next day the front page of the local paper reads "BIGCO Inc. to Acquire SmallCo, LLC, for $5 million!" Oops.

How Do You Discover Metadata?

There are a number of tools available to discover Metadata, but the simplest is Word itself. With a Word document open and Track Changes turned on, go to the Review tab and make sure under Tracking that you have "Final Showing Markup" selected in the Display for Review field. Then you should be able to see the edits and changes made, if any were preserved in the document.

Alternatively, you can use third-party tools like Metadata Assistant or Doc Scrubber (see Figure 11.1) to analyze your document (and remove potentially damaging metadata).

FIGURE 11.1

How Do You Clean/Prevent It?

There are a number of methods available to clean metadata out of a Word document and a few ways to prevent it in the first place. The method you use to clean it should depend upon what the document is ultimately intended to do.

If the intention is to print the document and provide it in hard copy, then your metadata worries are few. Very little metadata would appear in a printout—in fact, you would have to deliberately set the print options *to* print the metadata (such as comments and other markup) for it to appear (see Figure 11.2). By default, Print Markup is *not* checked in Word 2010.

FIGURE 11.2

So if your intent is to print the document and provide it only via hard copy, then don't worry about the metadata. Print your document, proof-read it, and then rest assured that your recipients aren't getting anything you didn't intend to give them (unless they're going to be testing your printout for incriminating fingerprints or DNA).

If the intent is to send the document electronically, as it so often is these days, then you have to make another determination before you pro-ceed: do they need to edit it? If the party you're sending to doesn't need to edit the document, then the preferred way to send the document—and for the recipient to receive it, in many cases—is as an Adobe PDF file. PDF has a number of advantages:

First, the formatting is going to be consistent. The way the PDF looks on your computer is how it looks on the recipient's computer and printer. No questions about whether the other party has the right fonts or what version of WordPerfect he or she is using. A PDF is a PDF is a PDF. It's electronic paper. All the recipient needs is a compatible version of Acro-bat Reader, which is available from Adobe for free.

Second, it's portable. This relates a bit to the first advantage, but there are PDF readers for nearly every platform. So if you're dealing with an attorney who is still running Windows 98 or an attorney who has gone over to the Mac or a real propeller-head who insists that Linux is the only true operating system . . . it doesn't matter. All of these attorneys can read and print PDF files you send them. Heck, most mobile devices like Blackberries, iPhones, and Android phones can read PDF files now too.

Third, and most important for the purposes of Chapter 11 in this book, almost no interesting metadata goes with a PDF file. When you send a Word document to PDF, you're effectively printing it, and that means the same rules apply—unless you have explicitly told Word to include things like comments, tracked changes, or other markup in the PDF file, it won't. The worst you're likely to see in a PDF file is the document title, author, and perhaps some keywords. You'd have to try pretty hard to get significant metadata into a PDF file.

That said, Adobe does create a bit of its own metadata; like all files on a computer it will have an associated creation date, for example. But I'd suggest that if you're really concerned with the simple creation date of the document, you may want to reexamine the ethical issues of the matter.

So, let's examine the scenario where you need to send a document out that the recipient **does** need to be able to edit or where you are, for some reason, required to send it in Microsoft Word format.

Document Reuse

One thing that attorneys *love* to do, and we talk about it a little more in Chapter 12, is reuse existing documents. It's a big time saver and can help to maintain a high standard of quality. If you already know a document is good, why not use it as the basis for a future document? Well, the answer to that question can be found in Chapter 8. You're really better off using templates and/or document assembly software and building a fresh new document with those tools rather than using an existing, completed work product as the basis for a new one. Unfortunately, the practice of document reuse is widespread, and old habits are hard to break. When you reuse that old document, you risk also reusing the metadata from that document. So, in our scenario where you *have* to send a Word document and you've succumbed to the pressure to reuse an old document, then you want to try to minimize the chances that any metadata is transferred from the original document.

To do that, open your old document. The very first thing you want to do is make sure Track Changes is turned *on* in that document. Then go to File and click New to start a new, blank document. In that document make sure that Track Changes is turned *off*. (Yes, *off*.) Now go back to your original document (sometimes referred to as the "Donor Document") and press CTRL+A to select all of the text. Go to the new document (sometimes referred to as the "Recipient Document") and press CTRL+V to paste that text in. Now save that new document with a new file name. Close the old, or donor, document. Now you can go through and make any edits or changes you need to make to the new document. When you have it finished, go to File, click Check for Issues, then Inspect Document, and let Word's built-in Metadata Inspector take a look at your document.

If you haven't saved the document lately, the metadata inspector will prompt you to save. That's a smart move. Then it will ask you what data to check for (see Figure 11.3). Generally speaking, I would let it check for everything—except perhaps for headers, footers, and watermarks, there probably isn't any of that other data that your recipient should have. Besides, the metadata inspector will ask you before it removes anything, so I'd just leave them all checked.

FIGURE 11.3

After it's done inspecting, you'll get a report, like in Figure 11.4. You can see here in our example that there were comments, personal information, and custom XML data found. Word's tool is reasonably primitive in two respects:

FIGURE 11.4

1. It's not going to show you the specifics of what it found. It just tells you it exists; that's all.

2. It doesn't let you selectively remove it. If you have Word remove comments, for example, it's going to remove all of them. If you want to selectively remove some, you'll have to go back through the document yourself and delete just those comments you don't want to retain.

Configure Word to Warn You

If you use Track Changes a lot, then you might want Word to warn you if you go to save or send a file that has tracked changes in it—if nothing else, it's a good reminder to run the built-in metadata inspector. To enable that, just go to File | Options | Trust Center and click Trust Center Settings. In the Privacy Settings group, halfway down the page, you'll see what I have in Figure 11.5.

FIGURE 11.5

The first option lets you turn on the warnings that you want, and I encourage you to enable it; again, just to be on the safe side.

The third option is another one you'll want to enable. It makes sure that if you open a document that has tracked changes in it, the tracked changes are shown—even if you changed the Display for Review setting to be "Final" only the last time you worked on this document. It may seem like a nuisance, but it's a valuable reminder that there are markup and tracked changes in the document that you may need to deal with before passing it along.

If you're collaborating on a document with others, you may not even realize that a document has Track Changes turned on. It's possible that somebody else has enabled Track Changes without your knowledge—or even theirs. Better safe than sorry.

The final option here, "Remove personal information from file properties on save," will change the author, manager, and company names, as well as dates and times associated with comments or tracked changes. That sounds really useful! But it's unavailable in Word 2010 . . . it'll be grayed out unless you're working on a document that was created in an earlier version of Word and you had this option turned on in that earlier version. Too bad.

Summary

Word seems like a pretty simple tool, but it's a powerful one as well. As any first-semester law student can tell you, documents are a critical part of the practice of law, and the word processor is an important tool for the law firm. There are a number of mistakes that lawyers and their staff can make with Word—some of them are merely efficiency issues, but others can be very serious. Leak the wrong metadata to the wrong person and the consequences could be as severe as disbarment. And that's really not the way to move your practice forward.

Tricks to Impress Your Law School Classmates With

12

Word 2010 has a surprising number of great tricks that can be used to improve your productivity, and considering that law is such a document-intensive field, anything that helps improve your effectiveness in this product can directly translate into your practice. In this chapter we'll take a look at some of those nifty tricks you can use to get even more out of Word 2010.

Mark as Final

Want to pass your document to somebody for review but discourage them from editing it? Mark it as final. That will set the document to be Read-Only and marked for review only. Is it foolproof? No, not really. The other person can just click the "Edit Anyway" button that Word presents, but that's actively defeating your clearly stated desire that the document be final.

Mark as Final is just a handy way to flag a document so that others know that it *shouldn't* be edited any more. It doesn't prevent editing—there are other mechanisms for that, if that's what you're after.

Note: I occasionally mark my own documents as Final as a reminder to myself that the document shouldn't need to be edited any further.

Open Multiple Files

If you need to open two or more documents at once you could open one, then open the next, then open the next. Or . . . you could click File | Open and then hold down the CTRL key and click on each of the documents you want to open. Once you have them all selected, let go of CTRL and click the "Open" button. All of the documents you selected will open in one step.

Note: the one catch is that all of the documents have to be in the same folder or library.

Minimize the Ribbon

One of the first comments folks have when they see the Ribbon is that it takes up a fair bit of screen real estate at the top of the screen. If you'd like to minimize it to give yourself more room to work, just right-click anywhere on the tab line and choose "Minimize the Ribbon." To get it back . . . repeat that process. Alternatively, you can double-click any of the Ribbon tab labels to minimize, and subsequently restore, the Ribbon.

Publishing to PDF

Attorneys love to save and send PDF files. There are some good reasons for that:

1. PDF files are difficult to surreptitiously modify. Saving to PDF effectively "finalizes" the document.
2. PDF files contain only minor amounts of relatively harmless metadata and thus are safer to send to clients or opposing counsel.
3. PDF is a nearly universal format. Virtually everybody has the ability to read and/or print PDF files—even users who work on Macs or Linux machines.

Office 2010 will let you save your documents as PDF files without having to purchase and install Adobe's Acrobat program. Of course, the PDF files you can create with this are fairly basic—you don't get the advanced features of Acrobat—but for most users that's sufficient.

Saving to PDF in Word is simplicity itself. With your document open click File, choose Save and Send, and

▼

Want to know more about Adobe Acrobat? Pick up a copy of David Master's book *Adobe Acrobat for Lawyers* from the American Bar Association.

then "Create PDF/XPS Document" from the menu that appears. You'll see a single button on the right that reads "Create PDF/XPS." Click that. If you want to keep it simple you can just click the "Publish" button on the next dialog box. There are a few options you can configure, if you'd like:

- Open File After Publishing: checking this box will open your document in Adobe Reader after your save completes.
- Optimize For – Standard: this creates a larger, but better quality, PDF file.
- Optimize For – Online publishing: this creates a smaller, tighter file but sacrifices a bit of quality.

For extended options click the "Options" button to get the dialog box you see in Figure 12.1. Here you can select the page range (in case you only want certain pages), whether or not you want the markup (comments, tracked changes, etc.) to show, and other such settings.

FIGURE 12.1

One setting here that may be important (and we mentioned it back in Chapter 5) is the setting that lets you create this PDF file in PDF/A format. That's the format the federal courts seem to prefer for e-filing. So if you're preparing this document for filing, you will probably want to go into Options and check that box.

Once you've set your options, just choose a file location to save to, give it a file name and save it. Voilà!

Outlining

Outlines are a powerful way to create new documents (it's how I started this book, for instance) as well has a handy way to organize your thoughts. Word is a very good outlining tool, even if you never take your outline all the way to a full document. Word is even smart enough to recognize an outline when you start one. Just type an "I" (like a Roman numeral 1) followed by a period and then your first heading. Word will automatically jump into Outline mode for the succeeding text.

Use TAB (and Shift-TAB) to move items up and down levels (left and right), but you can also use your mouse to drag items up and down within your outline.

Generally, I'll start with my major level items (I., II., etc.), go back through and fill in the second-level items, then go back through and flesh those out with third- and fourth-level items, and . . . next thing you know I have a fairly detailed outline. From there I can start writing the text to explain each of the items.

As I mentioned in Chapter 7, I will often do my outlining in Microsoft OneNote and then send that nearly completed outline to Word to finish the document. If you haven't looked at OneNote yet, you really should check it out. Great stuff for lawyers; it does a lot more than just outlining and note taking.

Word 2010's Outliner view is actually pretty nice and has some good outlining tools. If you're a hardcore outline user, you may want to give that a try. On the View tab of the Ribbon, click "Outline" to see your document in outline format.

AutoCorrect

AutoCorrect is great for correcting spelling errors, but did you know you can also use it to speed up your typing? Create custom AutoCorrect entries that replace shorthand acronyms with full text. We talked about that a bit in Chapter 8 under automating Word.

Navigation Pane

When you're creating a lengthy and extensive document—a book on Microsoft Word 2010, for example—it can be handy to see all of your headings in the style of a table of contents so that you can make sure your content is complete and in a logical order (see Figure 12.2). The navigation pane shows you the headings in your document and provides an easy way to navigate up and down in the document. This is especially important when your document is more than 200 pages long and your "Page Up" button is getting a bit worn down.

You can also use it to reorganize your content. Grab a header in the navigation pane and drag it up or down. Word will reorder your text accordingly.

FIGURE 12.2

Search

The navigation pane also includes a really good search capability. Click in the "Search Document" field at the top of the navigation pane and press ENTER. Word will find all of the instances of that search term, tell you how many there are, and give you a few of those search results, in context—as you see in Figure 12.3. Click any of the contextual results and Word will take you to that place in the document and highlight your searched for term in yellow (see Figure 12.4).

 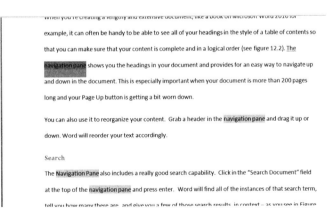

FIGURE 12.3   **FIGURE 12.4**

The only bit of the navigation pane that I don't find wonderful is the Thumbnails tab—which I think is moderately useless unless you're looking for something that you can't find with Search and that is plainly visible with the page 4 feet away.

Encrypt Document

There may come times when you'll want to protect the content of your document—perhaps you're collaborating with co-counsel and you want to use Information Rights Management (see Chapter 6) to control who can access your document and what they can do with it. Sometimes you want a simpler solution, though, and there are two of those:

Encrypt with Password

If you just want to keep unauthorized eyes off the document, you can choose to encrypt the document with a password. Just go to File | Protect | Encrypt with Password. When you do that, Word will ask you to give the document a password or pass phrase. When somebody (including you) goes to open the document, they'll be asked to provide the password. Without it . . . no document.

Of course, if you're planning to share this document with others, you'll need some way to safely get them the password. It's not really a good idea to e-mail them the document with the password in the e-mail. Anybody who intercepts the e-mail has the document and the password. Better to somehow get them the password through a different channel— phone call, face to face, SMS text message, perhaps? Or you just pick a password that has some shared meaning for each of you and give them a hint: "name of the restaurant where we met."

This is a good solution if you just want to protect the document at a basic level. Beyond that though—once they're in the document, they're in. This method doesn't stop them from editing or printing or anything like that.

Digital Signatures

You can use a digital signature in much the same way you use a printed signature—to lend authenticity to your document. Digitally signing a document is not a new feature in Word 2010 but it's a lot easier in 2010 than it was in previous versions. Digitally signing a document requires a digital certificate that verifies your identity. There are two basic classes of digital certificate:

1. Third-party certificates: these are certificates that you obtain from a trusted certificate authority like VeriSign, Thawte, or others.
2. Self-signed certificates: these are certificates that you generate yourself.

The self-signed certificate has several big advantages and only one real drawback. On the plus side, it's free and you can generate one and use it immediately. You know who provided the certificate, you don't have to jump through many hoops to create one, you don't have to break out your credit card, and you can start to use your certificate right away. The only real downside is that it's almost useless.

Self-certifying a certificate is like letting people print their own driver's licenses. Without an independent authority, there's almost no way to confirm that a signature is authentic or that the sender is who he or she claims to be. What stops me from creating a self-signed certificate that claims that I'm you? Nothing.

The only thing self-signed digital signatures will do for you is confirm that the version of the document hasn't changed since it was signed. If a signed document is changed, the signature is invalidated. Of course, somebody can intercept your document, change it, and *re*-sign it with a forged digital signature. Again, this applies only if you're self-signing.

To do digital signatures correctly you need to get a real certificate from a third-party authority. It's not hard to do; when you go to digitally sign your document for the first time (File | Protect Document | Add a Digital Signature) you'll be offered a button that will take you to the Office Marketplace online, where you can get a digital signature from one of a variety of digital signature providers. If you already have one, then you can just use that, of course.

Either way, if you're self-signing or using a third-party certificate, you'll get the Sign dialog box that you see in Figure 12.5. You have an optional field that asks for the reason you're choosing to sign the document, and you'll have a chance to choose which certificate (if you have more than one) to sign with. Assuming it's already signing with the certificate you want to use, you can just click the "Sign" button and your digital signature will be affixed.

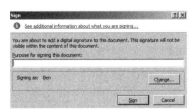

FIGURE 12.5

If you're using a third-party signature, when you send this document to others and they open it in Word, Word will verify, in the background, that the signature is authentic by contacting the third-party provider— and yes, the recipient will have to be connected to the Internet to do that verification. If you're using a self-signed signature, then it will just indicate that there isn't any way to verify the signature.

Research Tools

Most people seem to think that the pinnacle of Word document creation assistance is the real-time spell checker that puts a red, squiggly line under words it thinks you've misspelled. Actually, Word offers a far richer set of tools than that. If you're like me, you probably are used to having a dictionary and maybe a thesaurus close at hand when you work. You just may not have realized quite how close at hand they are. Select any word you've typed, right-click it, and choose "Look Up." The research pane will appear on the right side of your screen, offering you dictionary, thesaurus, encyclopedia, and even a translator that will translate the word to and from about fourteen languages.

> **Tip**
>
> Some of these features, like the Thesaurus, will work even when you're disconnected, but most of them will require you to be connected to the Internet.

Legal Research

The folks at LexisNexis have even gotten on the bandwagon. If you go to http://www.lexisnexis.com/msoffice you can download a free research pane tool that connects to LexisNexis so you can Shepardize cases, access the LexisNexis Bookstore, and even find LexisONE (if you're a LexisONE user).

NOTE: The research pane tool is free and some of the LexisONE services are, as of this writing, free. I can't say for sure if everything accessible through the LexisNexis research pane tool is free, but if you're already a LexisNexis user then it makes sense for you to add this research pane tool to your arsenal.

Watermarks

One of those features that many users didn't realize Word has had for quite a while is the ability to add a watermark to your document. A watermark is a bit of text or an image that is in the background, behind your text. It's a fairly subtle effect—subtle enough that I can't even screen capture it and have it look decent for this book. It can say or be just about anything you want and is a really handy way to mark a printed document with an indication of the document status—for instance "Draft" or "Confidential" or "Client Copy." To use the Watermark feature just go to the Page Layout tab and click the Watermark tool. (see Figure 12.6). You'll get the Watermark gallery, which has twelve sample watermarks you can use. If you don't like any of those you can create your own by clicking the

"Custom Watermark" command you see toward the bottom of the gallery. Clicking that will get you the Printed Watermark dialog box that you see in Figure 12.7.

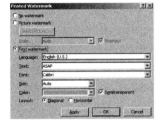

FIGURE 12.6   **FIGURE 12.7**

In the Printed Watermark dialog box you can create a picture watermark by selecting that radio button, then selecting the image you want to use. Word will automatically scale the picture so that it aligns on the page properly, but you can customize that if you like.

If you don't want to use a picture watermark, you can type your own custom text, complete with custom layout, color, font, and everything. Watermarks can be a nice way to add a stylish and functional element to your printed or PDF'd documents.

Full-Text Search

One of the big trends in desktop computing in recent years is the move toward powerful full-text search engines. Google Desktop, Copernic Desktop, and, of course, Windows Desktop Search all let you index your workstation, server, and even external hard drives to make searching for files and documents faster and easier. If you're not using a Full-Text Search tool, you really should be. It can help you find documents and files including documents and files you might not have thought about. Full-text search is different from what you may be used to in that it searches the *content* of the document, not just the name. Any words or phrases you've got will be found. And the full-text search tool will search not just Word documents but also PowerPoint, Excel, Outlook e-mails . . . all sorts of documents.

Run a full-text search for a particular citation and you may discover other documents in your document library that refer to it that you hadn't thought of. Doing conflict checks? How about a quick full-text search on the name; who knows what you may discover?

Windows Desktop Search is built into Vista and Windows 7. Just hit the "Start" button, begin typing in the search box, and Windows Desktop Search will do the rest. It's also available for Windows XP, though you'll have to download it and install it. Google Desktop and Copernic Deskop are the same—available for XP, Vista, or Windows 7. As of this writing, all of these tools are free. If you have a version of Windows older than Windows XP . . . well, then you're not running Office 2010 anyhow so you've probably bought the wrong book. (But thanks!)

Redaction

Every now and then you may want to send out a document with parts of it blacked out, to obscure particular facts the other party (or the public) shouldn't read. As you probably know, that's called "redaction," and there are a couple of ways to do that in Word.

First off, it once again comes back to knowing the medium in which your document is going to be transmitted. If it's going to be printed or sent as an image-only PDF file, then you could just select the text you want to redact and use the highlighter tool in Word to redact those words you want hidden (see Figure 12.8) by highlighting the black text with black highlighter.

transmitted. If it's going to be printed or sent as a PDF file then you could just select the text you want

to redact and use the highlighter tool in Word to redact ██████████████

FIGURE 12.8

That works fine if you're transmitting in a format where the end user can't access the actual document data. You can't use that, though, if you're going to be transmitting the document as a Word document— because the recipient could just turn off the highlighting. If you're PDFing the document as an *image* (not a searchable file), then all the recipient is going to get is a picture of the text, and it will be obscured. If you're going to print the document, then the printer will just print your redactions, and that will work OK.

There are some other creative ways to redact text, but really . . . if it's text that needs to be redacted, then it's probably important that it be done right. If you go to http://www.codeplex.com/redaction you can find the Word 2007 Redaction tool. It's made by the team at Microsoft but not officially supported by Microsoft. Yes, I know . . . but it works in Word 2010 too.

When you install it—which can take quite a while, by the way, so be sure you don't wait until five minutes before the document is due—it adds a "Redact" group to the Review tab of the Ribbon, as you see in Figure 12.9. To use the tool, you just go through your document, marking text that you want

As with any URL I give you in this book, I can only vouch for its accuracy as of this printing. The Internet is sort of like a river: you step in, but the water has moved on. If you try one of the URLs I've posted and it doesn't work, I'd suggest Googling for the content. Perhaps it has merely moved somewhere else.

redacted. When you've marked everything you want to redact, you can click the down arrow on the "Mark" button and have it redact the entire document. Figure 12.10 shows you that menu. The redaction tool will then go through your entire document and replace all marked text with black bars.

FIGURE 12.9   **FIGURE 12.10**

Caution: *This can't be undone*. I strongly suggest that you save a copy of your document *un*-redacted first, then do your redaction. That way if it turns out that you inadvertently redacted something, you can go back to the pre-redaction copy. After you finish the redaction, the tool will suggest that you run Word's metadata inspector (remember Chapter 11?), which is a good idea.

One other thing you'll notice on the menu in Figure 12.10 is a "Find and Mark" command. That lets you search the document for all instances of a string (a client's name, for example) and have all of those instances marked for redaction automatically . . . so you don't have to search it manually.

Publishing to Web

These days it's all about the Web, of course. Microsoft Word has long been "capable" of generating Web content in that you could put together a basic Web page and have it generate the HTML (HyperText Markup Language) for that page. Did it look OK? Sure. But there's a reason why professional Web designers don't use Microsoft Word for that task. The HTML code it generated was widely derided as being fairly sloppy. Still, if you just need a quick and simple page and Word is the tool that you're comfortable with, you can use it for that purpose. Just lay out your page, do a File | Save As, and choose "Web Page" to save your document in the right format. Upload it to your Web site and you've got a basic Web document.

The more interesting new feature in Word, however, is the ability to use it as a blogging client. Blogging has really taken off in the last year or two, not only as a way to get information but also as a marketing tool for lawyers. More lawyers have blogs today than ever before. Word is a powerful tool for creating text, so there's no reason why you shouldn't use it to author your blogs as well.

To get started, go ahead and create your first article. Go to File, click "New," and you'll see an option in the New Document dialog box called "Blog Post."

The first time you select that template, you will have to register your Blog with Word . . . which is to say, tell Word where and how to send the content. You'll be prompted to register your blog, as in Figure 12.11. Click the down-arrow next to Blog and choose your blog provider. Chances are pretty good that it's one of those listed there, but if it's not you may still have some hope.

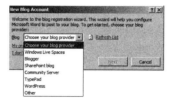

FIGURE 12.11

Select your blog provider from the list and click "Next." Word will then lead you through a short wizard that asks you to give it the URL, username (if applicable), and password for posting to your blog. Depending upon your provider, it may ask you for one or two other bits of information or tell you to make one or two minor adjustments to your blog configuration (such as configuring Live Spaces to accept E-mail publishing).

Once you have it set up, though, posting new entries is as simple as starting a new blog post (File | New | Blog Post) and publishing it to your blog (File | Save and Send | Publish as Blog Post | Publish as Blog Post).

The best blogs are the ones that are updated regularly. If you post to your blog only a couple of times a year, then you won't get many readers. Try to post at least once a week. Consider repurposing some of your other writings for your blog—maybe that great article you wrote for the local bar journal three years ago could be updated and posted as a blog entry? Or maybe it could be broken up and posted as a series of blog entries?

Speech Recognition

For years attorneys have been asking for a good speech recognition application, and many attorneys have spent a lot of money trying various products with varying degrees of success. Vista and Windows 7 offers a free, built-in speech recognition module that is really pretty good. In Vista it's called Vista Voice (you may find it in the Programs list as Windows Speech Recognition). In Windows 7 it's got the less fanciful (or at least less alliterative) moniker of "Windows Speech Recognition." Can you use it to dictate text into Word 2010? Well, I'm dictating this sentence right here. Is it perfect? No. But it's good. Really, I think it's better for voice control of your system. I can be working away and suddenly realize that I want to switch to another program on my system. I can just say "Switch to Inbox" and Outlook pops up with my Inbox displayed.

It's just another way to interact with your system, but I think it's worth a shot.

▼▼▼▼▼

TIP #1: Get a good headset if you're going to give speech recognition a try.

TIP #2: Speech recognition works best in a quiet environment. If you have the TV on in the background, you're likely to get a phrase like "Next week on *The Real Housewives of New Jersey* . . ." in the middle of your brief. And you really don't want to have to admit to that. Any background noise can affect the accuracy of speech recognition, though, so if your neighbor is having fun with the leaf blower or your office is right next to the copier, you may not have that much success with the tool.

Calculate

One of the most surprising features of Microsoft Word 2010 is a feature most people have no idea even exists: Calculate. I'm not talking about your run-of-the-mill, add-a-column kind of calculate. That's just so 1993. I'm talking about calculating off numbers in sentence format. Yes, it's a little primitive, but it's still pretty cool.

To use it, first you have to configure access to it. This feature isn't on any of the Ribbon tabs so you'll need to add it to the QAT. To do that, click the down-arrow to the right of the QAT and click "More Commands." Set the list of commands on the left side to "All Commands" and scroll down that list to find "Calculate." Click "Add" and then "OK" to close the customize dialog. You'll now see a curious green sphere on your QAT—that's the button for calculate.

So, now that you can access it, what can you do with it? Type a sentence that has some numbers in it; such as "Carrie has 5 apples and Emily has 3." Then click the "Calculate" button. Nothing happened? Look at the status bar at the bottom left. This feature is still fairly primitive and it tends to prefer addition, but if you use symbols such as "32,213-11,235" that will work for subtraction and other basic mathematical functions too.

Fancy Replacements

The replace tool from the Editing group of the Home tab can do more than replace "Jerry" with "Gerry." It can actually be used to make some more sophisticated replacements—of font elements, for example. Maybe you mistakenly used superscript throughout your document and you meant it to be subscript.

Click "Replace" and then the "Format" button. Choose Font from the list that appears, and you'll get a dialog box that looks like Figure 12.12. Select Superscript. Then click the "Replace With" field and go back to Format | Font. Select Subscript. Click "OK" and have it replace all.

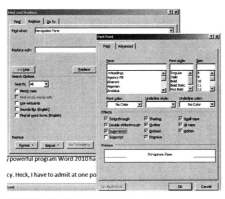

FIGURE 12.12

Of course . . . it would have saved you the hassle if you'd just applied that superscript with a style like I told you to in Chapter 4. Then you'd just have to change the style from superscript to subscript and it would have been instantly fixed throughout the document. But some lessons have to be learned the hard way.

Summary

Like any powerful program, Word 2010 has a lot of potential for tricks to improve its utility and efficiency. Heck, I have to admit at one point I had about twenty-five different sections in this chapter and finally had to whittle it down a bit (though some of those tips found their ways into other chapters of the book).

Some of the tricks, like minimizing the Ribbon, using speech recognition, or using the navigation pane, are ways to make Word a more productive environment to work in. Others, like encryption or Web publishing, are about new ways to produce content that you might not have thought of before.

Getting the most out of Word requires constantly learning—we've barely scratched the surface of what Word is capable of.

Keyboard Shortcuts

13

Like most of Office 2010, Word has a number of great and useful keyboard shortcuts that can really help the fast typist who resents having to use the mouse to get things done.

One important thing to remember is that, despite the Ribbon interface, the keyboard shortcuts that you learned for Word 2003 are still going to work in Word 2010. They may *look* a bit different, but they're still there.

Almost all of the commands on the Ribbon can be accessed via keyboard shortcuts; it's just that many of them are actually a sequence of keystrokes as opposed to a HotKey.

To see the keyboard shortcuts that activate a command on the Ribbon, just press (and release) the ALT key.

A hotkey is a single key or a combination of keys pressed at once to activate a command or feature. WINDOWS KEY+S is a hotkey. As opposed to a sequence of keys like "WINDOWS KEY, S," which tells you to press and release the Windows key and then press and release the S key. If you see the plus sign ("+") that means press this key *and* that key at the same time by pressing the first key and holding it down while you press the next key. A comma means press and release the first key, then press the next key.

In Figure 13.1 you can see that pressing the "F" will activate the File menu, pressing numbers 1 through 6 will activate the corresponding shortcuts on the Quick Access Toolbar, and pressing the letters that correspond to the tabs on the Ribbon

FIGURE 13.1

will activate those features. Pressing the "H" key to activate the Home tab gives you what you see in Figure 13.2.

FIGURE 13.2

If we were to press ALT followed by H (to activate Home), and then the number 5, that would set the font of the selected text to Subscript. Alt, H, 7 activates the Change Case feature. ALT, H, A, R sets the alignment of the current paragraph to the right. And so forth. . . .

Hotkeys in Office are almost always either function keys (F1–F12) or combination keys where you press and hold the SHIFT, ALT, and/or CTRL ("Control") keys in combination with one or more function keys or letter keys.

For example, pressing F4 will repeat the last action. Need to type "I have no recollection of that at all, Senator." over and over again? Just type it once, then press F4 as many times as you need to.

Pressing and holding CTRL+ALT+F1 (and then letting go of all of them) will launch a very handy tool most users never realized was there: System Information.

Those are both hotkeys. The first keyboard sequence I'm going to teach you here is to press F1 to launch the help system, and then type "Keyboard Shortcuts" in the search window. That will get you a list of articles and resources on the subject right on your screen. You can readily find any shortcut in the program that way. In this chapter I'm going to give you a few tricks to using keyboard shortcuts, as well as highlight my favorite keyboard shortcuts and how you might use them. A full list of shortcuts would just be cheating on my page count, and since I don't get paid by the page, I think I'll just be a little green here and not waste the paper on a simple list of shortcuts you can readily get elsewhere.

Navigating and Managing Word

First of all, there are a few good shortcuts for getting around in Word that you may like. I juggle dual monitors in the course of my work, and as such I frequently find myself windowing and maximizing windows so that I can move them around my screens and then work with them.

ALT+TAB is a well-known keyboard shortcut that isn't really a Word 2010 shortcut but rather a Windows shortcut that launches the Task

Switcher. It can be a quick way to switch between running programs, including multiple Microsoft Word 2010 instances. Hold down ALT, and then press TAB. As long as you hold down the ALT key, the list of applications will be displayed on screen as a set of icons or thumbnails. Each time you press TAB the focus will change to the next application on the list (clockwise). Let go of Alt, and Windows will switch system focus to that application (in other words, put it in the foreground so you can work with it). **ALT+SHIFT+TAB** does the same thing but goes counterclockwise through the list. As long as you don't let go of the ALT key, the list will stay up, so if you're a little dexterous you can go back and forth between ALT+TAB and ALT+SHIFT+TAB to move back and forth through the list without having to start over.

If you happen to be a Vista or Windows 7 user and have the Aero interface enabled (which most of you probably do), you can get the Flip 3D version of ALT+TAB. Press the **WINDOWS KEY+TAB** (or **WINDOWS KEY+SHIFT+TAB**) to see the fancy version and cycle through (or backwards through) the list of running applications. Functionally, it does the same thing as ALT+TAB . . . just prettier.

Windows 7 has a new feature called "Snap" that lets you dock your windows to the left or right side of the screen. This is pretty handy, especially with the newer wide-screen monitors, if you want to see two windows side by side. To snap a window to one side of the screen, just select that window and press **WINDOWS KEY+←** or **WINDOWS KEY+→** to snap to either the left or right side of the screen, respectively.

If you have multiple monitors, pressing **WINDOWS KEY+←** (or →) repeatedly will step the window across the screens. For example, if you have a Word 2010 document open on the right-hand monitor and you press **WINDOWS KEY+←**, the document will snap to the left side of the right-hand monitor. Press that combo again and it will snap to the right side of the left-hand monitor. Press it one more time and it will snap to the left side of the left-hand monitor.

These keyboard shortcuts for snap are handy because it can be tricky to snap a window to the side of multiple monitors.

If you want to close your current Word 2010 window, you can press **CTRL+W** or **CTRL+F4**. This is one of those curious instances where the same command can be accessed from two key combinations.

It's handy to know what keyboard combinations are duplicates because it gives you an idea of a key combo you can remap to some other function if you want or need to. We talked about customizing the keyboard and third-party applications like AutoHotkey in Chapter 8.

Don't worry about hitting those keys accidentally and losing all of your data; if you press those keys while you have unsaved changes in your document, Word will pop up a dialog box prompting you to save, discard, or cancel, like you see in Figure 13.3.

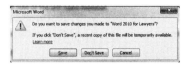

FIGURE 13.3

If you hit the key combo for close accidentally, just click "Cancel" and Word will return you to your document without any ill effects.

You can quickly window or maximize the current Word 2010 window just by pressing **ALT+F5** (to window it) or **CTRL+F10** (to maximize it). **WINDOWS KEY**+↑ also maximizes the current window. **WINDOWS KEY**+↓ windows it again.

You probably already know that you can copy a picture of the screen to the Windows clipboard by pressing **Print Screen** (PRTSCN on many keyboards) but I'm going to show you two better ways to do it:

1. You usually don't want the *entire* screen, but rather a selected part of it. To capture just the active window to the clipboard, press **ALT+PRINT SCREEN**. That will crop off all of the other stuff on the screen and grab only the active window.

2. If you have Microsoft OneNote installed (and if you have Office 2010, you do), it has a terrific screen grab tool in it. Just press **Windows Key+S** and you can select any part of your screen to copy to the clipboard, as big or small as you want. There are other third-party utilities that can do this as well, like Snagit, but OneNote is one of the best I've seen.

Word 2010 has a built-in Screenshot feature as well, but in my experience it's a little flaky. You can find it on the Insert menu in the Illustrations group, if you want to try it out.

If you want to open an existing document, you can get to the File Open dialog box by pressing **CTRL+F12** or **CTRL+O.** For a fast typist this is a lot quicker than mousing up to File, clicking that, then choosing Open or pressing ALT, followed by F, followed by O.

If you want to create a new document **CTRL+N** gets you started on that.

Pressing **F12** will display the Save As dialog box. That, along with **CTRL+S** to save, is a hotkey you definitely want to know about.

For printing documents, **CTRL+P** launches the print dialog. **ALT+CTRL+I** used to give you just a print preview of the current document—handy for seeing what you're going to get before you use the paper—but now it does the same thing as CTRL+P . . . since Print Preview is built into the Print dialog.

CTRL+← or **CTRL+→** will move you one word left or right. **CTRL+↑** or **CTRL+↓** moves one paragraph up or down. **CTRL+HOME** or **CTRL+END** will take you to the beginning or the end of the document. **HOME** and **END** go to the beginning or end of the current line. Use the **SHIFT** key in conjunction with any of those to select those things. **F8** is a handy tool for selecting as well. Pressing it twice selects a word, three times selects the current sentence, four times selects the current paragraph, and five times selects the entire document. (It's easier to press **CTRL+A** to select the whole document, I think.)

Speaking of selecting—this is actually a mouse trick—if you click once, you put your cursor on that spot to type. If you click twice, you select that word. Click three times to select the entire paragraph. Didn't see "select the sentence" in there, did you? **CTRL+Click** does that.

▼▼▼▼▼
The Coolest Feature That Works Again!

One of the niftier Word shortcut keys is one that was sort of broken in recent versions: **SHIFT+F5**. It returns you to the last place in the document you edited. In fact, it will step you back through the last three edit points if you continue pressing it. (Pressing it a fourth time will return you to where you started this exercise.) Unfortunately, in Word 2007 that functionality was broken. So, while you could still use SHIFT+F5 within an open document to go back to recent edit points, you couldn't use it on a freshly opened document to pick up where you left off. That bug is fixed in Word 2010!

Bonus Tip: If you occasionally find yourself accidentally skipping to another part of the document (as I do when I brush the wrong key on the keyboard) SHIFT+F5 is an easy way to navigate yourself back to where you were a moment ago.

The **F5** key will launch the GOTO dialog box—which you can then use to navigate to just about anywhere in the document. It's handy if you want to go to a specific page number, or if you want to advance a certain number of pages. One feature of GOTO I also want to call to your attention (you have to scroll down to find it) is the Table option. If you press F5, then pick "Table" in the left-hand pane, you can have Word automatically take you to the next table in the document. This is helpful if you have quite a few and you want to step from one to the next.

The last operational hotkey I want to bring to your attention is one you may find yourself using a lot: **CTRL+Z**, or Undo. It will undo whatever your last action was, at least within some reason. If you deleted some text and didn't mean to, CTRL+Z is your hero. If you lent your car to a teenager, CTRL+Z doesn't really help.

Working with Text

There are several hotkeys available for setting the format of your text. Some of them you may be familiar with already, like **CTRL+B** to turn on boldface, **CTRL+I** for italics, or **CTRL+U** to underline. Others may be a pleasant surprise. Did you know that **CTRL+SHIFT+C** will copy the formatting from a piece of text and **CTRL+SHIFT+V** will paste it? Yes, just like the format painter. Of course, don't let your giddiness at the idea of these hotkeys shake your resolve to make better use of Styles instead of direct formatting. . . .

Maybe you need to select all of your text before applying (or removing) a particular bit of formatting. **CTRL+A** is your shortcut for that.

Want to increase the font size of your text? **CTRL+SHIFT+>** is the answer. (That's a "greater than" sign, probably on the same button with the period on your keyboard.) **CTRL+SHIFT+<** reduces the font size of the selected text. The increments are the same as the increments in the font size drop-down (12, 14, 16 . . . 28, 36, 48 . . .). Or you can go point by point: **CTRL+]** increases the font size by 1 point while **CTRL+[** reduces it by 1 point.

In Chapter 4 we talked about direct and indirect formatting. There may be times when you want to strip the direct formatting off of a paragraph to clean it up or troubleshoot an issue. To reset the formatting to the underlying style, just select the affected paragraph and press **CTRL+SPACEBAR** to remove the character formatting. **CTRL+Q** removes any paragraph formatting. **CTRL+SHIFT+N** returns the current selection back to the Normal style.

Sometimes when I'm typing I create a section title but forget to capitalize the first letter of each word. Or maybe I was typing too fast to notice that I accidentally activated my CAPS LOCK key for the last sentence. Either way, I may want to quickly change the case of my text. To do so I need only select the text and then press **SHIFT+F3** to toggle between the different case settings in word.

While I'm creating that section title, I usually want to assign a heading style to it. **CTRL+ALT+1** will assign Heading 1 style. **CTRL+ALT+2** will assign Heading 2, and so forth. If I want to adjust it after I've assigned the heading style, then **CTRL+SHIFT+←** and **CTRL+Shift+→** will promote or demote through the heading styles.

Summary

Fast typists often find the keyboard to be preferable to the mouse. Taking your hands off the keyboard to use the mouse can slow you down and break your train of thought. Learn the keyboard shortcuts for the five or ten most common commands you use, and you may find that you save quite a bit of time over the course of your day. Not to mention the value of a regular CTRL+S. There, I just pressed it again myself!

Index

Virtual Law Practice: How to Deliver Legal Services Online
By Stephanie L. Kimbro

The legal market has recently experienced a dramatic shift as lawyers seek out alternative methods of practicing law and providing more affordable legal services. Virtual law practice is revolutionizing the way the public receives legal services and how legal professionals work with clients. If you are interested in this form of practicing law, *Virtual Law Practice* will help you:

- Responsibly deliver legal services online to your clients
- Successfully set up and operate a virtual law office
- Establish a virtual law practice online through a secure, client-specific portal
- Manage and market your virtual law practice
- Understand state ethics and advisory opinions
- Find more flexibility and work/life balance in the legal profession

The Lawyer's Essential Guide to Writing
By Marie Buckley

This is a readable, concrete guide to contemporary legal writing. Based on Marie Buckley's years of experience coaching lawyers, this book provides a systematic approach to all forms of written communication, from memoranda and briefs to e-mail and blogs. The book sets forth three principles for powerful writing and shows how to apply those principles to develop a clean and confident style.

iPad in One Hour for Lawyers
By Tom Mighell

Whether you are a new or a more advanced iPad user, *iPad in One Hour for Lawyers* takes a great deal of the mystery and confusion out of using your iPad. Ideal for lawyers who want to get up to speed swiftly, this book presents the essentials so you don't get bogged down in technical jargon and extraneous features and apps. In just six, short lessons, you'll learn how to:

- Quickly Navigate and Use the iPad User Interface
- Set Up Mail, Calendar, and Contacts
- Create and Use Folders to Multitask and Manage Apps
- Add Files to Your iPad, and Sync Them
- View and Manage Pleadings, Case Law, Contracts, and other Legal Documents
- Use Your iPad to Take Notes and Create Documents
- Use Legal-Specific Apps at Trial or in Doing Research

Find Info Like a Pro, Volume 1: Mining the Internet's Publicly Available Resources for Investigative Research
By Carole A. Levitt and Mark E. Rosch

This complete hands-on guide shares the secrets, shortcuts, and realities of conducting investigative and background research using the sources of publicly available information available on the Internet. Written for legal professionals, this comprehensive desk book lists, categorizes, and describes hundreds of free and fee-based Internet sites. The resources and techniques in this book are useful for investigations; depositions; locating missing witnesses, clients, or heirs; and trial preparation, among other research challenges facing legal professionals. In addition, a CD-ROM is included, which features clickable links to all of the sites contained in the book.

How to Start and Build a Law Practice, Platinum Fifth Edition
By Jay G. Foonberg

This classic ABA bestseller has been used by tens of thousands of lawyers as the comprehensive guide to planning, launching, and growing a successful practice. It's packed with over 600 pages of guidance on identifying the right location, finding clients, setting fees, managing your office, maintaining an ethical and responsible practice, maximizing available resources, upholding your standards, and much more. You'll find the information you need to successfully launch your practice, run it at maximum efficiency, and avoid potential pitfalls along the way. If you're committed to starting—and growing—your own practice, this one book will give you the expert advice you need to make it succeed for years to come.

Social Media for Lawyers: The Next Frontier
By Carolyn Elefant and Nicole Black

The world of legal marketing has changed with the rise of social media sites such as Linkedin, Twitter, and Facebook. Law firms are seeking their companies attention with tweets, videos, blog posts, pictures, and online content. Social media is fast and delivers news at record pace. This book provides you with a practical, goal-centric approach to using social media in your law practice that will enable you to identify social media platforms and tools that fit your practice and implement them easily, efficiently, and ethically.

ABA LawPracticeManagementSection
MARKETING • MANAGEMENT • TECHNOLOGY • FINANCE

30-Day Risk-Free Order Form

Call Today! 1-800-285-2221

Monday–Friday, 7:30 AM – 5:30 PM, Central Time

Qty	Title	LPM Price	Regular Price	Total
_____	The Lawyer's Guide to Collaboration Tools and Technologies: Smart Ways to Work Together (5110589)	$59.95	$ 89.95	$_____
_____	Google for Lawyers: Essential Search Tips and Productivity Tools (5110704)	47.95	79.95	$_____
_____	The Lawyer's Guide to Adobe Acrobat, Third Edition (5110588)	49.95	79.95	$_____
_____	The Electronic Evidence and Discovery Handbook: Forms, Checklists, and Guidelines (5110569)	99.95	129.95	$_____
_____	The 2011 Solo and Small Firm Legal Technology Guide (5110716)	54.95	89.95	$_____
_____	The Lawyer's Guide to LexisNexis CaseMap (5110715)	47.95	79.95	$_____
_____	Virtual Law Practice: How to Deliver Legal Services Online (5110707)	47.95	79.95	$_____
_____	The Lawyer's Essential Guide to Writing (5110726)	47.95	79.95	$_____
_____	iPadin One Hour for Lawyers (5110719)	19.95	34.95	$_____
_____	Find Info Like a Pro, V1: Mining the . . . (5110708)	47.95	79.95	$_____
_____	How to Start and Build a Law Practice, Platinum Fifth Edition (5110508)	57.95	69.95	$_____
_____	Social Media for Lawyers: The Next Frontier (5110710)	47.95	79.95	$_____

*Postage and Handling	
$10.00 to $49.99	$5.95
$50.00 to $99.99	$7.95
$100.00 to $199.99	$9.95
$200.00+	$12.95

**Tax
DC residents add 6%
IL residents add 9.75%

*Postage and Handling $_____
**Tax $_____
TOTAL $_____

PAYMENT

❏ Check enclosed (to the ABA)

❏ Visa ❏ MasterCard ❏ American Express

_____
Account Number Exp. Date Signature

Name _____ Firm _____

Address _____

City _____ State _____ Zip _____

Phone Number _____ E-Mail Address _____

Guarantee

If—for any reason—you are not satisfied with your purchase, you may return it within 30 days of receipt for a complete refund of the price of the book(s). No questions asked!

Mail: ABA Publication Orders, P.O. Box 10892, Chicago, Illinois 60610-0892
♦ Phone: 1-800-285-2221 ♦ FAX: 312-988-5568

E-Mail: abasvcctr@americanbar.org ♦ Internet: http://www.lawpractice.org/catalog

Are You in Your Element?

Tap into the Resources of the ABA Law Practice Management Section

ABA Law Practice Management Section Membership Benefits

The ABA Law Practice Management Section (LPM) is a professional membership organization of the American Bar Association that helps lawyers and other legal professionals with the business of practicing law. LPM focuses on providing information and resources in the core areas of marketing, management, technology, and finance through its award-winning magazine, teleconference series, Webzine, educational programs (CLE), Web site, and publishing division. For more than thirty years, LPM has established itself as a leader within the ABA and the profession-at-large by producing the world's largest legal technology conference (ABA TECHSHOW®) each year. In addition, LPM's publishing program is one of the largest in the ABA, with more than eighty-five titles in print.

In addition to significant book discounts, LPM Section membership offers these benefits:

ABA TECHSHOW
Membership includes a $100 discount to ABA TECHSHOW, the world's largest legal technology conference & expo!

Teleconference Series
Convenient, monthly CLE teleconferences on hot topics in marketing, management, technology and finance. Access educational opportunities from the comfort of your office chair – today's practical way to earn CLE credits!

Law Practice Magazine
Eight issues of our award-winning *Law Practice* magazine, full of insightful articles and practical tips on Marketing/Client Development, Practice Management, Legal Technology, and Finance.

Law Practice Today
LPM's unique Web-based magazine covers all the hot topics in law practice management today — identify current issues, face today's challenges, find solutions quickly. Visit www.lawpracticetoday.org.

Law Technology Today
LPM's newest Webzine focuses on legal technology issues in law practice management — covering a broad spectrum of the technology, tools, strategies and their implementation to help lawyers build a successful practice. Visit www.lawtechnologytoday.org.

LawPractice.news
Monthly news and information from the ABA Law Practice Management Section

LawPractice.news
Brings Section news, educational opportunities, book releases, and special offers to members via e-mail each month.

To learn more about the ABA Law Practice Management Section, visit www.lawpractice.org or call 1-800-285-2221.

MARKETING • MANAGEMENT • TECHNOLOGY • FINANCE

Join the ABA Law Practice Management Section Today!

Value is . . .

Resources that help you become a better lawyer:
- Up to 40% off LPM publications
- Six Issues of *Law Practice* magazine, both print and electronic versions
- Twelve issues of our monthly Webzine, *Law Practice Today*
- Your connection to Section news and events through *LawPractice.news*
- Discounted registration on "Third Thursday" CLE Teleconference Series and LPM conferences

Networking with industry experts while improving your skills at:
- ABA TECHSHOW
- ABA Law Firm Marketing Strategies Conference
- ABA Women Rainmakers Mid-Career Workshop
- LPM Quarterly Meetings

Opportunity given exclusively to our members:
- Writing for LPM periodicals and publications
- Joining ABA Women Rainmakers
- Becoming a better leader through committee involvement
- Listing your expertise in the LPM Speakerbase

**Members of LPM get up to 40% off publications like this one.
Join today and start saving!**

www.lawpractice.org • 1.800.285.2221

LawPracticeManagementSection

MARKETING • MANAGEMENT • TECHNOLOGY • FINANCE